ROUTLEDGE LIBRARY EDITIONS: ECONOMICS AND SOCIETY

Volume 32

STATE ENTERPRISE

STATE ENTERPRISE

Business or Politics?

DAVID COOMBES

Routledge
Taylor & Francis Group
LONDON AND NEW YORK

First published in 1971 by George Allen & Unwin Ltd.

This edition first published in 2026
by Routledge
4 Park Square, Milton Park, Abingdon, Oxon OX14 4RN

and by Routledge
605 Third Avenue, New York, NY 10158

Routledge is an imprint of the Taylor & Francis Group, an informa business

British Library Cataloguing in Publication Data
A catalogue record for this book is available from the British Library

ISBN: 978-1-032-97576-4 (Set)
ISBN: 978-1-041-13122-9 (Volume 32) (hbk)
ISBN: 978-1-041-13125-0 (Volume 32) (pbk)
ISBN: 978-1-003-66815-2 (Volume 32) (ebk)

DOI: 10.4324/9781003668152

STATE ENTERPRISE
Business or Politics?

David Coombes

Professor of European Studies
Loughborough University of Technology

PEP
12 Upper Belgrave Street, London

LONDON · GEORGE ALLEN & UNWIN LTD
Ruskin House, Museum Street

First published in 1971

ISBN 0 04 338047 6

Printed in Great Britain
in 10 point Times Roman
by Alden & Mowbray Ltd
at the Alden Press, Oxford

Acknowledgements

This book is the result of one of a series of studies of the control of public expenditure in Great Britain undertaken by PEP with the help of a grant from the Wolfson Foundation. In the course of making the study the author received invaluable help from the staff of various government departments, boards of nationalised industries, and other public bodies, as well as from many other people currently or previously engaged in the business of state enterprise. He wants to take this opportunity to thank them for the loan of their wisdom and patience. In addition, his thanks are due to the *Studieforbundet Naringsliv och Samhälle* in Stockholm, and to the *Istituto Affari Internazionali* in Rome, for arranging visits of Study to Sweden and Italy respectively. Officials, politicians, commentators and industrialists in both those countries also gave generously with their time and advice. Naturally none of the organisations or persons mentioned here is responsible for any opinions or errors contained in this book, which belong to the author himself.

PEP, London
August 1970

Contents

Part I

THE POLITICS OF STATE ENTERPRISE

Chapter 1

INTRODUCTION

For much of the present century it has been taken for granted that people's view of business was a condition of their political views. Conversely party politics in most western democratic countries has been based on a distinction between economic collectivists and liberals. Central to this distinction has been the question of state enterprise. In Britain for many years nationalization was considered decisive—at least among domestic policies—in separating one set of political leaders from the other. According to election studies and opinion polls it separated the mass of the voters as well.

At one stage this seemed to have changed and it was assumed that most conservatives or liberals had moved closer to collectivists or socialists in their attitude towards the organisation and conduct of business. Mainly as a result of changes in the policy of the Labour Party it seemed that nationalization itself was going to lose its importance in British party politics. Government policy for industry came to be regarded increasingly as a technical subject, on which the views of accountants or economists were more valuable than those of MPs or political commentators. The attitude of the new Conservative Government returned in 1970 (as this book went to press) seems to suggest that the old divisions might be renewed. In any event it would be no surprise to those entrusted with running the nationalised undertakings in this country to find themselves once more the pawns of political conflict. It is one aim of the present book to see whether some means could be found of giving them a role which is less exposed to the disruptive effects of political change: whether the business of managing these large and vitally important undertakings can be separated from the fluctuating and doctrinaire demands of party politics.

One does not have to follow the public debate for long to realize that there is confusion about the criteria by which the performance of state enterprises should be assessed. In our opinion this is still an enormous problem and we hope that in this book, although we cannot solve it, we can at least make clearer what it is the disagreement and misunderstanding are about. In spite of the difficulties this presents for those running the industries, much of the problem arises from political disagreement about the role of state enterprise. To put it crudely, there are those who start from the assumption that state enterprises should be judged in the same way as privately-owned undertakings, or on 'business' or 'commercial' principles (the language is imprecise and varies), and there are those who emphasize social and economic ends which the 'market' does not serve. The two have moved strikingly together and most informed observers today would probably maintain that both sorts of criteria should be applied. Some economists have argued forcibly that there would be no disagreement here if only people understood each other better. Our inquiries have led us to believe that the misunderstanding may go much deeper than some would like to think.

Books by professors of politics and reports from parliamentary and departmental committees usually treat this problem of criteria under the name of 'public accountability'. This sounds, and invariably is, an appallingly dull subject. Often it involves fruitless and painstaking search for new relationships between institutions and new rules of decision-making. But it ought to raise vital questions about the role of the state, and about the nature of political processes and political opinions. Public accountability is, after all, being answerable for decisions to legitimate political authorities, such as Parliament or the Executive. It is, therefore, to do with the role of government itself. Most people in democratic countries would probably agree that people should be publicly accountable for decisions which are politically important. The problem is to decide which decisions are politically important and here economists or other technicians are not much help. There is not even much point in discussing institutional relationships unless the purposes to be served and the nature of the subject are clear. Does everyone agree that state enterprise is simply another form of business and, more importantly, do they share the same view of what 'business' is?

How does the job of the chairman of a nationalized board differ from that of a minister in the government or that of the chairman of the board of a private firm? Who is at fault when a service of a nationalized industry is inadequate or inefficient – the board, the minister, civil servants, the workers in the industry – or perhaps no one? Do the relations between a coal-miner and his employers differ from those between a car-worker and his? What qualifications should be sought from a civil servant in a department dealing with nationalized industry and how should these differ from those of an executive in a nationalized undertaking or in a private business? Certainly innumerable questions are bound up in the subject of state enterprise and one has only to mention some of these to see the relevance of the question posed in the title of this book.

Apart from the problem of deciding what is success and failure in state enterprise there is that of how to organize government in the interests of effectiveness and efficiency. There is a growing interest in Britain in this problem and the Fulton Report on the civil service seems to be associated in many minds with a trend of questioning the rationality of the machinery of government. The Fulton Committee only touched on some of the relevant questions. In view of the functions of modern government, are responsibilities allocated among different levels and units in the most effective way? What do we expect of existing structures and personnel in government and are our demands reasonable? Could the same ends be served in different, less expensive ways? State enterprise accounts for a large and important chunk of the machinery of government in Britain and a study of the rationality of organization in this sector is long overdue. How much of the responsibility for state enterprise can be 'taken out of politics'? How far are civil servants engaged in 'business'?

A lot of attention has been paid just recently to the idea of devolving tasks from central government departments to autonomous boards or regional bodies. The nationalized industries should provide a case of devolved authority in that they are already vested in what might be called autonomous boards. But the reality is probably different from this and we should ask why. The most valuable studies of public administration seem to result from case studies, for theory is best when it is tested by study of some actual experience. What we are really doing in this book is testing theory by studying part of the process of government. What sort of tasks have civil servants and their ministers acquired as a consequence of nationalization and what problems do they meet in carrying them out? More importantly, why do certain functions fall to central administrators in the first place? Is there any reason to think that the present functions could be changed with gains to efficiency or effectiveness?

Although in these ways we set out to be original, we shall make some limiting assumptions which have already been made in comment and research on the subject. In each case, however, our assumptions will be a little less limiting than usual.

In the first place we shall maintain the academic convention of keeping out of the controversy of public versus private ownership. Indeed we shall emphasize that many of the problems of the nationalized industries are really problems common to all large-scale industry in the modern economy. However, we shall argue that some recent writers have gone too far in treating ownership as irrelevant.

We have come to the conclusion that in some respects (in particular where the efficiency of industries is concerned) public ownership makes a substantial difference to our ability to assess performance. We have been unable, within the scope of this book, to reach any conclusions about the relationship of different kinds of economic system to industrial efficiency. There are basic differences of approach to this question. For example, from certain points of view public ownership is a prerequisite for achieving social and economic ends and efficiency is a secondary problem. We shall go no further in this study than to try to make existing arguments more explicit and to illustrate some of the problems raised by public ownership. We are aware that often the same problems arise in the private sector of industry. We shall be unable to look for solutions within the framework of the present study and, indeed, we hope to show that one's approach to solving the problems often depends on one's evaluation of different kinds of ownership and on one's view of ownership in relation to the economic system as a whole.

Again, we shall not recommend changes in the political system and any conclusions we reach about the machinery of government or parliamentary control will take the existing system of government as given. However we believe that it is important to point out the limitations of the political system and to show where necessary that some demands placed on it involve changes which may not be acceptable. Thus, for example, the increasing concern of modern governments for industrial and commercial matters might require increasing independence of the executive from parliamentary control.

Furthermore we shall not attempt to evaluate the decisions of state enterprises or to assess their performance. We shall not even be able to recommend changes in organization and structure designed to improve performance. These are fields we leave to the economist and the specialist in management. Nevertheless, the problem of public accountability is bound up with that of performance in that experts disagree about the effects of accountability on the efficiency and effectiveness of undertakings. The relationship between an organization's ability to perform in certain ways and its public accountability is certainly relevant to our main theme.

In this respect particularly we have been fortunate in being able to draw on the great deal of work already carried out by other scholars in the field, by the House of Commons Select Committee on Nationalized Industries and by numerous departmental and other official inquiries. The subject of public accountability has certainly not been overlooked in recent years, although past studies may well have failed to go sufficiently deeply or widely into the question. We are concerned here directly with state enterprise in Britain and have limited ourselves to the so-called nationalized industries, namely, those brought into public ownership mainly by Acts of Parliament under the Labour Government of 1945–50. We have kept the title and some of the language of the book more general because we hope that we have been able in places to cover somewhat broader ground than this. In particular, it is our aim to raise questions and to test theories rather than to make specific recommendations so that we have not been all that inhibited by this limitation. But we recognize that the problems of different undertakings vary. Had we set out to make more concrete findings we would have had to carry out a much more extensive study. As it is, in our research we have concentrated on three particular industries: electricity supply, railways and coal. What we call 'research' was mainly interviewing officials in certain government departments (the Treasury, the Ministry of Transport and what was then the Ministry of Power) and also representatives of boards (the Electricity Council, the National Coal Board and British Rail). In addition we received a great deal of help from officials of the National Board for Prices and Incomes. In fact our inquiries ranged much more widely than this and the author has held conversations with a number of people who were students of and participants in the activity of holding nationalized industries publicly accountable.

Parts II and III present a fairly detailed analysis of the public accountability of the nationalized industries up to about the autumn of 1969, relying on the author's existing knowledge of the subject, on the published findings of parliamentary and other inquiries, on existing privately published comment, and on the research just described. It will be noticed that three particular problems of decision-making at this time are used as case material in Chapters 3, 4 and 6: uneconomic railway services, the contraction of the coal industry (and the related problem of ordering new electricity generating stations), and forecasting of demand in electricity supply. In some important respects this case material is now historical in that policy or the facts have changed; we have referred to some of these changes but we do not believe that any of them weaken the value of the material in its use here, namely, as an illustration of general features of certain kinds of institutional relationship. At the end of Part III there is an analysis of recent proposals for reforming the relationship between government and nationalized industries, particularly those contained in a report of the Select Committee on Nationalized Industries in 1968.

Part IV is much more general in subject and in relevance and tries to take up the questions arising from the empirical analysis of the British nationalized industries presented earlier. The leading problem which emerges from this analysis is how far state enterprises can be expected to behave as business concerns and what institutional arrangements are best suited to ensuring that they do. The most interesting examples in Europe of state enterprises which are meant to be run on business lines are in Sweden and Italy and the author made special studies of the public accountability of state undertakings in both these countries. The findings are presented as the first two chapters in Part IV. The author visited both countries in the summer of 1969 and carried out an intensive programme of interviews with government officials, representatives of state undertakings and expert observers. The rest of Part IV seeks to draw together and generalize what seem to be the main obstacles to treating state enterprises as businesses. It then suggests how, in spite of the political differences which are likely to continue, means could be found of setting up the nationalised industries on a less politically exposed and more efficient basis.

For the rest of Part I we feel it is necessary to set the scene for what follows in as straightforward a manner as possible. First, we attempt to summarize as concisely as possible the motives which have led to public ownership in Britain and, secondly, we try to identify the defining characteristics of the British nationalized industries in terms of their formal relationship with government. Most students and practitioners of state enterprise in Britain will already be familiar with most of this material and might prefer to move on to the beginning of Part II. Our interpretation of the motives leading to public ownership is fairly original, however, and arises again later so that it probably deserves scrutiny at this point.

Chapter 2

THE ORIGINS OF THE NATIONALIZED INDUSTRIES

Even if we confine ourselves to Britain, various purposes have been sought through public ownership. State enterprise in Britain is normally identified with the undertakings called 'nationalized industries' set up mainly by Acts passed under the Labour Government of 1945–50. It has never been clear what the objects of those Acts were. Moreover, the model of public ownership chosen after 1945 would by no means have been widely accepted before that date.

In the first place, many socialists in Western Europe have seen public ownership as a means of radically changing the structure of industry. Thus particularly in Britain in the late nineteenth and early twentieth centuries proposals for public ownership were strongly influenced by syndicalist ideas of workers' control. Viewed from the Left public ownership has frequently been sought for *political* reasons. From this view the purpose of state enterprise would be not so much economic, in the sense of improving the performance of the undertakings concerned or serving national economic policy, as political, in the sense of changing the existing control of industry. Sometimes workers' control has not been so explicit as an objective, and there has been a vague commitment to increasing public participation. In this respect one of the main purposes of public ownership must presumably be to ensure greater political control.

In very few cases in Western Europe, however, has this influence had a significant effect on the eventual organization of state enterprises. It is remarkable perhaps that in most countries in Western Europe public ownership before 1945 was justified overwhelmingly on pragmatic, and mainly economic, grounds. State enterprises were set up chiefly as part of specific government policies to protect or promote particular undertakings in the public interest. For this purpose public ownership has rarely if ever been the only tool available to governments. When state enterprise has been created to serve some specific social or economic objective in this way we shall describe it as *contingent*. Invariably public ownership on contingent grounds proves acceptable to political parties of whatever colour. Most acts of public ownership in Britain before 1945 were contingent in this sense and were taken by Liberal or Conservative governments. In some countries this type of state enterprise can be associated with public ownership of individual undertakings rather than of whole industries and with a decentralized and competitive form of organization.[1]

Contingent motives like this were certainly present when the Labour Government, elected in 1945, came to nationalize the coal, gas, electricity supply and inland transport industries and the air corporations. These industries had for a long time been accustomed to a lot of intervention aimed mainly to ensure safety, to maintain adequate supply in times of crisis, to compensate for occasional shortages of capital, to improve labour relations and so on. With certain important exceptions (such as road transport) public ownership was accepted on all sides of politics as a logical continuation of this intervention. In each case there were compelling practical social and economic reasons for some form of public ownership. In the case of electricity supply and the air corporations there already was substantial public ownership.[2] The main controversy then and since has been about the scope and the form of public ownership introduced by Labour's Acts of nationalization. Moreover what consensus existed in the case of power and transport certainly did not extend at all to the nationalization of the steel industry in 1949.

The prevailing interests of the Labour Party at the time could probably have been served only by acquiring whole 'industries' placed under more or less centralized control. Although the earlier *political* objectives of public ownership, especially workers' control, had become less influential, there were overriding motives which seemed to make abolition of private ownership and competition essential and other instruments of government action inadequate. For example, it was strongly believed that in most respects competition was harmful in the industries nationalized. It is not entirely clear how far this view was shared in other parties. 'Rationalization' and large-scale organization were promoted in many parts of industry before the war by Conservative-dominated governments as a means to greater efficiency. What really worried Labour leaders and supporters, however, was the effect of leaving large-scale undertakings in private hands. 'Rationalization' or 'co-ordination' were supported by Labour on grounds of efficiency and economic necessity long after enthusiasm cooled elsewhere and were regarded as inseparable from greater public participation. Moreover, there was unmistakeable antipathy in the Labour Party to the profit motive. To solve the problems created by private control of monopolies and by the allegedly selfish and wasteful principles of private enterprise, therefore, everything was now staked on the policy of abolishing private ownership in certain basic industries (including steel where there was little record of state intervention). There was little idea how public participation would in fact be increased.

There was another important motive for Labour's nationalization of 1945–50, also rarely articulated. This was the belief that nationalization of basic industries was needed for effective economic planning. It was said that the government should obtain control of the industries most vital to the economy and furthermore that adequate control could be obtained only by nationalization on the 1945–50 model. It has never been clear whether public ownership of whole industries combined with centralized direction was really considered necessary. Indeed, recent Labour writers have argued that it is not necessary and have recommended different forms of state enterprise for extending the influence of the central government in the economy (such as ownership of a percentage of shares in different undertakings). However, at the core of the Labour Party's thinking about public enterprise has always been a feeling that public ownership is an indispensable means of socialist economic policy. In this sense it can be distinguished from the contingent approach to public enterprise in that the latter admits that other instruments are available and uses public ownership as a device specific to the problem of a particular industry at a particular time.

We shall call the approach to state enterprise embodied in Labour's Acts of nationalization between 1945 and 1950, the *positive* approach. This is because in this approach public ownership seems to be a unique instrument. First, it is a means of abolishing private ownership, which for various reasons is considered immoral or inefficient. Secondly, it is seen as an indispensable means of central economic planning.[3]

As we have remarked these principles are not always clear from the statutes of the nationalized industries. Moreover, there are some statutory differences and enormous physical ones between one nationalized industry and another. Nevertheless, the British nationalized industries constitute a special type of state enterprise, and the general characteristics of this type will now be stated. We should stress, however, that we have abstracted from reality here and have deliberately overlooked minor differences not relevant to our main theme.

The first characteristic of the 1945–50 model of state enterprise worth noting is that for the most part the Government sought to take whole industries into public ownership and to set up some form of centralized organization. For example, the state acquired virtual or complete monopolies in coal, gas, electricity supply, railways and steel. The nationalized gas and electricity supply industries were both organized on a federal basis, responsibility being divided between a central authority (there are now two of these in electricity) and area boards. When steel was first nationalized in 1949 the former private companies retained their identity and were not abolished as happened in the case of other acts of nationalization. Moreover, in the case of civil aviation there were three, then two, separate undertakings with no central authority (apart from the Minister). In spite of these variations, however, the essential principle was the same: acquisition of whole industries and the creation of substantially centralized authority; (the air corporations are separated on the basis of providing services over different areas).

Secondly, there are no shareholders in nationalized industries; equity belongs, it is said, 'to the nation'.[4] Until 1956 all undertakings except the Coal Board issued fixed-interest and fixed-term stock, but did so with Treasury guarantee with the result that the stock was treated as gilt-edged security. After 1956 it was decided that it would be more convenient and would require no change in principle for the industries to borrow directly from the Exchequer.

The industries are not vested in companies but in public corporations created by statute. Each corporation (or 'board') is given certain fixed financial and economic rights and duties by statute and we shall discuss these later. In most cases these obligations are the same for all the industries. (They are in fact vaguely worded and, as we shall see, little practical meaning can be read into them.)

In many respects, however, the public corporations are like joint-stock companies in that they are separate legal entities which can sue and be sued in the courts, which keep commercial accounts, and which hire and fire their own staff. Public corporations are not directly accountable to Parliament (or thereby to the electorate), their staff are not members of the Civil Service, and they do not need parliamentary approval before spending money as does a government department. They are not headed by a minister but by a board of independent members appointed on the basis of their qualifications. However ministers (who are accountable to Parliament) may possess statutory powers over public corporations. In the case of the nationalized industries these ministerial powers follow a pattern and the most important can be paraphrased and summarized as follows:

1. The minister specified appoints the members of the board and (with Treasury approval) fixes their salaries and pensions (which are, however, charged to the board). The members may in some cases be dismissed or 'not re-appointed' by the minister.

2. The minister may give directions to the board 'of a general character' as to the exercise of its functions in relation to matters affecting the national interest.
3. The minister must approve general programmes or proposals involving expenditure of large sums of capital.
4. The board has to provide the relevant minister with whatever returns, accounts and other information he may require, and the latter presents an annual report and accounts from the board before Parliament. The minister also appoints auditors to inspect the board's accounts.
5. The minister must authorize borrowing by the board and can make directions about the management of reserves and the disposal of surplus revenues.

In addition there are a vast number of detailed ministerial powers varying in form from statute to statute concerning such matters as the relations between different boards in the same industry; the right to diversify activities, lend money, develop property and so on; the role of consumers' councils; pension funds; and so on. The minister specified in the relevant statutes as exercising these powers is known generally as the 'sponsoring' minister for, in addition to carrying out the powers given him by the nationalization statute, he is expected to keep a general watch on the industry's performance and welfare and to administer other legislation affecting it. The same minister invariably has sponsoring responsibilities towards some private firms as well (for example, the former Minister of Power's sponsoring functions included the oil industry as well as coal, gas and electricity).

These then are the main principles of the type of state enterprise adopted by the Labour Government of 1945–50 and known as 'nationalized industries'. They have continued to apply with only slight changes ever since in the case of coal, electricity supply, railways, canals and inland waterways, London Transport, British European Airways and the British Overseas Airways Corporation.[5] The Labour Government had little opportunity to develop its ideas about the role of state enterprise in the economy or in the political system before a Conservative Government was returned in 1951. Thus for most of their existence the nationalized industries have been run under Conservative governments. It is perhaps remarkable that in their years of power after 1951 the Conservatives made so few fundamental changes in the constitution of these industries and showed what might be considered disappointing lack of imagination. Certainly special efforts were made after about 1960 to re-think the role of the industries in the economy and the policies then adopted did diverge in some important respects from those adopted by the

Labour Government, as we shall see later. Private competition with the air corporations was also greatly facilitated by the Conservatives and some extensive changes in the organization of some nationalized industries were carried out (in particular in the electricity supply industry in 1957 and in transport in 1962). Road transport was returned to private ownership in 1953 and in 1962 those road services which remained in public ownership were vested in a Transport Holding Company (an experiment which deserved more public attention and a better fate – the Company was abolished in 1968). Meanwhile the steel industry was de-nationalized without ever having effectively become a nationalized industry. However, apart from the cases mentioned, there was no attempt to reduce the state's owning interest in the nationalized industries or to change the basic principles on which they were set up. The Conservatives did not add to the scope of state enterprise properly so called, although some new public corporations with mainly promotional, financial or regulatory powers were established, such as the Independent Television Authority, the Sugar Board, and the Atomic Energy Authority.

Probably the most boring aspect of the subject of state enterprise in this country is the relentless lack of variety in the principles on which the existing nationalized industries are constituted and in the way this type of state enterprise has been adopted here to the exclusion of almost any other. There certainly are cases of state ownership of a percentage of shares in otherwise private undertakings (as in the case of British Petroleum); there are a number of promotional, regulatory and financial bodies and some publicly-owned research organizations; and there are noteworthy public enterprises run by local authorities. The model represented by the nationalized industries, however, is identified more or less justifiably in the minds of people in this country with state enterprise itself. The consitution of the original nationalized industries has been virtually frozen and has sometimes been treated as almost undebatable. This is all the more surprising in that Conservatives hardly shared the positive approach to state enterprise of the Labour Government of 1945–50. Their own approach in office can only be described as a *negative* one, regarding public ownership as a necessary evil, not even supported particularly on contingent grounds. Only this can explain the Conservatives' failure to make greater changes in the constitution of the industries.

In recent years there has been increasing support within the Labour Party for a more contingent approach. This has arisen mainly as a reaction to the results of the nationalization carried out between 1945 and 1950. Greater flexibility and variety in state intervention have been recommended, and some writers have emphasized the limitations of public ownership as an instrument of socialist objectives. In the late 1950s and early 1960s an attempt to revise Labour's thinking on public ownership produced a serious schism within the Party. It could be said that the Party's attitude to economic affairs is generally far less doctrinaire now than it was in 1945. Competition and the profit-motive are more acceptable than they were. (This has even affected the Party's attitude towards the existing nationalized industries, as we shall see below.) However, it is not easy to tell whether the positive approach has been abandoned in favour of something else. Thus, although many so-called 'Revisionists' argued for abandoning the 1945–50 model of state enterprise, many of the earlier attitudes against profit-making and competition were retained.[6] Moreover, although after 1951 the Labour Party showed increasing interest in other forms of state enterprise, it continued to be firmly committed to the objectives sought by nationalization between 1945 and 1950, such as destroying private control of large-scale undertakings and ending 'wasteful competition'.[7]

Indeed the recent Labour Government reaffirmed its faith in the nationalized industries by passing legislation on the 1945–50 model to re-nationalize the steel industry in 1967 and to change the Post Office from a government department into a public corporation in 1969. Although it would have been premature to have tried to draw any major conclusions from the experience of the steel industry since 1967, it must now be added to the list of nationalized industries and we believe our conclusions will be relevant to it in future. Similarly the Post Office has not usually been included in strict definitions of the nationalized industries (although postal and telecommunications services have been in public ownership longer than any other industry). However, by an Act of 1961 the Post Office was given much of the same financial status as a public corporation responsible for a nationalized industry. The Act finally making it a public corporation was regarded as a culmination of an existing trend. Some of what we have to say here will therefore extend to it but we shall leave it to the reader's discretion to decide how much; certainly we think that many of our conclusions will apply to the new Post Office Corporation in a general way.

It is still too early to say how the new arrangements for road transport provided by the Labour Government's Transport Act of 1968 (setting up a National Freight Corporation and a National Bus Company) will work out and whether road transport should now also be included as a nationalized industry. (Practically all references to land transport in this book are to the railways.) At least the new organization of transport shows originality in the way local authorities have been used to create a new form of constitution for state enterprise. Other features of the Act, however, follow the conventional pattern.

Nevertheless, between 1964 and 1969 there were definite signs that the Labour Government was willing and able to experiment with new forms of state intervention in industry. In some respects existing institutions have been used in a different way, like the National Research Development Corporation. New institutions have been created, like the Industrial Reorganization Corporation and the National Board for Prices and Incomes. The use of promotional, financial and regulatory bodies for industry has in some cases been extended. There is also evidence that the notion of partial share-ownership as a substitute for nationalization began to gain official favour. There have been few signs, however, of a change of mind about the existing nationalized industries (including the two new ones added by the Labour Government). There have certainly been significant changes in policy towards these industries during Labour's latest tenure of office, as we shall show. However, it is still far from certain how far Labour are willing to forego the positive approach to public ownership conventionally associated with the nationalized industries or to move from a negative approach to a willingness to change.

This book was written before the policies of the new Conservative Government of 1970 could be fully known. However, it does seem that there is a new willingness on the part of the Conservatives to ask some basic questions about the existing nationalised industries, including a re-examination of their fundamental usefulness to government. This might represent a departure from the negative approach of previous Conservative administrations. If it does lead to a radical review of the organisation and methods of nationalized industries this will be the first time since the original statutes were passed. It will also mean that this book has proved to be unexpectedly prophetic.

REFERENCES

1. The best surviving examples can be found in Sweden, see below, pp. 179–86. In Britain between the wars the tendency was to create monopolies like the Forestry Commission, the Central Electricity Board and the British Broadcasting Corporation. One of the contingent motives at the time happened to be 'rationalization' and deriving economies of scale. Pre-war acts of public ownership were not carried

out as part of a general programme: in each case there were special reasons for acting; and the governments concerned were certainly hostile to public ownership. See J. W. Grove, *Government and Industry in Britain*, George Allen & Unwin, London, 1963, pp. 42–55, 297–307.

2. Before the 1947 Act electricity generation and transmission were already virtually nationalized, distribution being in the hands partly of private companies and partly of local authorities. The British Overseas Airways Corporation was set up under the National Government in 1939 and enjoyed a near monopoly of overseas air services. However the Labour Government sought to pool national resources in civil aviation in the Act of 1945 by extending public ownership to inland services and greatly expanding overseas operations.
3. D. N. Chester, 'Management in the Nationalized Industries', in *Public Administration*, vol. XXX, spring 1952, pp. 27–47.
4. W. A. Robson, *Nationalized Industry and Public Ownership*, George Allen & Unwin, London, 2nd edn 1962, p. 66.
5. The minister had no statutory power to approve programmes of capital expenditure in the case of BEA or BOAC until 1966. Responsibility for London Transport has now been handed over to the Greater London Council.
6. H. Gaitskell, *Socialism and Nationalization*, Fabian Tract No. 300, 1956, pp. 31–6.
7. Labour Party Publications Department, *Signposts for the Sixties*, 1961, pp. 13–18.

Part II

NATIONALIZED INDUSTRIES AND THE PUBLIC INTEREST

Chapter 3

SOCIAL AND ECONOMIC OBLIGATIONS

The boards of the British nationalized industries often seem to have had no clear idea about the purposes of nationalization and to have found no real guidance in the statutes about the principles on which the industries should be organized. In the first years the process of finding principles for running the undertakings – in particular how to arrange their relationship with government – seems to have been a circular one. The boards of the industries turned for guidance to ministers and their advisers while the latter based their instructions on what they thought the boards themselves wanted. It was probably not until the 1960s that government departments began to produce some articulate and original policies, and even then these policies did not constitute a coherent or consistent whole. Of course it is not necessarily the purpose of governments to produce comprehensive or changeless programmes setting out detailed means and ends of action (although many modern students of government would like to think so), nor is such a thing usually possible. On the other hand, whereas there are bound to be 'grey areas' of policy, in the case of the nationalized industries there was so little light that those responsible for the industries often had no idea at all, or at least had conflicting ideas, about fundamental questions of purpose and role. As a result it was impossible to sustain a meaningful discussion in Parliament or elsewhere about whether particular undertakings were successful or not: even the members of the boards themselves were uncertain. Furthermore, the industries were certainly nationalized on grounds of urgent public need. Nationalization, as we have seen, was a *positive* undertaking and was intended to achieve great things. All the more important to know what these things were meant to be.

It is for these reasons that the relationship between government and boards has been probably the most difficult and thoroughly studied aspect of the nationalized industries. The problem has been that, although the industries clearly had important rights and duties in the public interest, the public interest in this area was the very thing about which there could be no agreement – even among those who supported nationalization. Before deciding the role of the nationalized industries, it is essential to know the relationship between nationalized industries and the public interest. This chapter and the next will take up this question of the public interest in order to see how far a consensus has now emerged. The public interest is ultimately determined in Britain by the government of the day and is expressed in the way the government interprets legislation, in the way it announces its aims, and in the way it answers criticisms of its conduct. There are a number of reasons, which we can state straight-away, why the public interest should be difficult to define.

First, the main political parties have not taken up distinctive positions on the question. Public ownership has certainly been a major divisive issue in post-war party politics, but public ownership of concerns such as the railways, the nationalized air corporations, the postal services, and the domestic fuel and power industries has for a long time been an accepted fact of life. Usually these industrial activities have not been in the forefront of conflict between the parties. One's impression indeed is that most attention to the existing nationalized industries in Parliament has been paid, not to the problem of defining economic and social responsibilities, so much as to relatively isolated matters, such as: the appointment and payment of board chairmen, individual instances of alleged inefficiency (accidents on the railways or in the air, breakdowns in electricity supply, and so on), particular labour disputes, and the impact of particular decisions on regional employment. Moreover, these issues have been raised by backbenchers of both parties and both sides of the House have then been critical of the conduct of government and industry.

Another general observation is that changes which have taken place in government policy for the nationalized sector have issued not so much from changes of government as from the administration. In private those involved sometimes explain the stages in evolution of government policy as resulting from the posting of particular officials to key positions in the relevant ministries. This sector is one of many in modern government where normal inter-party conflict has not been particularly helpful in settling the differences involved. It is, in other words, a very important case where the public interest is confused yet where administrators have been left a lot of scope in interpreting it.

A further difficulty is that decisions in this sector are extremely complex and cannot be taken as choices between clear alternatives. A decision to construct a new electricity generating station, for example, involves a technical assessment in terms of thermal energy of the efficiency of different primary fuels; an economic judgement of the value of the resources employed; a financial estimate of commercial viability; numerous decisions about the employment of labour, relations with consumers and so on; not to mention consideration of broader social questions such as the effect on amenity of possible sites, and the rest. The rights and wrongs of decisions like this are far from clear to the general public. They are probably not even readily understood by those directly involved at an operating level, who will usually be specialists of one kind or another and thus have difficulty in taking a general view. Those at a policy-making level within the industries have been uncertain of the exact scope of the decisions they take. Many of the civil servants we have spoken to also admitted difficulty in taking a complete view of the subject.

However, during the last ten years or so there has been a growing attempt to distinguish and make more articulate the different functions of policy for the nationalized industries and to do so in public. More recently quite ambitious efforts have been made to quantify some aspects of decision-making in this field by the application of techniques such as cost/benefit analysis. As we shall see later, the bulk of recent academic work on the subject has been contributed by economists. The main contribution in government and Parliament has come from special committees of inquiry appointed by ministers or boards, the Select Committee on Nationalized Industries of the House of Commons, and the government departments themselves. The results can be found in the reports of the various committees, in government White Papers and in academic commentaries.

The most original and probably the most influential idea to emerge from this activity so far has been that the responsibilities of ministers on the one hand, and boards on the other, should be clearly demarcated from each other. In other words, the conflict and confusion in the minds of the boards should be settled by giving them a clear responsibility to act in their own 'commercial' interests and to leave all other considerations to ministers. The board of a nationalized industry should not take account of the 'public interest' of its own accord. The most famous statement to this effect is found in the Report of the Herbert Committee on the Electricity Supply Industry. Any departure from 'business principles', that Committee said, 'should be undertaken only on precise instructions' from a minister: 'The line between the Government and the industry should be a clear one for all to see'.[1] The reports of the Select Committee on Nationalized Industries have expressed a similar view over the years although not with total consistency. Certainly, however, under its two Conservative chairmen up to 1964 the Select Committee laid great emphasis on the need to draw a clear distinction in practice between what it called the 'commercial' interest of the industries and the 'national' interest of the government.[2]

It is far from agreed, however, that it is correct to interpret the aims of nationalization in this way. According to the earlier writings of Herbert Morrison (commonly regarded – and rightly so – as having had the greatest influence on the content of the nationalization statutes), the public corporations vested with the industries should take the public interest into account themselves.[3] This interpretation has been supported by a number of other authorities, in particular by Professor Robson.[4] In our own conversations with representatives of nationalized industries we have been struck by a widespread feeling that nationalized undertakings were bound to feel more conscientious about the public interest than any private firm. It certainly seems to be basic to the professional ethos of many managers in the nationalized industries that the ends they serve are wider in some way than those of a purely 'commercial' undertaking. This view is supported by the statutes, many of which place directly on the boards the duty to behave in ways which could hardly be described as 'commercial' and sometimes use the very words 'in the public interest'. For example, the National Coal Board is entrusted, among other things, with 'making supplies of coal available, of such qualities and sizes, in such quantities and at such prices, *as may seem to them* best calculated to further the public interest in all respects'.[5]

In this book we hope to show that there is little point in making a definition of the public interest which is based on a division of responsibilities between minister and board and which excludes the so-called 'commercial' interests of the industries themselves. Even if we ignore the statutes, it is quite evident, as we shall show, that in practice the responsibilities of minister and board overlap and necessarily so. Boards must form a view of the public interest just as ministers must take the financial results and efficiency of boards into account. Both would otherwise fail in their duty.

The public interest here is a vague and unreliable notion, which probably cannot be defined as a set of undisputed or internally consistent standards. In practice various obligations have been placed on the boards of the nationalized industries in the name of the public interest. It is essential to try to distinguish each of these obligations as far as possible so that the aims of public policy which they are meant to express can be better identified. Then (but only then) it should be possible to see what forms of organization would be best suited to achieving these aims. As we have said this task has never been seriously attempted before and is long overdue. We have implicitly accepted some separation into two main kinds of obligation by dealing with social and economic obligations in the rest of this chapter and leaving financial obligations and efficiency to the next.

SOCIAL OBLIGATIONS

The nationalization statutes state or imply that four types of social obligation should be placed on the boards of the nationalized industries. Two of these are straightforward and need not concern us greatly at this point, namely: the obligation to establish machinery for joint negotiation and consultation with employees on the terms and conditions of employment; and the need to establish, consult and inform consumers' councils. The other two types of social obligation are only implied by the statutes and are much less precise. First, most of the industries are affected by general or specific instructions to serve the public in certain ways. These oblige the boards concerned to carry on the activities vested in them 'economically', 'efficiently', and so on, and to make 'adequate' supplies available. They also oblige the boards to take special account of such questions as amenity and safety and in some cases to provide special services. Secondly, there are various provisions in the statutes which seem to be designed mainly to prevent industries abusing monopoly powers.

It has never been clear what these and other statutory provisions are intended to mean but they do confirm at least that the nationalized industries are expected to observe important social obligations in the public interest. To understand these obligations and to study their practical application the statutes are actually of little help and we must rely overwhelmingly on other sources. The most important type of social obligation to be met by the industries in practice is the performance of a variety of social services.

The industries seem to be obliged to perform the following social services (some of which are specifically required by statute):

1. Providing unremunerative goods and services which benefit a particular type of consumer directly, or benefit the general public indirectly (for example: running railway branch lines and commuter services; providing air transport to remote regions; supplying rural electricity; and running the inland telegram service).
2. Observing certain restrictions on their revenue-earning activities because otherwise some damage or offence might be caused either generally or to particular groups of people (for example: considering amenity in building gas-making plant and electricity-generating stations; avoiding air pollution and aircraft noise, and so on).

3. Employing certain factors of production mainly in order to benefit particular groups or to benefit the general public indirectly (for example: the burning of surplus coal by the Central Electricity Generating Board; the purchase of British manufactured aircraft by BEA and BOAC, and so on).

Two problems in particular have arisen from the performance of these services by the nationalized industries. The first is the problem of distinguishing what is a service provided out of social obligation as opposed to one provided in pursuit of profitability, larger markets, and so on. Many privately owned industries, it is well known, perform the kind of services we have just described, although probably much less than the nationalized industries. Little is known for certain about the behaviour of private firms in this country, but the tendency of modern industrial corporations of all kinds to accept social responsibilities has been widely discussed in the United States and now increasingly here.[6] What we have defined here as social services are sometimes found in private company policies under other names, such as 'public relations', 'labour relations', and so on. The Central Electricity Generating Board did for some years burn more coal in its power stations than it would have liked, because it wished to help the coal industry during a period of difficult adaptation. It was regarded as being in the electricity industry's own interests to provide for an efficient and profitable coal industry in the future. Similarly it is a major source of the National Coal Board's anxiety regarding the closure of uneconomic pits that too little regard for the welfare of redundant miners might worsen labour relations in pits in economic areas. Even in the nationalized industries therefore social services may sometimes be provided for a mixture of motives.

Perhaps the best means of distinguishing services provided out of social obligation is to treat them as compulsory, meaning that the board is required to provide them against its will. BOAC have complained from time to time that they have been obliged to buy British aircraft in the national interest. Sometimes the Coal Board has had to delay closure of pits longer than it would normally choose on account of a government's policy for regional unemployment. To regard social services as obligatory in this strict sense is certainly a means to greater clarity. However it does not solve the problem completely, for it could be difficult even to tell what is compulsory. A board might 'bluff' the government into making compulsory what the board would probably do otherwise of its own accord. Moreover it is sometimes impossible to measure separately the different benefits to be derived from a particular service so that one could say in advance what were sensible reasons for providing it. For instance, the benefits to the undertaking itself from providing consumers with a particular good or service are not always measured by the immediate financial return.

The second crucial problem in the performance of social services by nationalized industries is deciding who shall pay for these services and by what means. This important decision is often overlooked altogether, with unfortunate consequences. One possibility of course is that the consumer of the service or the beneficiary of it could pay a price sufficient to cover the total cost of providing it. Leaving aside the question of how these costs could be calculated, this solution is seldom found to be satisfactory. For one thing, it is not always possible to make the main beneficiary pay since many of the services we are considering are designed to produce an indirect benefit either to particular groups or to society in general. Providing services of public transport and fuel supply to remote areas might, for example, be considered desirable in the interests of avoiding congestion and overcrowding in heavily populated areas. Another reason why this is often an undesirable method of financing social services is that the consumer is frequently a member of a group which is being specially favoured by the provision of the service concerned. For this group to pay the full costs of providing the service would not be consistent with the decision to give it special treatment: in other words, the service would cease to be a social one. On the other hand, it should be remembered that there is one enormous advantage in the beneficiary paying as far as is possible the full cost: this is, other things being equal, the best means of equating supply and demand. Usually, however, this method cannot be adopted (wholly, at least) because of important disadvantages like those we have mentioned.

Another method might be called indirect subsidy. Some surplus from the industry's ordinary goods and services could be made to subsidize the beneficiaries of the social services. This will only be practicable, of course, if demand for these other services is inelastic enough; and in any case, the board of an industry may not wish to risk losing competitive flexibility or may not wish to follow what some would regard as an unfair pricing policy. Alternatively an enterprise could simply make a loss on its trading account and make this up by drawing on reserves, if these exist, or by borrowing from outside. In fact, in nationalized industries indirect subsidy has generally meant increased borrowing from the government. It has recently been argued with some force that, rather than make an indirect subsidy of this kind by increased lending to a nationalized industry, it is much better for the government to recoup the cost of providing a social service directly. Then, of course, it is the taxpayer who finances the social services provided by the industry concerned.

However, there are a number of arguments in favour of the method of indirect subsidy. In particular, establishing a direct subsidy is extremely difficult because of the problem we have already met of defining a social service. Quantifying such a subsidy is even more difficult, since the exact cost of providing a service is uncertain: yet it is usually extremely important to be accurate in the interests of effective parliamentary supervision and Treasury control. At the same time direct subsidies are easily related in the public mind to increased government spending and higher taxation, and governments are usually unwilling to incur disfavour by providing them.

For many years now the Select Committee on Nationalized Industries has been illustrating in its reports that a number of social services of the kind we have described are provided by the nationalized industries. In the vast majority of cases the provision of such services has necessitated some form of indirect subsidy. The Committee (along with many other commentators) has repeatedly criticized this arrangement, arguing that it confuses responsibility and makes it impossible to assess the financial results of the industries. In its place the Committee and others have recommended a system of direct subsidy, intended to settle responsibility for deciding the social obligations of the industries on the ministers concerned, where it is said to belong.

The famous statement of policy for the nationalized industries made in the White Paper of 1961, Command 1337, while announcing a new policy to treat the industries as 'commercial' bodies expected to earn a 'commercial' rate of return, made no reference to the responsibility for providing social services or to paying for these. It did recognize that individual boards carried on a number of 'commercially unprofitable activities' which might affect the level of their total costs. A small concession was made to the opponents of charging an indirect subsidy to an industry's ordinary consumers:

> 'These activities will, so far as practicable, have been taken into account in fixing the financial standard for each undertaking. To the extent that commercially unprofitable activities are subsequently imposed from outside, a Board would be entitled to ask for an adjustment of its financial objectives.'[7]

In other words boards would not be required by the government to use revenue from ordinary goods and services to provide social services. But it was still not explicit that these services would have to be paid for by the taxpayer instead.

Later the case for direct subsidies became more popular in government circles and in some cases such subsidies have been paid out to boards to cover the cost of specific services performed out of social obligation. Thus the Labour Government paid a grant to the CEGB to recoup additional costs of burning coal in power stations in place of oil, and compensated the Coal Board for losses arising from delays to the closure of pits imposed at government request. A new White Paper in 1967, Command 3437, announced this change in the Governments' policy:

> 'Where there are significant social or wider economic costs and benefits which ought to be taken into account in the industries' investment and pricing these will be reflected in the Government's policy for the industries, and if this means that the industry has to act against its own commercial interests the Government will accept responsibility. (Where necessary the Government will make a special payment to the industry or make an appropriate adjustment to its financial objective.)'[8]

There were probably two reasons for this change. First there had been increasing support for the argument that social obligations should be treated separately from the other duties and objectives of the nationalized industries, and should be clearly imposed by the government. Secondly, identifying and measuring the various benefits derived from social services provided by the industries had been made much easier by the development of new techniques of economic analysis, in particular by what is now widely known as *social cost/benefit analysis*.[9] However the Treasury was still not convinced that direct subsidies were altogether desirable and, as we shall see later, its doubts were well grounded.

However, quite apart from the provision of these social services, the nationalized industries seem inevitably to have wide social consequences. These social consequences seem not to be related to the form of ownership or control but to the nature of the activities in which the industries are engaged. It is difficult, for example, to see how the employment policy of the coal industry could have been treated other than as an issue of national importance, and much the same can be said for the commercial policies of the railways. Practically all of the nationalized industries perform activities which are vital to the general welfare of the country. Most are moreover public utilities in the traditional sense, and even the steel industry and the air corporations are engaged in activities which make a vital and substantial contribution to the gross national product. In most western capitalist countries, industries of this size and importance have been given extensive social obligations.

If we were to pursue the topic further now, we would become involved in very far-reaching issues concerning the effectiveness of different kinds of economic system. The most we shall conclude here is that many of the same qualities are shared by some industries which are not publicly owned in Britain, such as oil extraction and distribution, electrical engineering, shipping and so on. For an industry to have wide social consequences has not been regarded as a sufficient condition for nationalization, and public ownership is in itself no solution to the problems raised by the need for social obligations.

Indeed, one social obligation of the nationalized industries seems to be to avoid abusing their position as monopolies. The nationalization statutes give no explicit guidance in this respect apart from making instructions not to show 'undue preference', and using such words as 'economical', 'adequate' and so on to describe how goods and services should be provided. However it is obvious from government publications over the years that the element of monopoly in the industries has been one of the main grounds for government intervention. This was borne out by conversations with officials in the relevant departments, who still placed this very high on the list of motives for putting obligations on the industries in the public interest. However, it seems that public monopoly was to be treated differently from private monopoly, for the nationalized industries were not subject to the same machinery for control of restrictive practices as firms in the private sector. The control of both types of monopoly has nevertheless proved to be a general problem for postwar governments. More recently the pricing policies of both private and public industry have been referred to the National Board for Prices and Incomes (of which more below).

These social obligations of the nationalized industries are not firmly and unambiguously established (except perhaps those concerning consultation with workers and consumers). For the main part, they are at best mutually understood by government and boards, but there are considerable problems of definition and measurement and it is not clear who should be responsible for determining what social obligtions should be accepted. The obligations have ramifications for the general financial and economic policies of the boards and of the government as well. The fact that the industries are publicly owned has little or nothing to do with their existence, since most of them arise from the nature of the industries themselves. Some privately owned firms have similar obligations in varying degrees.

In fact it has been left very much to professional economists to find means of solving the problems which arise from these social obligations in the nationalised industries. These so-called 'social' aspects cannot be understood on their own, and overlap with the much wider economic aspects of the public interest.

ECONOMIC OBLIGATIONS

The policy of nationalization in the postwar years was intended to increase the power of the State in economic affairs. However, the nationalization statutes provided no basis of an economic policy for the industries. They were concerned rather with giving ministers the power to direct the industries in the interests of national economic policy, whatever that might be. Just exactly how the 'commanding heights of the economy' should be used has never been very clear.

In the first place we can identify, for our own purposes at least, three senses in which economic policy might affect the nationalized industries:

1. Obligations will be placed upon the industries arising from the government's economic policy in the short term: that is, its policy for controlling the business cycle and the balance of payments, and for dealing with immediate crises.
2. A more general objective of economic policy is the efficient and equitable allocation of resources (overlapping almost indistinguishably with the social policies of the government), and for this reason governments are concerned with prices and investment in the nationalized industries.
3. Most governments today include among their economic responsibilities the duty to encourage economic growth and development, and to foster technological innovation.

We shall deal with each of these aspects of economic policy in turn.

1. *Short-term Economic Policy*

This has been a continuing influence on the boards of the nationalized industries. It has almost certainly had a more direct impact on them than on firms in the private sector. Naturally, in modern conditions all forms of economic activity are restricted at one time or another by government measures designed to manage the national economy in the short term. In the case of the private sector this influence has generally been felt indirectly through changes in the levels of taxation and interest rates. In the case of nationalized industry the effect has more often been felt in the form of direct government intervention on pricing and investment policies.

Ministers are given no power in the statutes specifically to control prices in the nationalized industries. On only one occasion in the past has a minister taken advantage of his power to give general directions to a board in the national interest for this purpose.[10] Otherwise, what are known as 'gentlemen's agreements' have operated, whereby no change in the general level of an industry's prices has been made by a board without first getting the relevant sponsoring minister's approval. The inquiries of the Select Committee on Nationalized Industries have revealed how, again and again, this has led to boards postponing price increases in the public interest. The White Paper of 1961 admitted that:

> 'Although the Government possess no formal power to fix prices in the nationalized industries, nationalized undertakings have, in fixing their prices, given great weight to considerations of the national interest brought to their attention.'[11]

The Government hoped that the new arrangements for financial objectives announced in the White Paper would imply 'greater freedom and flexibility in the pricing policies of nationalized industries'. The existing 'gentlemen's agreements' would continue to apply, but in future the Government would be more willing to take responsibility for delays in price increases caused by its own economic policy:

> 'If a board decided to modify their own proposals by reason of views expressed by the minister it would be open to them to require a written statement of these views, which could be published by the minister, or the board, and to propose an appropriate adjustment of their financial objectives where, in their opinion, this modification would significantly impair their ability to meet them.'[12]

This statement of intent was made partly in response to continued criticism by the Select Committee on Nationalized Industries. If ministers wished to influence the pricing decisions of the boards in the interests of economic policy, said the Committee, they should be clearly seen to do so, otherwise it would be impossible to assess the performance of the industries. After 1965 the pricing policies of the industries were made subject to the Labour Government's general prices and incomes policy, and in September 1967 the Government announced that in future all major price increases in the nationalized industries would be referred to the National Board for Prices and Incomes.

In the case of investment, on the other hand, there is a clear statutory basis for ministerial control, in that the nationalization statutes empower the sponsoring minister concerned to approve from time to time the board's general programmes of capital investment.[13] Ministers are also empowered to control the industries' borrowing, but economic control of capital expenditure has been exercised mainly by means of the right to approve investment programmes. All the same a government has a direct means of influencing the level of long-term borrowing in the industries in that, since 1956, the latter have derived the bulk of their capital funds from the Exchequer. The system of borrowing on the market with Treasury guarantee was brought to an end in that year, but the change was regarded mainly as one of convenience and the extent of the State's liability was said to be practically unchanged.[14] The Treasury have always argued that a government's concern with the level of the industries' investment does not arise from these borrowing arrangements, but from the fact that a group of industries with an annual investment of about £1,300 million is bound to receive special attention from those responsible for the economic stability of the nation.

It is evident both from the Select Committee's inquiries and from our own research that the boards accept the need to adjust their own price and investment policies according to the short-term economic policy of the government of the day. There is less agreement, however, about the frequency of such adjustments, the method by which they should be made and their relation to other aims and obligations of the industries. For example, should the nationalized industries be subject to greater controls on their pricing and investment policies than industry in the private sector? There is a great temptation for governments to answer this question affirmatively in view of the national importance of the industries. Moreover it is clear that there are special advantages for economic management in the existence of a large nationalized sector, and these advantages are recognized by the government and are bound to be taken into consideration when weapons of short-term economic policy are chosen.[15]

What are the effects of these short-term interventions on the financial performance of the industries? Will allowance be made for the fact that individual boards may be unable to make a profit, or even to break-even financially as a consequence of restrictions on their pricing policies? What if boards are unable to take advantage of promising investment opportunities because of cuts arising from the government's economic policy? These are important questions for the government to answer, if only because continuing losses by the nationalized industries must lead eventually to increased borrowing or even to the kind of indebtedness which necessitates writing off a board's capital debt to the Exchequer. Moreover, another reason why the pricing and investment policies of the nationalized industries must be of general interest to the government is that the latter is concerned in the longer term with the allocation of resources, as we are about to see.

It was the need to relate interventions arising from short-term economic policy to other aspects of the public interest that led the Select Committee to criticize the methods by which ministers sought to influence the level of prices in the industries, and that led also to a concerted attempt throughout the 1960s to draw up a consistent and articulate policy for prices and investment in nationalized industry. Before the history of this can be told, we must first examine those other aspects of the public interest in more detail.

2. *Economic Policy in the Longer Term: the Allocation of Resources*

The level of prices and costs in the nationalized industries and the extent of their borrowing and investment are important for the economic welfare of the whole community. We have already rehearsed some of the reasons for this, such as the significance to society of the goods and services provided by the industries, the very size of the industries, and the fact that in some respects the industries are monopolies and so have considerable freedom in determining their own prices and output.

As we have already seen, the nationalization statutes offer little, if any, help to the boards of the nationalized industries in deciding what economic objectives to pursue. The general objective given to the boards is to cover their outgoings with revenue 'taking one year with another' or 'on an average of good and bad years'. This does not prevent individual boards 'cross-subsidizing' from one activity to another if market conditions allow, for 'outgoings' refers to expenditure on board's total activities. We have already noted that there are statutory provisions restricting the boards from showing 'undue preference' to different consumers, although it is almost impossible to say what these provisions mean. However, the 'outgoings' which have to be covered are fairly well defined in the Statutes and include such things as depreciation or renewal of assets, and paying off capital debts. In other words, the boards are expected to make a profit of some kind, but exactly what kind of profit is far from clear.

For about a decade following nationalization most of the industries interpreted their duty to cover costs as referring to average costs and so widely adopted pricing policies which did not charge all types of consumer the exact cost of meeting their demand. It is now generally admitted that price levels in most of the industries were kept artificially low during the same period in the public interest. This policy led to a heated controversy among economists, carried on mainly between those who favoured a policy based on average costs and those who wanted one based on marginal costs. The way the industries made provision for capital expenses and for depreciation also led to criticism. Indeed two kinds of attack were made on the industries' financial policies towards the end of the 1950s, the first that their prices were too low, and the second (which was far from universally accepted) that there was considerable over-investment in the industries.[16] These criticisms, which were to some extent politically motivated, led to demands for more precise definition of economic objectives.

Some of the boards were certainly making annual deficits of alarming proportions and most of them had been unable to provide from their own earnings for the replacement of assets. The first important call for more financial discipline in the industries came from the Herbert Committee, which attacked the boards' woolly notions of serving the public interest:

> 'We state our view without any qualification that the governing factor in the minds of those running the boards should be that it is their duty to run them as economic concerns and to make them pay.'[17]

The Select Committee on Nationalized Industries unearthed one or two striking examples of bad investment decisions in particular industries and this helped to strengthen feeling that the industries were a drain on scarce resources. The use of words such as 'commercial', 'economic', 'business-like', and 'paying one's way' were used with more frequency than precision. However, they generally implied that some substitute was needed in the nationalized sector for the natural economic disciplines which the forces of the market were supposed to place on private firms.

The famous White Paper of 1961 was designed mainly as a response to these criticisms. The Government now announced new policies in three aspects of the industries' financial affairs. First, the requirement to 'break even' would be interpreted as meaning that the boards' surpluses on revenue account should be at least sufficient to cover deficits over a five-year period. These surpluses should provide, not only for paying the cost of interest and depreciation (charged on a historic-cost basis), but also for making reserves available to enable assets to be replaced at current prices, and to help finance future capital development. For this purpose the Government would proceed to agree with the boards on financial objectives for the following five-year period. Secondly, the Government codified the existing procedures for approving the industries' investment programmes. No specific rates of return were discussed in the White Paper but the Government announced that it would fix each year an upper limit on the amounts to be spent on investment by each undertaking during the two years ahead. The Government would also expect to be 'kept informed of the extent to which the undertaking is proposing to invest new capital in projects which are expected to yield a relatively low return'. Finally, the industries would be given a greater 'freedom and flexibility' in fixing prices where they found this necessary in order to achieve their new objectives.[18] In the few years following the publication of the White Paper financial objectives were settled for most of the industries and were expressed in most cases in terms of a percentage return on net or gross assets. The objectives varied from industry to industry and were reviewed annually.

Although they went some way to answer the demands for more financial discipline in the nationalized industries and did much to give clearer guidance to the boards, in fact these policies did little to satisfy the needs of economic policy. The financial objectives meant different things for different boards and in general the system did not lead to the establishment of clear economic criteria for the financial policies of the industries. It was insufficiently precise as a means of controlling prices and investment. In emphasizing the achievement of financial results, it reflected the principles of accountancy and management in private enterprise, but not those of the economist concerned with the optimum allocation of resources, and with the balance of the national economy over the longer term.

Gradually an alternative doctrine began to get the upper hand. This can be summed up in the words of the Select Committee on Nationalized Industries:

> 'financial results should be an expression of economic policies, and not an end in themselves. . . . much more emphasis is placed on achieving an optimum allocation of resources: pricing policies and investment criteria should be envisaged with this end in mind.'[19]

There was later a definite change of emphasis in government policy for the nationalized industries, reflecting increased support for this doctrine in government circles. Partly as a result of this the arrangements set up in 1961 were reconsidered and the results reported in the new White Paper of 1967. What this White Paper described, however, was a compromise between a number of different points of view within the administration. It indicated that the Government had not decided what its economic policy for the nationalized industries should be. Any compromise based on what are really rather complex economic arguments is bound to read rather oddly, and the 1967 White Paper certainly contained a number of contradictions. This is not surprising for the White Paper was a political document attempting quite properly to reconcile a number of different interests and was not an essay in economic theory. (Perhaps what its inadequacies illustrated above all were the limitations of economics as a guide to decision-making in government.) One voice which was trying to be heard through the 1967 White Paper seemed to be saying that the Government should as a priority see that resources were allocated 'upon an economically and socially rational basis'. Another voice was calling for more financial discipline as suggested originally by the 1961 White Paper. There were other voices as well which merged with each other and with those just identified, but it would be difficult and rather pointless to distinguish them all.

The main positive developments in economic policy which the 1967 White Paper announced affected the criteria for investment decisions and the system of pricing. In the first place, the Government now took upon itself the responsibility for laying down a particular *test rate of discount* to be used in calculating the return on new investment projects in the industries. The choice of a suitable rate expressed the government's view of the desirable allocation of investment resources. However, there were different views of how this choice should be made. Should one be guided by some estimate of the prevailing rate of return in the private sector? Or should one devise some special rate to reflect the social objectives of the government?

It is now generally agreed that the government ought to arrive at some appropriate measure of the cost of investing in public undertakings. The orthodox view in the late 1960s seemed to be that the discount rate chosen for public investment should be based on the opportunity-cost of the investment, in other words: 'the value to society of the use to which the resources employed in the project would otherwise have been put'.[20] It was officially assumed that investment in public enterprise displaced at the margin investment in the private sector. Thus the discount rate selected for the nationalized industries was calculated from the marginal rate of return expected from comparable investments in private industry. By this means the Government sought to promote 'the most efficient distribution of goods and services in the economy as a whole'.[21]

One objection to this procedure is that it might prevent a number of 'socially-desirable' projects being undertaken. In the first place, why should it be assumed that investing in public enterprise displaces only investment in private industry? Should not governments reach some decision of their own about how much should be invested in general, as well as what forms such investment should take? Many economists would argue that the prevailing market rate of discount does not reflect the true cost to society of future, as opposed to present, consumption at the margin. They would suggest that the government should devise a rate of its own on the basis of its policies for such things as economic growth, income distribution, and so on.

A further difficulty is that the real benefits from a particular investment may well not be reflected in the cash-flows to the enterprise undertaking it. In the event that they are not, the profitability of the undertaking is no test of the desirability of the investment. Indeed, both the cost and benefits of investment in nationalized industries will often not appear in the accounts of the board concerned. For one thing, as we have already seen, the nationalized industries perform a number of social services, the net benefit of which cannot be measured in cash-flows to and from the board. This may be, for example, because the actual beneficiaries do not pay for the services provided. The pricing policy of an industry may also detract from economic efficiency, not for social reasons, but because the board seeks to maximize profits in a situation where marginal cost is below average cost.

Even if the pricing policy of a nationalized industry were designed to take account of these and other inconsistencies with economic efficiency, there would still be some costs and benefits associated with its activities which could not be expressed in cash-flows at all. As we have seen, the activities of the nationalized industries in this country are important for the welfare of the whole community and cannot be considered apart from matters of public concern such as regional employment, technological development, the balance of payments and so on. Some would say in addition that the financial policies of the industries should be deliberately used to support government policy for the distribution of income.

The new arrangements for investment in 1967 were not to preclude consideration of social costs and benefits. The Government had also been developing techniques of economic analysis to enable it to assess more accurately the wider social and economic consequences of the activities of public enterprises. In many cases all the net benefits expected from a project could be found in the net cash-flows to the undertaking:

'But where there are grounds for thinking that the social costs of benefits do diverge markedly from those associated with the alternatives the Government will take this into account when assessing the investment. Indeed it must take a wider view than that of the industry itself since the Government's objective is to secure the maximum social return on the capital invested while the industry's concern is properly with the financial return.'[22]

Moreover, the 1967 White Paper expressed the view that 'prices need to be reasonably related to costs at the margin and to be designed to promote the efficient use of resources within industry'. There was no explanation in the White Paper of what 'reasonably related' was intended to mean, but it was clear from this, and from the Treasury's evidence to the Select Committee on Nationalized Industries in 1967, that marginal-cost pricing had now been recommended to the industries as an economically desirable policy.[23]

It might seem from this that the Government had gone a long way to accept the optimum allocation of resources as its overriding objective and had relegated its concern about the profitability of individual boards in the industries where marginal costs tend to be less than average costs. This was far from being the case, however, and no such commitment was expressed in the White Paper:

'The Government's policy starts . . . from the principle that nationalized industries' revenues should normally cover their accounting costs in full – including the service of capital and appropriate provision for its replacement.'[24]

This would require in many cases – where increasing returns apply – a policy of making prices equal to average costs. Moreover, although pricing and investment policies were now intended to be the direct instruments of economic control of the industries, financial objectives continued to be set and were still necessary as a means of control 'over the return achieved on a very substantial public investment'. The system of setting objectives was to be much more flexible than before, allowing for a variety of types of objective, and the Government was willing to review targets in the light of changing circumstances. However, the financial objectives were not to be derived by 'an arithmetical exercise' from prices and the return on investment. The Government was clearly unwilling to face the prospect of industries earning deficits as a result of marginal cost pricing (as might happen for example, in industries such as the gas industry, following the discovery of North Sea Gas).[25] On the other hand, the Government was also clearly not prepared to see prices rise too rapidly, and by referring their increases to the National Board for Prices and Incomes intended that the industries cooperate in carrying out the prices and incomes policy.[26]

Government economic policy for the nationalized industries seemed in 1967, therefore, to be a mixture of sometimes incompatible objectives. The 1967 White Paper expressed rather than resolved these conflicting objectives. Thus, although it represented a step in the direction of making the optimum allocation of resources an overriding aim of economic policy, the White Paper did not say how far social costs and benefits should be taken into account in the management of the nationalized industries. It was significant, moreover, that the White Paper stated that the Government and not the industries should be responsible for taking social costs and benefits into account.[27] By its vague and sometimes contradictory wording it also failed to establish any kind of precedence among resource allocation, short-term economic management and the profitability of individual enterprises. These three objectives will often conflict. What is perhaps most serious is that it was unclear whether, where there was conflict, the boards themselves should pursue the policies suggested by those wider economic considerations, or should aim to earn a surplus on revenue account. Finally, it was still uncertain what role should be played by the Government's policy for the various sectors such as transport, and fuel and power. For it has become an increasing preoccupation of government to assist technological innovation and growth not only in individual sectors but in the economy as a whole.

3. *Economic Development and Technology*

The government's economic interest in the nationalized industries is not confined to short-term management of the economy or to ensuring an efficient allocation of resources. Particularly after 1964 the central government in Britain sought to develop long-term objectives for industry which aimed to increase productivity of both labour and capital, get the most technologically advanced equipment adopted, and encourage growth in key sectors. These have been general aims of industrial policy and produced in the late 1960s new government departments, such as the Ministry of Technology, and new kinds of contact between government and industry, such as the 'little neddies' and the regional development councils. The sponsoring departments concerned with the nationalized industries have had their part to play in this by expanding and elaborating industrial policy for their respective sectors. The investment plans of the nationalized industries have been seen as a principal instrument for this purpose. Indeed the 1967 White Paper made this a basic reason for the Government' concern with investment in the industries:

> 'The development plans for industrial sectors must greatly influence investment decisions made by individual public corporations, and, conversely, the pattern of investment decisions that is expected provides some of the basic information on which broad industrial policies are formulated by the appropriate Government Departments in consultation with the industries.'

The Paper also stated that prices 'need to be set in the framework of government policy for the sector as a whole'.[28]

In so far as the requirements of economic development impose obligations on the nationalized industries these might conflict with the industries' social obligations. For social obligations include a duty to protect the welfare of particular groups which society (or the government of the day) feels obliged to shelter from the direct effects of economic activity. It is possible to criticize such interference with the 'natural' behaviour of the market on the grounds that it slows down adaptation to change, weakens initiative, and thus in the longer run harms those it is designed to assist. Sometimes, indeed, when a government feels obliged to intervene in order to speed up change, its social and economic objectives conflict.

Quite apart from the broad objective of ensuring cheap and plentiful supplies of essential commodities, a policy for economic development may impose special measures on the nationalized industries in order to help particular industries in the private sector. The nationalized industries' vast capital expenditure on such things as nuclear power stations, aircraft, telecommunications equipment, and so on, means that a number of key industries in the private sector depend on the nationalized industries for a substantial amount of their income. In the past, governments have taken advantage of this fact to support British industries, for example, in persuading BOAC to buy British-made aircraft and in encouraging the electricity supply industry to commit itself to the first nuclear power programme. The full extent to which this aspect of public procurement is used by governments is not fully known. (Aspects of this are the subject of another current PEP study.) We shall say no more about it here, except to point out that this is clearly one other area of the industries' management where wider economic factors may be taken into account.

The development of technologically advanced methods and the adoption of policies to favour national economic growth will often, of course, be consistent with the undertaking's own profitability. It could be argued that the best conditions for achieving these aims are a competitive spirit and a determination to increase productivity. However, governments over the years seem to have doubted whether these conditions existed in the nationalized industries. They have generally felt it necessary to some extent to pay special attention to this aspect of the industries' management. Indeed, one aim of the previous Government's fuel policy was that the fuel industries should be 'technically progressive and viable'.[29] The efficiency of the industries and the general competence of their management is thus one aspect of their economic obligations in the public interest. This can lead to a lot of confusion about the role of nationalized undertakings, as we shall see.

One striking feature of the social and economic obligations of the nationalized industries, as these have been defined here, is that invariably they reflect general objectives of government policy for industry as a whole and are not peculiar to nationalized industry. Private firms sometimes perform social services – either of their own accord or at government request (although when the latter is the case they are usually compensated by some financial payment or concession). They are also required to refrain from certain restrictive practices and abuses of monopoly. They are clearly affected by the measures used by governments to manage the economy in the short term. They can, if it is thought necessary, be influenced to adopt pricing and investment policies designed to promote an efficient allocation of resources, and can be (and are) induced to contribute to technological advancement. The impact of a government's social and economic objectives may be felt differently in the private sector. Private firms are not actually given instructions by statute to serve the public interest. Nevertheless, for the main part, the social and economic obligations of the nationalized industries do not arise from nationalization and were not created by statute: indeed there is hardly any guidance in the statutes to what the specific obligations of the industries are. Moreover most of the problems raised by these social and economic aspects of the public interest are general problems of allocating resources in a large and complex economy.

How, then, was nationalization meant to help? In what way are the nationalized industries meant to make a special contribution to solving these problems? This is still far from agreed. It is still not decided how responsibility for social and economic objectives should be allocated between government and boards; and the associated difficulty of allocating the cost of undertaking obligations in the public interest remains. When should a nationalized undertaking take wider social and economic objectives into account, and how is one to know that it has done so adequately and properly? How should such wider obligations be allowed to affect an individual undertaking's financial results? What weight should be given to different objectives when they conflict?

As we have already seen the problem is complicated by the fact that governments are interested, not only in getting nationalized industries to agree to broad social and economic objectives, but also in seeing that narrower standards of performance are attained. In fact the public interest extends beyond the social and economic obligations which we have been discussing here. It also gives undertakings the duty to achieve a certain level of performance in their commercial operations, a level measured by financial results or by general standards of management and service. That duty imposes obligations which are mostly different from those we have dealt with here, for then the public interest is usually engaged precisely because the industries are nationalized.

REFERENCES

1. *Report of the Committee of Inquiry into the Electricity Supply Industry* (*Herbert Report*), 1956, Cmnd. 9672.
2. D. Coombes, *The Member of Parliament and the Administration*, George Allen & Unwin, 1966, pp. 132–54.
3. H. Morrison, *Socialization and Transport*, 1933, pp. 156–7.
4. W. A. Robson, *Nationalized Industry and Public Ownership*, George Allen & Unwin, 1962, 2nd edn, pp. 297–8.
5. Coal Industry Nationalization Act 1946. Italics added.
6. See, in particular: PEP *Security of Employment: A study in the Construction Industry*, Broadsheet No. 505, 1968; *Company Giving*, Broadsheet No. 511, 1969; Mrs B. Shenfield, *Company Boards*, George Allen & Unwin for PEP, 1971.
7. *Financial and Economic Obligations of the Nationalized Industries*, Cmnd. 1337, 1961, para. 32.
8. *The Nationalized Industries: A Review of Economic and Financial Objectives*, Cmnd. 3437, para. 37.
9. See, for example, M. E. Beesley and C. D. Foster, 'The Victoria Line: Social Benefit and Finance', *Journal of the Royal Statistical Society* (Series A) 1965, and 'Estimating the Social Benefit of Constructing an Underground Railway in London', *op. cit.*, 1963. See also, First Report from Select Committee on Nationalized Industries Session 1967–8, *Ministerial Control of the Nationalized Industries*, HC 371, vol. III, pp. 29–33 (Treasury memorandum on social cost/benefit analysis).

10. This was in 1952, instructing the British Transport Commission not to increase passenger charges for rail travel outside London. For a long time the rates and charges of the nationalized transport services were subject to approval by the Transport Tribunal. This body, which inherited its powers from similar bodies dating back to the middle of the nineteenth century, had its powers greatly reduced by the Transport Act, 1953, and was abolished altogether outside the London area in 1962. The Minister of Transport could, under Section 47(1) of the Transport Act, 1962, at any time require the Transport Tribunal to review the level of fares charged by the London Transport Board. An important exception to the general rule of formal freedom of boards to fix prices is the case of the air corporations. The international fares of BEA and BOAC are fixed by the governments concerned through their membership of IATA (International Air Transport Association). Under the Civil Aviation (Licensing Powers) Act of 1960 fares on BEA's domestic services are fixed by the Air Transport Licensing Board.
11. Cmnd. 1337, *op. cit.*, para. 29.
12. *Ibid.*, paras. 30–1.
13. With the exception of the air corporations. The same power was not extended to the Minister of Aviation until the Air Corporations Act, 1966.
14. Cmnd. 1337 *op. cit.*, para. 27.
15. *Ministerial Control of the Nationalized Industries. op. cit.*, vol. I, paras. 270 and 392, and vol. III, Evidence from the Chief Secretary to the Treasury, q. 2362.
16. For a discussion of these criticisms by an economist, see W. G. Shepherd, *Economic Performance under Public Ownership: British Fuel and Power*, New Haven and London, 1963.
17. *Herbert Report*, *op. cit.*, para. 507.
18. Cmnd. 1337, *op. cit.*, paras. 19–20, 24–6.
19. *Ministerial Control*, *op. cit.*, vol. I, para. 193.
20. P. D. Henderson, 'Investment Criteria for Public Enterprise', in R. Turvey (ed.), *Public Enterprise*, Penguin Books, London, 1968, p. 103.
21. Cmnd. 3437, *op. cit.*, para. 7.
22. *Ibid.*, para. 14.
23. *Ibid.*, para. 21. *Ministerial Control*, *op. cit.*, vol. II, pp. 4–7.
24. Cmnd. 3437, *op. cit.*, para. 17.
25. *Ibid.*, paras. 21–2, 33–5.
26. *Ibid.*, paras. 25–6.
27. *Ibid.*, para. 15.
28. *Ibid.*, paras. 6 and 22.
29. Ministry of Power, *Fuel Policy*, Cmnd. 2798, October 1965, para. 35.

Chapter 4

FINANCIAL OBLIGATIONS

It might be argued that the wider social and economic obligations of the nationalized industries were so important that the financial results of each individual undertaking should have no significance except as a reflection of a government's social and economic policies. In other words public ownership might be supposed to be a means of taking responsibilities for industrial decisions out of the hands of the directors of particular undertakings and giving it to ministers. Ministers could then delegate the taking of certain decisions to lower levels, whether these levels constituted 'autonomous boards' or degrees in the hierarchy of the civil service. To be more extreme the nationalized industries could have been simply included in the welfare services already provided by the central government. For example, instead of fixing a minimum rate of return for the industries' investment, the government could simply set a limit to each undertaking's capital expenditure each year following a decision in the cabinet about the desirable allocation of public expenditure. Prices could then be set according to what was considered desirable in social and economic terms. One suspects that some people might prefer arrangements of this type.

In theory this approach has been rejected. It has been the declared policy of all governments to treat the nationalized industries as 'commercial' undertakings. This practice is implied by the statutes and was strongly asserted by Morrison and other supporters of nationalization. In so far as standards such as profitability, financial viability, and 'commercial success' are commonly adopted by governments in judging the industries, then the achievement of these standards is clearly a duty in the public interest. So the nationalized industries were not – and are not in general terms – intended to accept social and economic obligations as a priority compared with achieving positive financial results.

The organization created by nationalization reflects this approach quite clearly, for the industries were vested in public corporations which retained their own commercial accounts and were given freedom to frame their own policies for pricing, employment, methods of production and so on. Indeed, unless the industries are 'commercial' the arrangements provided by the statutes were most inadequate for ensuring effective and efficient performance. Devolution to 'autonomous boards' is one thing, and there are enough examples of that being done with satisfactory results in British central government. But to assume that the corporations vested with the nationalized industries were intended simply to carry out approved social and economic policies would be to throw a completely new light on the relationship between government and nationalized industries. We shall return to this important question of assessing performance below. It is fairly obvious, however, that the nationalized industries were not meant to be extensions of government departments but 'commercial' bodies, and that their performance was to be judged by 'commercial' standards. The problem is that it has never been clear what this expression is intended to mean.

THE MEANING OF 'COMMERCIAL'

The original purpose of using this expression was most likely to emphasize that the public corporations vested with the industries were to be organized like private companies rather than like government departments or other public agencies. In this sense it still applies. For example, the boards of the nationalized industries are still required to break even financially over a period of years. They are more or less free within this framework and – subject recently to the Government's prices and incomes policy – to fix individual prices to their consumers and to negotiate wages and salaries with their staff. They are also free to invest capital (which is, however, expected to yield more than a certain minimum return). The Treasury does not allocate funds to the industries in the same way as it does to other parts of the public sector. Similarly, again with certain limitations and within this general framework, the boards are free to vary the quantity and type of service they provide to consumers and to hire and fire staff. No minister is answerable to Parliament for the day-to-day conduct of the boards and their staff are not members of the civil service.

As we have seen the term was not given any more precise meaning than this until the White Paper of 1961, which was itself a response to criticism of insufficient 'commercial' discipline in the industries. It now came to mean the obligation to achieve certain financial results on trading – results agreed in advance between ministers and boards. This definition did not go far enough to satisfy all the criticisms, as we shall see. Indeed what seemed to worry bodies like the Herbert

Committee was that the mechanisms assumed to operate in the private sector to provide certain financial constraints on the behaviour of an undertaking did not exist – at least to the same degree – in the nationalized industries. In particular, the nationalized undertakings did not compete on equal terms with private firms for capital on the market (and did not raise long-term capital on the market at all after 1956). Most of them have not faced full competition in the sale of their products and services. There is also little danger that individual undertakings will go bankrupt without being financially reconstituted by the government. In other words, the word 'commercial' has come to be used to represent an image of the checks and balances on behaviour which exist in the private sector. Whether this image is a realistic one need not concern us for the moment and we shall return to that later.

However, it is worth commenting now that in a more recent application the word 'commercial' seems to mean an economically optimum allocation of resources. In this sense it would be part of an undertaking's wider social and economic obligations to be 'commercial'. This is a weak use of the term, because commercial activities in general are not always thought to be economically efficient. It is not clear whether this usage is meant to imply that the checks and balances of the private sector do in fact lead to economic efficiency. To make such an implication would naturally be to beg the question. Even a policy of maximizing profits may not lead to an optimum allocation in all circumstances. Indeed, as we have seen, it is only as a result of tortuous study and argument that policies have been designed for the nationalized industries in the hope that their pricing and investment policies will lead to economic efficiency. It is still not clear what should happen when this objective conflicts with others, such as profitability, or serving some other social or economic obligation. A policy to promote economic efficiency should surely not be distinguished by the term 'commercial'.

Indeed, when the minimum return on any new investment and the system of pricing are determined in advance, it is quite legitimate to ask whether any scope is left for the boards to behave 'commercially'. Some economists would argue (as would now the Select Committee on Nationalized Industries) that the financial objectives of the industries should merely be calculated from a given test rate of discount on investment and prices which are equal to long-run marginal costs. If financial objectives were so derived, would any commercially important decisions be left for the boards to take?

There would certainly be important questions left to the board of the industry. First, there are the great variety of decisions associated with predicting the future, in particular forecasting demand and thus deciding how much to produce. In investment decisions the board would still need to be responsible for assessing risk. Secondly, there is the general aim of reducing costs and increasing productivity by means of encouraging technical innovation, improving labour relations, and developing new management techniques. Following from this in competitive conditions there is the challenge to win new customers by varying the quality and price of the product. Control of the investment by fixing a rate of return and of prices by laying down a rule about marginal costs, clearly leaves the board of a nationalized industry with a great deal of discretion in commercial matters. One of the main arguments in favour of this type of control is that it would leave the board better equipped to perform its essentially 'commercial' role, leaving the 'public interest' to the minister.

All the same, this is a rather emasculated concept of 'commercial' and it has none of the empire-building or self-aggrandizing connotations of the traditional image of the entrepreneur. Yet it is the notion of 'commercial' recommended by the Select Committee on Nationalized Industries:

> 'Being enterprising in seeking markets, discovering and exploiting technical advances, reducing unit costs wherever possible, and generally . . . adopting a "business-like" attitude.'[1]

This comes very close to some modern paradigms of administrative efficiency, and even to some more traditional ones as well. The characteristics described would not be out of place in many modern government departments (although 'seeking new markets' would clearly be out of place in defence and the hospital service, for example!). Is there a lot of difference between this definition of 'commercial' and one's normal expectations of competent, progressive and efficient administration? The Select Committee admits that in common use the word also refers to 'the main objective of the private business man, namely profit maximization and expansion into other fields of activity', but says that it does not wish to include these in its own definition. Perhaps the notion the Committee was really looking for was simply 'well-managed' or 'competent'. The question which really should be asked (but which the Select Committee has never put) is: under what conditions is one likely to get well-managed and competent industrial undertakings?

If the term 'commercial' were to be restored to its meaning in the dictionary ('of, engaged in, and bearing on commerce') then there would be no problem in applying it freely to the nationalized industries. The boards of these industries are evidently engaged in 'the exchange of merchandise especially on a large scale'.[2] It is clearly in the public interest that this should be done competently and efficiently. How to ensure that commercial undertakings are well and efficiently run is a question that is still largely unanswered in spite of the enormous time spent by accountants, economists, civil servants and others in looking for 'commercial' standards for the nationalized industries.

THE ROLE OF FINANCIAL OBJECTIVES

In fact the financial obligations of the nationalized industries are not simply deduced from social and economic obligations. In spite of being criticized for doing so, the last Government decided that financial objectives for the nationalized industries did have some value in their own right, even though economically justified investment and pricing policies might have been prescribed already. In so doing, what were they implying about the duties of the nationalized industries? It has never been very clear what the financial objectives fixed for the industries since 1961 are meant to represent and it was still far from clear at the end of the 1960s.

The original objectives, as we have already mentioned, meant different things for different industries. In the case of London Transport, the financial objective was: 'simply an accountant's measure of the minimum the industry should earn if they were to fulfil their statutory duty of paying their way'. In the case of BEA, it represented: 'what was considered to be an attainable return' which, it was recognized, was not 'the rate of return which a fully commercial undertaking would expect to attain in the private sector generally'. The objective of the Post Office was based largely on past results projected into the future. The actual objective for the National Coal Board has fluctuated over the years and was overshadowed by the writing-off of £415 million of the Board's capital debt in 1965. Basically it was to break even over the five-year period of the objective while at the same time paying for the replacement of fixed assets. Only in the case of the gas and electricity supply industries and telecommunications did the original financial objectives provide for the earning of a sizeable surplus towards financing future capital requirements.[3]

There seem to be three main purposes for financial objectives at present. The first is simply to give the undertakings some yardstick of performance to use as a guide to management, both as a control and as an incentive. There is general agreement about their value in this respect. They are a means here to ensure the managerial competence and efficiency to which many people refer by using the term 'commercial'.

Although it was never admitted, this particular reason for setting financial objectives was probably the most important of all when they were first conceived. The 1961 White Paper appeared after a long period in which the financial performance of most of the industries had been severely criticized from business circles and from the back-benches of the Conservative Party. The National Coal Board had made a loss on revenue account in every year but one, between 1954 and 1959, and the British Transport Commission had made a loss in every year during the same period, having an accumulated deficit of £350 million in 1959. As the 1961 White Paper took pains to point out, in most cases the low return on capital earned in the public, as opposed to the private, sector could be explained by the many social and economic obligations which the boards had accepted. At about the same time, however, the Select Committee castigated the British Transport Commission, the Ministry of Transport and the Treasury in a report on the railways which revealed accounting methods which would have been quite unacceptable in private enterprise.[4] It is now widely argued that, for at least the first ten to fifteen years of nationalization, most of the boards of the nationalized industries placed insufficient emphasis on financial results. In the structure of their formal organization, in the qualifications of the men appointed to the boards, and in the outlook of senior management staff, the main priority in most cases was output or the provision of a service. As we have seen this was not incompatible with the statutes. Indeed, the structures, methods and attitudes associated with private commercial enterprise have been acquired slowly, if at all. 'For the greater part of the period since the outbreak of the Second World War the object of the industry has been to increase or maintain output; output rather than price has dominated the minds of its management.'[5] This remark on the coal industry could apply to a number of cases (and particularly to the railways before the appointment of Dr Beeching as Chairman).

The worst problems were not solved by the system of financial objectives. We have already remarked on the decision to write off £415 million of the Coal Board's capital debt in 1965. BOAC had £110 million of its capital debt written off in the same year. The British Transport Commission was abolished in 1963, and replaced by separate boards for each of the main transport undertakings. At the same time, £1,192 million of its capital debt was cancelled. However, the Transport Act of 1968 has already written off another £557 million of debt of the Railways Board. Following that experience it is not surprising that, quite apart from any economic considerations, governments should be anxious to ensure financial discipline. Just what financial discipline means, how far it can be said to exist in an undertaking making continuing losses, and whether it means the same thing as competent and efficient management, are questions to which we shall return.

The government's concern with financial results is all the greater in that it is obliged to act as the industries' 'banker'. Since 1956 the industries have borrowed straight from the consolidated fund and even before that most of them borrowed on the market only with Treasury guarantee. This brings us to a second motive for setting financial objectives for the industries, namely the government's interest as 'banker' and source of long-term funds to a very sizeable, and sometimes extravagant, customer. This motive has been underplayed, even in the 1961 White Paper, in an attempt to give wider economic objectives more prominence. However it is still an important underlying force in the government's relations with the nationalized industries. Our own conversations with departmental officials suggest that it is much more strongly felt than published statements of government policy would suggest (although strangely enough this seems to be more so in the sponsoring departments than in the Treasury). This impression could be supported from a variety of published sources.

We have already remarked that there is not complete agreement about the general pricing rules recommended by the 1967 White Paper. There is especial anxiety about observing such rules in cases where they would lead to deficits. As representatives of the Ministry of Power told the Select Committee:

> 'Our enthusiasm for marginal-cost pricing has to be matched against our enthusiasm for a reasonable degree of financial probity.'[6]

The Permanent Secretary to the Ministry of Transport told the Committee that the Government's concern with pricing and investment in the railways and London Transport was bound to be predominantly financial rather than economic, the immediate and urgent aim being to reduce deficits in face of competition:

> 'If you are pursuing a practical objective of that kind, . . . trying to get your prices as near to the point of what the market will bear as you can, then the more theoretical and abstract considerations about what pricing policy ought to be do not really apply.'[7]

The Head of the Government Economic Service said that financial objectives were required among other things to guide the boards in fixing prices in the short run, since 'the long-run marginal cost formula is not one that gives a precise price in every set of circumstances', while some consideration should be given to the 'eventual surplus' which the industry was expected to earn. (In the same way the test rate of discount would not give 'a precise amount of investment'.[8]) This view was supported by the Permanent Secretary to the Ministry of Power. Financial objectives could not be simply derived from a particular pricing policy, he said, because the Treasury 'are interested in the amount of new investment which is financed by surpluses in a very straightforward and necessary way.'[9]

The idea that the industries should finance more of their investment from their own resources was particularly influential when the system of financial objectives was introduced in 1961. However, the Treasury's views about self-financing were far from settled even as late as 1966.[10] To set financial objectives for this purpose may well tend to conflict with other needs of the public interest. In the first place, although governments might be anxious to limit the borrowing of the nationalized industries in order to control inflation, objectives designed to provide for self-financing might require increases in prices in the nationalized industries which themselves produce inflationary pressure. Secondly, self-financing is not always a sign of competitiveness and cost-consciousness in the nationalized industries, for many of the undertakings enjoy a considerable amount of monopoly so that they can achieve objectives simply by raising prices in conditions of inelastic demand. There are examples where both these consequences have come about as a result of a policy of self-financing.[11] In other words, there is no magic in financial objectives and it is important to be clear exactly what aspect of the public interest – short-term economic policy, financial probity, economic efficiency, lower prices – is being promoted in setting them.

This brings us to a third purpose for financial objectives, which is again not always as articulate in public statements of policy as it is influential on the actual thinking of administrators: namely that maximization of profits cannot be allowed in the nationalized industries. In view of this the financial objective agreed between government and board is a means of fixing price levels (in the long- and short-term) which are 'reasonable' and which do not exploit monopoly. In the words of the Permanent Secretary to the Ministry of Power before the Select Committee, they provide 'an appropriate return for a public utility' in the absence of maximization of profits. This was expressed even more precisely by the same witness when he was asked whether the financial objectives represented a maximum, so that the Government would be 'very distressed' if it were exceeded: 'Not if it did so by reducing its costs, but very much if it did so by increasing the cost of fuel to the consumer'.[12]

It is obviously quite inadequate to describe the role of financial objectives as being to make the nationalized industries 'commercial'. In the first place they are not intended to produce a copy of what happens in private enterprise. Of course not enough is known about what does happen in private enterprise and that is one source of the difficulty of determining the obligations of the nationalized industries. However it does not seem to be considered in the public interest for the boards of the nationalized industries to adopt entrepreneurial attitudes such as profit maximization and expansion. The financial objectives are intended above all to provide financial restraint, whether as a means of preventing loose financial control of management, or as a prevention of abuse of monopoly. In these respects some kind of control is clearly essential in the public interest. The ideal competitive forces, which are meant to control markets for both capital and consumers in the interest of efficiency in private enterprise, do not exist in the case of nationalized industries. Because the industries are nationalized, financial obligations must be placed on them in the public interest. The question is: what kind of obligation?

Since the nationalized industries are apparently meant to be organized as commercial undertakings on a model more or less close to that of private firms, then there are good grounds for using financial results as a measure of managerial performance. But who should decide what results are satisfactory? In so far as the financial objectives are really aimed at ensuring good management, what is 'good management', what are the purposes of these undertakings and who decides them? It could be argued from the statutes that the answer to all these questions is that the boards of the industries are responsible for setting objectives and controlling management. Indeed in the present system financial objectives are said to be *agreed* between ministers and boards, not fixed by the government. What purposes are the boards supposed to seek in this process, apart from seeing that the undertakings for which they are responsible conform to the objectives set? This has never been made clear. What is the board's duty in the public interest? Is it to maximize profits as it is said a private entrepreneur would seek to do, or to aim at expansion, or what?

Now there is clearly a strong feeling that financial objectives are more than a means of controlling management. Already they have been used in some ways to express social and economic objectives; it was the original intention that allowance should be made for the boards' obligations in this respect in setting the financial objectives.[13] As we have seen, there are some who want the objectives simply to reflect optimum pricing and investment policies, optimum in the economists' sense of an efficient allocation of resources. Others place less emphasis on this, doubting whether it is desirable to go so far, and seek rather to use the financial objectives to control the supply of capital to the industries, whether from some vague concern for financial probity, or in the interest of short-term management of the national economy. Financial objectives seem to be used to take account of the problem of monopoly as well. In fact none of these purposes is sought exclusively and, as we have just seen, some conflict with others. What is most likely is that those responsible for setting the objectives are not clear in their own minds at any one time what the objectives really represent.

One problem seems to be that nationalization, having made a clean break with those ideal competitive forces which are thought to act on private firms, has made it necessary to place certain artificial financial obligations on the nationalized undertakings. Governments may have come to realize this too slowly, but there can be no mistaking that they have realized it now. They are very aware of their responsibilities as 'bankers' to the industries; of the need to extend to these industries a form of control, such as the monopolies legislation affecting the private sector; and above all, of the fact that since there are no private shareholders someone has to hold the boards accountable for the performance of the management.

There is another problem and this is that some people would reject the model just used of an ideal state of competition and accountability to shareholders and bankers. There is, for example, a view that theoretical pricing and investment policies can be laid down which take care of the anxieties just expressed and go further by ensuring an optimum allocation of resources. Again it could be argued that the object of nationalization was above all to make the achievement of certain public social and economic objectives easier, and that the commercial policies of nationalized undertakings should be designed to serve those objectives and no others. The objectives might, as we have seen, be various, including the provision of social services, the redistribution of income, or assisting the short-term management of the economy. As we have also seen, these objectives themselves sometimes conflict with each other. Financial objectives could still be used from all these points of view, but their function would be essentially to provide some means of controlling management. The setting of the objectives would result from the decision to impose social and economic obligations. The boards of the industries would then not be in much doubt about what the public interest required.

If the public interest were defined so extensively in terms of social and economic policies of government, however, the question might then arise whether the boards of the industries had much part to play in the process at all. As we said at the beginning of this chapter, perhaps it would be just as well under these circumstances to absorb them into the central government and for ministers to take responsibility for the nationalized industries.

In fact there would be widespread opposition to such a step if it were proposed. The postwar commercial public corporation is still an object of pride to many supporters of public ownership. Although some would like to get even closer to the model of a private company, few would wish to move in the other direction towards that of a government department. In so far as the nationalized industries are organized on commercial lines, then this is widely considered to be essential for purposes of management and administration. Indeed all the different approaches to financial objectives have one thing in common: they are all concerned with improving or maintaining the performance of management. It is necessary to ask therefore, in what ways nationalization was meant to affect the management of the industries.

DIFFERENT APPROACHES TO MANAGEMENT

What are the functions of management in a nationalized industry? In the first place, as in all industrial concerns, there is the need to ensure efficiency within the undertaking. In its pure sense efficiency is simply the achievement of maximum output with a minimum input, within the framework of existing decisions about consumer preference, risk, social obligation and so on. Engineers, accountants, industrial psychologists, management scientists and other specialists have found a number of ways of measuring efficiency in this sense: by studying such things as how the resources of skill, time, manpower and capital are deployed within an undertaking. The function of management goes beyond this to include such intangible and unquantifiable things as interpreting consumers' demands, predicting the future, noticing and using technical innovations, sustaining morale and so on. There is probably no adequate definition of the functions of management and it is also difficult to know how these functions should be allocated among different levels, for example between the board of directors of a company and the executives.

It is certain, however, that management cannot be an end in itself. There has to be some overall purpose for the undertaking, whether that is maximizing profits, seeking some point of expansion or serving some social or economic objective. Moreover, this purpose needs to be expressed in a strategy which can be communicated to all the various levels and parts of the undertaking so that their decisions make sense when taken together. The strategy is not relevant only as a means of conveying purpose downwards or outwards. Whatever the skills and other resources belonging to an undertaking may be, and however well-versed in the principles of technical efficiency its managers may be, these assets would be worthless unless they were harnessed to a strategy which was designed to take advantage of them. The same can be said for the environment of an undertaking. Management becomes 'competent' or 'efficient', and resources are valuable, only when connected to some end of achievement. The task of giving meaning to industrial activity in this way can be called, for want of a better word, the task of *direction*.

The relationship between purposes and management is clearly a two-way relationship but its exact nature is far from clear and this is a subject about which there are many different points of view. It is not known whether any special relationship was intended as a result of nationalization. Attitudes still tend to form into roughly two distinct kinds. There is a liberal point of view emphasizing the value of competition, automatic checks and balances, financial incentives, and so on; and there is a more collectivist attitude which stresses the need for co-ordination and getting agreement to predictions and other judgements. This second attitude tends to prefer co-operation to conflict as a means of control. The liberal view is associated readily with the conventional approach of the business-man and objectives such as profit maximization or growth come more readily to this sort of mind than broader considerations such as social and economic policy. The collectivist view belongs traditionally more to government and public administration, and takes more readily to generalized aims in which conflicting interests and desires can be reconciled. It is well known nowadays that the two attitudes are not mutually exclusive and are probably not really incompatible. They have, moreover, moved closer together and this may be both inevitable and desirable. For the moment we are concerned with the differences between them, for this has been a source of some difficulty in deciding how nationalized industries should serve the public interest.

Paradoxically, in the first decade after nationalization, the argument for providing greater opportunities for parliamentary and administrative control of the boards of the nationalized industries came from those taking a predominantly liberal attitude in the Conservative Party and financial and business circles. However, the argument then was that nationalization had destroyed two essential conditions prevailing in the market, namely, competition and accountability to shareholders. In later years the Treasury sought more precise and sophisticated control in the narrow sense of financial prudence. Over the whole period since nationalization, and with increasing authority in the last decade, professional economists of all political leanings have argued that the nationalized industries cannot be expected to achieve efficiency of their own accord, and that governments need to lay down general principles of pricing and investment decision for the boards of the industries to follow. In some cases, particularly on the political Left, it is argued that economic efficiency should be qualified by giving priority to social obligations and to long-term economic strategy. In other cases, the need to intervene in the interests of economic efficiency is seen as simply promoting or facilitating market forces.

Thus the stress on government controls has been made from both a liberal and a collectivist point of view. However an important (though often unclear) distinction must be drawn between the positive approach of collectivists and the negative approach of liberals. The distinction is important because the liberals would no doubt argue that the nearer one gets to the natural competitive conditions of the market the more governments should leave the boards alone – the rewards and penalties being built into the system. On the other hand, the more the boards' strategy needs to be laid down positively at a government level, particularly in order to temper it with special social and political objectives, the less they would be willing to rely on market forces, and the more they would resort to administrative devices such as artificial checks and balances, inspection and public accountability.

The leading supporters of nationalization sought to give as much freedom as possible to the boards of the nationalized industries in what was known as 'day-to-day management'. Their reason is put succinctly by Professor Robson:

> 'It is impossible to conduct even the most successful business enterprise without a considerable amount of expenditure which turns out to be wasteful. If the management is over-fearful of spending money unless it is absolutely certain to obtain a safe return on the outlay, the result is bound to be a highly conservative, excessively prudent, and technically backward undertaking, such as the British railways have been for the past thirty or forty years.'[14]

Lord Heyworth's remarks to the Select Committee on Nationalized Industries in 1951 on the more general aspects of business management have been quoted over and over again in this context:

'No one can tell at the point of time of having made a decision whether it is going to prove wrong or right. The point is that decisions have got to be taken. That is the thing which matters. It is dynamic. You have got to do something . . . Therefore, if people came to looking at everything I did in a year, after the event the shareholders would be horrified because they see that some of those decisions were quite wrong in the light of after events. The mere fact, therefore, that I felt someone was looking over my shoulder all the time and was going to examine these things at any time, the less I would be inclined to take action on a decision, and the less would be the result.'[15]

Arguments like these were used in the late 1940s and early 1950s against extending the incidence of Parliamentary Questions and against setting up a select committee to inquire into the affairs of the nationalized industries. Labour supporters of the public corporation were joined by representatives of both private and public industry in putting them forward.

Equally influential on thinking in the Labour Party, however, was the rather sentimental theory, associated particularly with Tawney and the Webbs, of 'disinterested professional' management in a socialist commonwealth. This had an important influence in the first place on Labour's conversion to the public corporation as a means of controlling and managing publicly-owned industries and its withdrawal from schemes for workers' control or for vesting industries in government departments. Industrial management came to be seen as a profession in its own right, but one which was frustrated by the profit motive of private ownership in 'the acquisitive society'. Following nationalization the managers would work for the good of society as a whole and not for their own self-aggrandizement.[16] The performance of the managers would be controlled by means of 'measurement and publicity'. Efficiency would be achieved by disinterested codes (in other words, presumably by administrative or bureaucratic means).[17] This approach is of course perfectly compatible with the view of economic efficiency held by those economists who would give priority to wider social and economic objectives and it can be regarded as supporting this view.

This attitude to management was prevalent in what we have called the positive approach to state enterprise which influenced the form given to the nationalized industries. In this sense, many socialists clearly intended that nationalization would change the nature of management in the industries. This ideal was no doubt related to a desire to make these industries more subservient to general social and economic objectives of government. Nationalization went a long way towards these aims by abolishing private ownership, replacing competition in many places with 'co-ordination', and substituting boards appointed by ministers for those accountable to shareholders. If we have described the aims correctly, however, then it is surprising that so little has been done since nationalization to make social and economic obligations of more overriding importance. Why for example has there been so much prevarication and uncertainty about the nature of the industries' financial obligations? One reason is obviously that not every one agrees with the positive approach, either about the primacy of broader social and economic obligations, or about the need for collectivist principles of management. In other words there seems to be basic disagreement about the public interest, even among supporters of state enterprise. Secondly, as we shall explain in greater detail in the rest of this book, the supporters of a positive approach really had little idea about the conditions necessary for achieving their aims, and so re-organising the industries. Much more can now be done to express social and economic objectives in strategies of direction for individual undertakings. The main contribution here has been by welfare economists working on pricing and investment decisions and developing social cost/benefit analysis. A significant gap, however, has been in understanding how social and economic strategies affect management.

In fact, whereas what we defined as the social and economic obligations of the nationalized industries seem to have general incidence for industry, the financial obligations we have been considering here apply particularly to the nationalized industries. Nationalization removed the context for industrial management provided by ownership and competition. Perhaps this context had already disappeared or was ineffective; in any event nationalization certainly did not provide a substitute on its own. That still had to be found. From a liberal point of view the substitute has been creating artificially as much as possible the same checks and balances and incentives as are thought to exist in the private sector. From this point of view the opportunity to create new forms of strategy and control seemed something of an embarrassment. From a collectivist position, however, it was anything but this and was rather a challenge to find new and supposedly better types of business strategy. Yet the hiatus still has to be filled with some new strategy and control and this was not sufficiently recognized at the time of nationalization or later. The main replacement that has been proposed so far is public accountability: new forms of institutional relationship and allocation of responsibility. We are about to study the nature of this solution more closely.

It is evident that analysing the public interest provides no ready-made role for the nationalized industries. We are now in a position to understand more clearly the different elements which make up the public interest but we have seen that there is no articulate consensus to guide the policy maker. There is broad agreement about the need for certain social and economic obligations and for providing management in the industries with some kind of direction and control. There is disagreement, however, about the relationship between these two needs of the public interest. Some would say that the second should derive from the first and that the two are inseparable in practice; others that they must be separated as far as possible. Some would regard the need to find new strategies for managements as a desired challenge and opportunity; others view it reluctantly as an inconvenience. Perhaps the opposition here is not the consequence of basically different values and aims but rather a result of failure to distinguish different levels and types of action. Could it be indeed that the existence of financial obligations in the public interest actually impedes the achievement of social and economic objectives and, if so, could the two be made separate?

REFERENCES

1. First Report from the Select Committee on Nationalized Industries. Session 1967–8. *Ministerial Control of the Nationalized Industries*, HC 371, vol. I, para. 63.
2. H. W. and F. G. Fowler (eds.), *Concise Oxford Dictionary*, 4th edn, Oxford, 1951, p. 238.
3. *Ministerial Control, op. cit.*, paras. 220–37, 482–504.
4. Report from the Select Committee on Nationalized Industries, Session 1959–60, *British Railways*, HC 254, paras. 384–90.
5. National Board for Prices and Incomes, Report No. 12, *Coal Prices*, February 1966, Cmnd. 2919, para. 33.
6. *Ministerial Control, op. cit.*, vol. III, Evidence from Mr M. V. Posner, qu. 1388.
7. *Ibid.*, vol. III, Evidence from Sir Thomas Padmore, qu. 1911.
8. *Ibid.*, vol. III, Evidence from Sir Alexander Cairncross, qu. 2093.
9. *Ibid.*, vol. III, Evidence from Sir David Pitblado, qu. 1790.
10. First Report from the Select Committee on Nationalized Industries, Session 1966–7, *The Post Office*, HC 340, paras. XV, 21–43.
11. *Ibid.*, the Herbert Committee recommended that the electricity supply industry should go to the market for its capital, partly in order to prevent the inefficiencies arising from self-financing. Report of the Committee of Inquiry into the Electricity Supply Industry, Cmnd. 9672, 1956, para. 507.

12. *Ministerial Control, op. cit.*, vol. III, Evidence from Sir David Pitblado, qq. 1361 and 1370–1.
13. See above, pp. 38–39.
14. W. A. Robson, *Nationalized Industry and Public Ownership*, George Allen & Unwin, 2nd edn, 1962, p. 196.
15. *Report from the Select Committee on Nationalized Industries*, Session 1951–2, HC 125, pp. 739–42.
16. See, for example, R. H. Tawney, *The Acquisitive Society*, London, 1921, p. 108.
17. Sidney and Beatrice Webb, *A Constitution for the Socialist Commonwealth of Great Britain*, London, 1920, p. 195.

Part III

POLITICAL CONTROL OF THE NATIONALIZED INDUSTRIES

Chapter 5

THE ROLE OF PARLIAMENT

One purpose of nationalization was to sharpen the response to demands in the public interest. In this part of the book we shall ask how control by political institutions has been used to realize this purpose. We shall try to judge the adequacy of political control as a means of supplying the discipline and incentive not otherwise provided under nationalization. We shall also inquire how political control designed to further social and economic objectives of the public interest is aided by the financial and structural conditions of nationalization. The fact that the public interest is inconsistent and inarticulate will underlie both these tasks and we shall need to draw repeatedly on what we have already said about that.

'Political control' is ambiguous and it is always difficult to distinguish control which is political from other kinds, such as administrative, commercial, judicial and so on. However, this need not prevent us from making good use of the expression here, because we are trying to find out how far a distinctly political kind of control can be identified. We also want to know when accountability to political institutions is necessary and, when it is not, what are the alternatives and how they differ from political control. So we shall include here accountability to organs which do not seem at first sight to have exercised political control at all, such as the National Board for Prices and Incomes, and representatives of an industry's workers and consumers. Relationships between nationalized undertakings and political institutions are often called 'public accountability' but that expression is even more ambiguous and clumsy than 'political control'; it does not, for example serve to distinguish political from other kinds of accountability.

It is appropriate that we should begin with the institution most associated in Britain with accountability of a political kind, namely, Parliament. There is not, however, a great deal to say about parliamentary control of the industries.

The main function of Parliament is to provide support for a government which is acceptable to the majority of the Members of Parliament returned at a general election. As a consequence of this Parliament is the centre of political life in the country. Thus it is the best place for presenting alternative policies to those of the government of the day, airing the grievances and claims of individuals and groups, and scrutinizing the administration and conduct of government. At the same time one of the means by which the government of the day seeks to remain in power is by listening and replying to criticism in Parliament, attending and responding to particular claims put by Members, and describing and explaining to Members its own activities. The main interest and duty of Parliament (in particular, the House of Commons) is therefore providing the country with a representative government. So much of the time and effort of Members of Parliament needs to be devoted to this that there is not much left over for the other things.

It is the government (in the person of the ministers of the Crown) and not Parliament as a whole which is made responsible for the conduct of government (and thereby for the administration as well). Parliament can control the administration but only by means of the control directly exercised by ministers over the various departments, boards and other bodies for which they are responsible. It is an unwritten law of the constitution that ministers must answer to the House of Commons for their policies and actions, including their control of the administration, and can be forced to resign if the House is not satisfied. However, the only matters for which the House of Commons as a whole is directly responsible are its own procedure, its own facilities and its own staff. The role of Parliament in holding the nationalized industries publicly accountable depends therefore on the role of ministers.

There is a vast area of publicly-owned and publicly-managed activity in Britain for which ministers are not directly responsible, for example the work of local authorities and the nationalized industries. In the case of activities like these, ministers are not answerable to the House of Commons in the way they are for their own departments. However, individual ministers have certain fixed powers in relation to the nationalized industries. They are responsible to Parliament for their exercise of these powers as well as any action their departments might take involving the nationalized industries. The nationalized industries were vested in public corporations in order to avoid certain forms of parliamentary control. As we have already explained, the reason for this was basically that the industries were seen as commercial undertakings which could not be treated like typical government departments and needed freedom of manoeuvre as well as financial independence. In other words the boards of the industries would be answerable to their customers, their employees and their creditors rather than to the House of Commons. Ministers were empowered only to appoint competent members to the boards, give them formal directions when the public interest so demanded, and keep an eye open to see that they lived up to expectations.

This arrangement probably over-estimated the impact of parliamentary accountability on ordinary ministerial departments just as much as it under-estimated the extent to which the industries were thought to engage the public interest. As a result the institutional relationship between Parliament, ministers and industries which it intended was much more unusual than the relationship which has evolved in practice. It is doubtful whether government departments suffer in modern times quite so much as is often claimed from the effects of parliamentary accountability. There has indeed been general criticism of the House of Commons for failing to provide adequate facility even for dealing with those matters for which ministers are directly responsible. At the same time ministers have been willing to admit more and more responsibilities involving the nationalized industries, although ministerial departments have acquired more functions towards the industries than ministers have liked to admit. There is in fact probably not all that much difference between the difficulties faced by Parliament in dealing with the affairs of the nationalized industries and those faced in dealing with any equally important aspect of modern government.

PARLIAMENTARY QUESTIONS

One important deficiency of parliamentary control of the nationalized industries (and of many other sectors of modern government) is that the procedures of debating are not suited to this kind of subject. As we have already seen, the issues involved are often complex and technical. Not only do members tend to lack information and understanding but the usual confrontation between front benches is seldom relevant. We have already mentioned our general impression that debates on the nationalized industries tend to deal with topics of rather transient and superficial interest. This is less so when special debates are set aside for discussion of an industry's report and accounts, or of a report of the Select Committee on Nationalized Industries, as has happened about once a year during the last decade. However, attendance at these debates tends to be poor because they lack current political importance. On other occasions, such as debates on the motion for the adjournment, the topic chosen is usually either one which concerns a particular interest group (say, the coal-miners), or one which touches some local grievance or alleged inefficiency in the industry concerned.[1]

For raising this kind of topic, written and oral Parliamentary Questions are much more appropriate than the various forms of debate. However, the vesting of the nationalized industries in public corporations was intended to protect them from the frequent incidence of Questions, and in the late 1940s and early 1950s ministers generally refused to reply to Questions on 'matters of detail' in the industries, on the grounds that they were not responsible. This principle was eventually upheld by a Select Committee in 1952 and has since become an accepted rule of the House. But ministers have in fact become more willing to answer Questions on the nationalized industries and members themselves have employed more dexterity in phrasing them to overcome procedural obstacles. Few Questions on the subject are nowadays ruled out of order and members seem to be satisfied on this score. This is, however, partly because a number of inquiries on detailed matters do have to be dealt with by boards.[2]

One reason why the problem has become easier is the general flexibility of the rule that ministers may only answer Questions on matters for which they are responsible.[3] Another is that ministers have been much more involved in the affairs of the nationalized industries than was apparently intended originally. Without wishing to enter into an argument about the chicken and the egg, it should of course be said that more flexibility in allowing Questions can itself increase ministerial involvement. Perhaps the best moral for us to draw is that the nationalized industries are believed by many politicians to have extensive social, economic and financial obligations in the public interest. Clearly, however, there must be limits to the extent to which Parliament can expand its interests in this way. Certainly, any further relaxation of the present rules would lead to congestion at Question Time and even more pressure on departments and boards. Although the boards of the industries are sometimes reluctant to admit it publicly, there is evidence that they are given a lot of work in dealing with Members' Questions. Although we have not tried to establish any definite relationship between the number of Questions and ministerial intervention in the industries, one must suspect that Questions can be, and are, sometimes used by civil servants as a pretext.[4]

It was largely because these shortcomings of the Parliamentary Question were acknowledged that in the early 1950s a rather bold step was taken in experimenting with a select committee to inquire into the nationalized industries.

THE SELECT COMMITTEE ON THE NATIONALIZED INDUSTRIES

Many argued at the time that this device had the same disadvantages as the Parliamentary Question, but in general this did not turn out to be the case. The Select Committee has been appointed in each parliamentary session since 1956 and has proved such a useful experiment that it has been taken as a model for similar committees on other subjects. However, this has been largely because the Committee did not fulfil the hopes of some of its original supporters. It has not really substituted for Parliamentary Questions, for it provides no kind of continuous opportunity to scrutinize particular industries and tends not to deal with detailed matters (although its inquiries do produce masses of detailed information about whatever industry happens to be studied). The general pattern of the Committee's work up to now has been to hold an inquiry into one industry at a time, taking usually at least a year to do so, and issuing a comprehensive and largely descriptive report at the end.[5] Although some people wanted the Committee to set up a sort of regular 'audit' of the industries and even to try to ensure that they did not abuse their powers as monopolies, the Committee does nothing approaching this and has always been an informative rather than an investigatory body. Its most important recommendations and conclusions have concerned the social and economic obligations of the nationalized industries and how these relate to the boards' other responsibilities. The Committee has from time to time surveyed important technical developments and has usually examined the organization of the industries, but it has not generally offered definite conclusions of its own on these subjects.

The reasons for this are straightforward enough. At a superficial level they are that the Committee does not have the kind of staff which would be required to carry out full investigations or 'audits', and that its own membership is anyway too small.

The real reason, however, is that the Committee could not have done much more without fundamentally changing the relationship between Parliament and the nationalized industries, and for that matter, between Parliament and the executive as well. As long as ministers did not take responsibility for the day-to-day management of the industries, the Select Committee could not have justified any attempt to control this management on the pretext that ministers should be made fully accountable to the House of Commons. On the other hand, deliberately to extend the role of ministers and civil servants to provide such a pretext, would have made the public corporations vested with the industries more or less redundant. It would not have met with support anyway, even from those who wanted more parliamentary control of the industries. Yet, without such a pretext, the Select Committee could have become responsible for reviewing pricing and investment decisions and for 'measuring' the efficiency of management, only by assuming executive powers which did not already belong officially to any minister of the Crown, and thus only by undermining the principle of government by majority party. Some people might desire this to happen as a general rule but, whatever one's wider beliefs about the political system, it is quite clear that such an outcome would be at least highly improbable with the present party system and with prevailing political attitudes in this country.

What the experience of the Select Committee on Nationalized Industries has illustrated is that it is possible for a select committee of back-bench MPs to do something valuable in this sector without undermining the system of public corporations, on the one hand, or that of ministerial responsibility, on the other. As it happens this consists, not so much of substituting for Parliamentary Questions, as of making up for the deficiencies of debating procedure. The Committee does this, first, by providing for serious and extensive study of the complexities of its subject – something which cannot be done in debates. Secondly, the deliberations of select committees are conventionally non-partisan. The temptation on the floor of the House to treat most things in terms of a clash of front benches tends to distort the problems of the industries and to emphasize relatively superficial topics of short-term significance. The Select Committee cannot altogether substitute for full-scale debates on the industries and the problems of this sector arise fundamentally from very real differences of approach to the role of government in the economy. It does, however, provide valuable preliminary clarification and agreement. If party leaders fail to take advantage of this to distinguish matters of principle on which a clear stand needs to be taken before the House, then the Committee is not to blame.

This function of the Committee is typified by the preoccupation of its reports with the scope and nature of the role of ministers in the industries. Its most effective recommendations have been designed to achieve a clearer demarcation of responsibilities between ministers and boards and to strengthen the role of the boards in 'commercial' matters. In this sense the Select Committee is a means of underpinning the independence of the boards and a safeguard against excesses of muddled ministerial thinking. This is not only because it acts as a pressure group for a greater degree of articulation of government policy, but also because the members of the boards can – and do – use it as a court of appeal against those government actions and policies which they dislike or regard as obstructing their own efforts. In this way the Select Committee is much more a specialized committee attached to the ministries concerned with the nationalized industries than a committee investigating the industries themselves.

These were the main conclusions of a thorough study of the Committee carried out by the author of this book in 1963–64.[6] Nothing has happened since then to change the author's general impression that the Committee is an extremely valuable (not to say indispensable) parliamentary device within the unavoidable limits which have already been described. However, since that original study was completed, the Committee's scope and resources have been extended considerably. Its membership has increased from thirteen to eighteen and it now has the right to appoint sub-committees. (It usually appoints two sub-committees per session of ten members each, and is thus enabled to increase the number of inquiries undertaken.) The Committee has also broadened the scope of the subjects it can inquire into, partly by including a larger number of bodies under its terms of reference (which have been amended by the House accordingly), and partly by undertaking inquiries on general topics as they affect a number of different industries. Moreover, in March 1967 the Committee was given the power in its terms of reference:

> 'to appoint persons with specialist knowledge for the purpose of particular inquiries, either to supply information which is not readily available or to elucidate matters of complexity within the Committee's order of reference.'

This addition to the Committee's previous staffing of two clerks of the House of Commons has taken the form of a senior academic economist working on a part-time basis. Finally, the Committee now takes evidence from a wider range of witnesses than it did before 1966 having decided, with the Government's encouragement, to call ministers before it and not just civil servants. Another change in practice is that the Committee now takes oral evidence from ministers and board members in public session.

Not all these changes have necessarily been improvements. With the exception of the use of sub-committees and the increase of membership the more ambitious efforts of later years have not proved very successful, and in some respects have been altogether damaging. This is particularly true of some aspects of the inquiry into ministerial control undertaken between the spring of 1967 and summer of 1968.

We make a number of criticisms of this inquiry elsewhere. In brief what happened was that the Committee took on the impossible task of defining the proper relationship between ministers and boards without articulating the questions of principle involved. The final Report contained some highly speculative economic theorizing and some rather ill-considered proposals for structural reforms based on inarticulate assumptions about the role of the nationalized undertakings. On the economic side, as Professor Robson has quite rightly said:

> 'It is difficult to avoid a suspicion that the members of the Select Committee were taken for an intellectual ride and being on unfamiliar ground they lost their way and were over ready to accept simple solutions to complex problems.'[7]

Other aspects of an apparent change in the Committee's style are its new practices of calling ministers as witnesses and taking some evidence in public. On the whole these changes have done neither harm nor good. As the author warned in 1966, evidence taken from ministers will probably be less useful than that taken from senior civil servants, since in practice the latter generally know more about the sort of things the Committee wants to inquire into, and discuss, than do ministers. This has now been confirmed by experience as a reading of the evidence since 1966 will show. The main disadvantages of these new practices are that they can engender a false impression among journalists, civil servants, MPs and board members that the Committee's real function is to play party politics, and can inflate expectations about its performance. No select committee of the House of Commons can take on Parliament's primary function of providing support for a representative government.[8] During the recent years of enthusiasm for parliamentary reform, select committees have been seen by many as a means of substantially increasing the power and independence of the back-bench MP to threaten the authority of the government of the day. The contest over parliamentary reform has tended to run very much on the lines of back-benchers versus front-benchers in the House of Commons, and the Select Committee on Nationalized Industries has been caught up in this contest.

It is certainly true that the Committee was recommended as a model for similar committees on other subjects. But this was not always intended to imply that any significant shift in the balance of power between legislature and executive could, or should, be achieved by this means. Retrospectively it seems that the Committee suffered from being caught up in this debate which took place on a different dimension altogether from that on which the Committee's real contribution should be judged. The wider debate about the balance of power in Parliament is much more relevant to discipline inside the political parties or to the role of party leadership.

While so many back-bench Members of Parliament have been preoccupied with asserting their independence from the party leaders it has been difficult for the Committee to recruit adequate members without advertising itself as a champion of back-bench prerogatives. Thus many of the changes introduced after 1964 were designed to make committee work more 'interesting' for members. (It could be argued, on the other hand, that the real cause of back-bench dissatisfaction was not the shortcomings of the Select Committee on Nationalized Industries so much as the ineptitude of party managers, a change in the general character of MPs, or simply a rupturing of the solidarity of one or other of the two main parties.) The net result seems to have been the loss of a lot of valuable time spent in wresting more powers from the Leader of the House without contributing anything of great significance to the Committee's real functions, at least as they are described here.

A glaring example was the Committee's campaign in 1967–68 to increase the number of bodies it could inquire into under its terms of reference. This required a twenty-seven page Report[9] and led to at least one four-month delay in getting the Committee appointed in a new session. The main object seems to have been to hold an enquiry into the Bank of England, and to move into the politically fissionable area of the relations between the Bank and the government in managing sterling. Naturally enough this was resisted by the Government. It might, or might not, be a good idea to set up a select committee in the sector of financial and economic policy in general to perform a similar function there to the Select Committee on Nationalized Industries. But there seems to be little excuse for the existing Nationalized Industries Committee getting involved in such questions. The Committee should certainly not have been distracted in this direction when its own inquiries into the bodies already included in its terms of reference were so 'behind schedule'. The Committee undertook no full inquiry into the affairs of the Coal Industry between 1958 and the spring of 1969, and was so preoccupied with other matters that it never got round at all to examining such an interesting body as the Transport Holding Company before it was abolished in the autumn of 1969.

The main limitation of the Select Committee on Nationalized

Industries is that the chief function of Parliament in this country is to provide support for a government, as we have repeatedly emphasized. Little time and energy is left over for the kind of activity which the Committee performs. This activity can therefore never be much more than subsidiary to parliamentary affairs (however vital it may be) and any attempt to bring it more into the centre of party political conflict must fail. The affairs of the nationalized industries do not lend themselves readily to full-scale debate, although the role of the government in these affairs (and indeed the basic principles of managing the industries) may invariably rest on important political differences. The Select Committee (assuming that it survives its awkward experience of the past few years) can continue to perform a valuable function of testing whether the affairs of the industries touch the public interest itself. At the same time the Committee provides a unique opportunity for the boards of the industries to explain their point of view and to justify their own actions. In these respects the Committee is a most desirable acquisition to the British system of government and when it is working normally it means that parliamentary control of the industries is probably more effective in this country than in many others (in Italy, for example, there is at present no parallel to the Select Committee and there is currently some pressure to find one).

The role of the Select Committee on Nationalized Industries illustrates that the role of Parliament itself in relation to the nationalized industries must be confined. Parliamentary control of these industries cannot be effective without ministerial control because of the system of representative government adopted in this country. Moreover, Parliament as a whole cannot make regular decisions about matters such as investment, pricing, employment, technical innovation, and so on. However, the more it delegates such decisions to ministers the more it needs select committees to sift through the work of government departments and to distinguish issues which Parliament itself should decide. On the other hand, the use of select committees cannot permit Parliament to extend its scope indefinitely, and in this sense the executive's independence from the rest of Parliament is probably bound to grow so long as the role of modern government continues to expand.

REFERENCES

1. The normal opportunities for debating the affairs of the nationalized industries up to 1969 were as follows:

Motions for the Adjournment (14 of these concerned nationalized industries between May 1966 and June 1967); Motions on Supply Days (about one of these a year concerns nationalized industries).

Motions to accept reports from Select Committees or the report and accounts of the board of a nationalized industry (sometimes taken on a Supply Day).

Motions to accept government policy as set out in a White Paper.

Debates on Bills and Statutory Instruments designed to reorganize industries or to alter their powers. See First Report from the Select Committee on Nationalized Industries, Session 1967–8, *Ministerial Control of the Nationalized Industries,* HC 371, vol. II, Memorandum submitted by the Clerk of the House, pp. 472–86.

2. *Ibid.*, vol. I, paras. 850–3, vol. II, pp. 472–6. See also A. H. Hanson, *Parliament and Public Ownership,* London, 1962, pp. 51–79.
3. See D. N. Chester and Nona Bowring, *Questions in Parliament,* Oxford, 1962, p. 305.
4. *Ministerial Control of the Nationalized Industries, op. cit.*, vol. I, paras. 856–63, vol. II, Evidence from Mr R. D. Barlas, qq. 1126–8. Professor Hanson held a different view, see *ibid.*, vol. II, pp. 529–31.
5. In addition it has regularly published sets of replies to its reports from ministers and boards, and has on two occasions followed up earlier reports with short inquiries into progress following its original recommendations. In 1968 the Committee published two reports based on inquiries made 'across the board', i.e. dealing with one subject as it affected a number of different industries, viz. *Ministerial Control of the Nationalized Industries, op. cit.*, and *The Exploitation of North Sea Gas,* HC 372, Session 1967–8.
6. David Coombes, *The Member of Parliament and the Administration,* London, George Allen & Unwin, 1966.
7. W. A. Robson, 'Ministerial Control of the Nationalized Industries', *Political Quarterly* Vol. 40, No. 1, January–March 1969, p. 108.
8. Coombes, *op. cit.*, pp. 16–29, 214–16.
9. Special Report from the Select Committee on Nationalized Industries, *The Committee's Order of Reference,* 26 June 1968, HC 298.

Chapter 6

THE ROLE OF MINISTERS

It is possible to make some generalizations at once about the role of government departments in controlling the nationalized industries, thanks to all the research and discussion on the subject in recent years (carried out mainly by the House of Commons Select Committee on Nationalized Industries).

First, a reading of the nationalization statutes gives only a slight impression of the role of sponsoring ministers in relation to the nationalized industries. In addition to the responsibilities given them by those statutes,[1] ministers exercise a wide range of powers derived from other Acts of Parliament, some passed before nationalization and some after it. Moreover on some aspects of policy 'gentlemen's agreements' are in force obliging the boards to seek ministerial approval before taking decisions. The famous White Paper of 1961 (Cmnd. 1337) announced that, if a board decided to modify its own proposals, 'by reason of views expressed by the Minister, it would be open to them to require a written statement of those views'. A letter from the Minister could be published by the board if they wished, and a board could also propose that its financial objective should be adjusted if it was affected by ministerial intervention. Quite apart from these formal arrangements regular discussions on a wide variety of topics take place at all levels between departments and boards. The sponsoring departments concerned with nationalized industries have the policies and programmes of the boards under continuous review and can make contact with representatives of the boards on a day-to-day basis. This relationship has been given the rather ugly, but now generally accepted, name of 'general oversight'.

There is nothing particularly surprising or questionable about this. Ministers have become more and more liberal before the House of Commons in interpreting their powers over the nationalized industries. Moreover the growing financial dependence of some industries on the government combined with the vagueness of the relationship implied by the nationalization statutes provide adequate justification for ministerial action, even if it has no direct statutory basis. Indeed informal, and even formal contacts of the type described are a normal part of the relationship between a ministerial department and sponsored industries. However Members of Parliament (particularly on the Select Committee on Nationalized Industries), while not disputing this, have repeatedly complained that ministers might be able to evade responsibility for intervention in the industries by using non-statutory contacts. Ministers have certainly evaded responsibility in the past and this has tended to make them less careful in considering their motives for acting.[2]

A second generalization which can be made about the role of ministers is that, although the industries have been vested in public corporations, nevertheless ministers and civil servants make vital decisions affecting many aspects of the industries' management. The distinction recommended by Herbert Morrison between 'general policy' and 'day-to-day administration' has never been maintained in practice. For the most part the civil servants concerned are ordinary members of the generalist administrative class of the civil service. In this respect one of the chief aims of the public corporation, namely, to keep business decisions in these industries out of the hands of civil servants has failed. Moreover the industries have become much more liable to Treasury control of their financial policies than was intended. Again there has not been any kind of conspiracy. Indeed one of the main causes of departmental intervention has been to rescue boards which were insolvent.

Thirdly, it is evident that there has never been any rational allocation of functions among the various government departments concerned with the nationalized industries, and that this reveals basic confusion about the purposes of government policy. There has been a gradual improvement since 1945, but the same applies under governments of both parties. Given the basic structure of central government between 1964 and 1968 an ideal allocation of functions would probably have given the Treasury the role of 'banker' to the industries along with responsibility for short-term economic policy, the Department of Economic Affairs responsibility for economic policy in the longer-term and the sponsoring departments the dual task of encouraging efficiency and defining the industries' social obligations. This does in fact come close to what seems to have been the official view of things.[3] In practice departments' functions have been far more complex than this and it is difficult to see how it could have been otherwise in view of the government's responsibilities in this sector.

The Treasury has not only concerned itself with short-term economic policy as it affects the industries but has also been the prime mover in paying more attention to efficiency (including the efficient allocation of resources in a global sense). Indeed the lines of demarcation between the Treasury and the DEA fluctuated right up to the time of the latter's disappearance in 1969, and it would be safer for us not to go into this wide topic here. The sponsoring departments (that is, before 1970 the Ministry of Transport, the Board of Trade, and the Ministry of Power—the last two now form part of Trade and Industry and a Ministry of Posts has been added) seem to have been responsible for far more than social obligations and managerial efficiency. They have also taken responsibility for the government's position as the main source of the industries' capital (the 'banker' role) and for articulating the policies which flow from the Treasury's view of the optimum allocation of resources. Only these departments are regularly in direct contact with the boards of the industries and some of the boards (in particular, the National Coal Board) have complained bitterly at times that, although the most important decisions seemed to be settled in the Treasury, they themselves had little or no direct contact with that department. Indeed a senior official of one of the boards described his sponsoring department's representatives to us as 'amateur Treasury men'.

Thus the real allocation of functions seems to have been that the sponsoring departments interpreted the whole range of government policies for the industries and took immediate responsibility for getting these policies accepted, while the Treasury (and to a lesser extent the DEA) has acted as general co-ordinator and source of policy over the longer term.

One difference between the Treasury and the sponsoring departments has been that the latter, unlike the former, were bound to act as spokesmen of their particular industries. But the attitude of these departments has been ambivalent on a number of levels. While acting on behalf of particular industries (for example, coal, gas, electricity, steel, and oil as in the former Ministry of Power), a sponsoring department has also been obliged to produce a co-ordinated policy for its sector, even though the industries concerned might have considered themselves to be in competition with one another, and even though one task of the department might have been to encourage a competitive spirit. Then again the department has tried to get technically advanced methods of production adopted while at the same time representing the 'banker's' interest in short-term financial probity. The department has expressed the social objectives of the government (which have sometimes coincided with an industry's own desire for growth or survival), while ensuring that the economic policies pursued in its sector were consistent with an overall efficient allocation of resources. Ambivalence of this kind is probably inherent in the sponsorship system and has not been peculiar to departments concerned with nationalized industries. For example, the Ministry of Agriculture, Fisheries and Food promotes the interests of British farmers while at the same time taking the consumer interest into account and must encourage the farming industry to invest in modern methods and techniques while keeping down the costs of subsidization.[4]

Most criticism of the system of accountability of nationalized industries has focused on these three general aspects of the relationship between ministers and the boards of the industries, namely: the confusion of responsibilities; the involvement of generalist civil servants in business decisions; and the unclear allocation of functions. There has been less objection to the actual scope of ministers' involvement. Reforms have been proposed on a number of different levels and we shall consider these at length in a later chapter. There has also been a concerted attempt within government over at least the last five years to move towards a clearer allocation of responsibilities between ministers and boards, and to re-state policy in such a way that the functions of government departments can be made more articulate and the making of decisions generally more rational. The White Paper of 1967, Cmnd. 3437, is the main official published account of this attempt to improve the instruments of political control. Analytic techniques – such as cost/benefit analysis, discounted cash flow, and economic rules for pricing and investment – have been intensively studied and are being increasingly applied. In its important report on ministerial control published in 1968 the Select Committee on Nationalized Industries paid special attention to the development of these techniques and recommended their further application. We shall now ask how much has been achieved by this activity by examining the relations between ministers and boards in some important aspects of decision-making in the industries.

CONTROL OF PRICES

The need for governments to exercise a broad, strategic control of the prices charged in the nationalized industries has never been seriously questioned. Government control tends to be restricted to changes in the general level of prices charged by a board, and in recent years it has not often extended to detailed price changes. Indeed the sponsoring departments are simply not equipped with knowledge or manpower to be able to exercise any kind of control over individual prices.

One justification for giving ministers the right to approve changes in the general level of prices is that the latter can be an important instrument in the government's short-term policy for managing the business cycle and balance of payments. On the other hand the boards are naturally afraid of being singled out for special treatment compared with private industry and the evidence collected by the Select Committee suggests that their fears have been justified on some recent occasions. In general, the prices and incomes policy of the Labour Government led between 1965 and 1969 to inconvenience and delay for the boards of the industries, and they were probably affected more than privately-owned firms in this respect.[5] The Select Committee thought that the system of five-year financial objectives introduced in 1961 had done a lot to inhibit ministers from encouraging a board to charge prices which might prevent it from breaking even financially, but not all the boards have the same favourable impression.[6]

Another reason for ministerial control of prices is that the industries are to some extent monopolies, so that the prices they charge may not be consistent with economic efficiency. Indeed there are various means (including the Monopolies Commission and the National Board for Prices and Incomes) by which governments have regulated the commercial activity of privately-owned enterprises on similar grounds. It has never been clear just how far governments do regard the nationalized industries as monopolies and most of the boards would protest that they do face severe competition in one form or another: for example coal from oil and nuclear power; electricity from gas and oil; and railways from road and air transport. A lot of the blame attaches to post war governments for failing to take a clear and consistent position on the subject of industrial monopoly and restrictive practices, whether in private or public sectors. The White Paper of 1961 (Cmnd. 1337) was itself quite incoherent on the subject but the existence of an element of monopoly was one justification for the system of financial objectives announced at the time.

However, these objectives were felt to be insufficiently precise and in 1967 the new White Paper (Cmnd. 3437) announced that, as an additional instrument of government policy, a precise strategy on pricing would be laid down. This was not intended to deprive the boards of any more autonomy in fixing prices:

> 'In so far as the industries observe the principles set out in the White Paper, the Government does not intend to interfere in the day-to-day responsibility of management to propose increases, and will endeavour to leave management the maximum discretion in

adjusting their price structure to meet competition and to take advantage of commercial opportunities.'[7]

As we explained in an earlier chapter, one of the principles which was laid down in the White Paper was that 'prices need to be reasonably related to costs at the margin'.[8] According to the White Paper this principle will be applied gradually and a number of qualifications will be made to it, the most important being that boards will not normally be expected to follow it if it is likely to lead them to make deficits.

The Select Committee, while making some of the same reservations in its 1968 Report, criticized the White Paper for being 'ambiguous' and warned against too much flexibility in applying the principle. The Committee was prepared to go so far as to say that 'marginal-cost pricing' should be part of the 'standard' policy for economic control of the nationalized industries, and that any departure from it should be discussed by minister and board, and the conclusions made public. Marginal-cost pricing would thus be the strategy laid down by ministers, while the initiative for specific prices and price changes would lie with the boards:

'So long as the industries accept the agreed pricing policy, then a large measure of discretion regarding the implementation of that policy, and the fixing and changing of prices within it, could and should be left to the industries – subject to quite separate early warning of price increases under prices and incomes policies.'[9]

In fact government departments were far less positive than the Select Committee about the extent to which marginal-cost pricing could be applied in practice. We also spoke to many representatives of boards who felt that the exceptions to the White Paper's principle would be more important than the rule itself. Clearly most changes in general price levels have continued to be considered on their merits and ministerial control has had to be rather more than strategic. For one thing it is rarely clear what this rule means when applied to business decisions. This aspect of the White Paper, and even more of the Select Committee's Report, seems to be particularly irritating to some boards. The misunderstanding partly reflects a typical difference of approach between economists and accountants, a difference which we are not qualified or willing to settle here. Accountants tend to argue (with the support of most business managers) that, in spite of the distinction which is drawn between short-run and long-run marginal costs and of the admission that the rule needs to be applied flexibly, marginal costs often simply cannot be calculated with enough certainty to act as a basis for pricing.[10] For example the Coal Board have explained in various memoranda to the Select Committee that a number of different results could be obtained in their own case by applying the principle.[11]

There is also a wide-spread feeling that, however flexibly expressed, the principle simply does not conform to the standards normally accepted in business. This means sometimes that it would lead to instability in prices and difficulties in distribution which would be offensive to consumers. Or sometimes it means that a board might be unable to take advantage of an opportunity to discriminate among consumers even when its private competitors were doing so. A typical reaction in the industries is that, in so far as the White Paper sought to encourage efficient production by getting prices related to the costs of different marginal outputs, then boards naturally try to take account of these in any case and would be open to criticism if they did not. But they would draw a distinction between trying to calculate marginal costs in the interests of efficiency and charging prices which endangered the viability and competitiveness of their enterprises in the market.[12]

As a means to a clearer understanding of economic efficiency and of the role of nationalized industries in promoting this, the principle set out by the 1967 White Paper may have its uses. (We do not intend to enter here the very complex argument among economists whether economic efficiency *is* more likely to be achieved if prices equal marginal costs, nor shall we do credit to the enormous problem of whether such a rule could really be applied in practice.) As an instrument in the government's general policy for making all industry more competitive and for reviewing all prices in the interests of economic efficiency, it could play some part in guiding officials who have to administer the policy and making their grounds for acting more precise and considered. However economic efficiency is not the only social and economic objective affecting nationalized industries. Moreover ministers are responsible for assessing the general competence and financial performance of the boards, which may not always mean the same thing as being efficient economically. It is not surprising, therefore, that the White Paper of 1967 was vague about the weight which should be given to its principle of marginal-cost pricing. Although there does seem to have been anxiety among the boards that governments would be dogmatic on the subject, there is no evidence yet that in any serious conflict of objectives a marginal-cost rule would (or could) be imposed against a board's own judgement. What government policy has never made clear, however, is what the general objectives of the boards in commercial policy should really be. Should they, for example, aim to increase the viability or size of their undertakings? If not, what kind of activity is it they are engaged in – should they regard themselves simply as instruments of a government's social and economic policy? These are the sort of questions to which the Select Committee should have devoted its attention.

In any event, both the commercial policies of the boards and the government's view of the allocation of resources have to be reconciled with the demands of national economic management in the short term. Clearly it is an improvement if economic policy takes the wider effects of the short-term intervention into account. But does it follow from this that price changes in the nationalized industries should be controlled according to some standard principle? The inquiries of the National Board for Prices and Incomes (which we shall consider more fully below) seem to have helped to reconcile the different requirements of short-term policy, social obligations, economic efficiency, and financial viability where these conflicted in individual cases of price changes by nationalized industries. However if the government has a policy on prices as part of its strategy for dealing with short-term economic fluctuations should this be applied with special force in the public sector? Should the public sector also be treated specially when the government has a policy for promoting efficiency? It could certainly be argued that there are important differences between the nationalized industries and the private sector. The boards of the nationalized industries do not have to compete with privately-owned firms for capital in the market. They are not accountable to shareholders and their financial solvency is taken as guaranteed by the government. It is far from certain whether they run the same risks of bankruptcy or take-over as the directors responsible for private enterprises. Before we can say any more on this subject, therefore, we must study the way in which decisions to borrow and invest are taken in the nationalized industries.

CONTROL OF INVESTMENT

Ministers' statutory powers over investment in the nationalized industries provide what are in practice their most important responsibilities in this sector. The wording of the relevant clause in the statutes seems to imply a strategic control over capital expenditure. In practice:

> '. . . through the attention they pay to investment programmes and projects, ministers and their officials are able to involve themselves

in almost as much of the detail of management as they wish, and to influence, directly, the operations of the industries.'[13]

The annual investment reviews (the various procedures for which were described in the Select Committee's 1968 Report)[14] provide an opportunity to go much deeper than 'major programmes of capital development' and are used by ministers among other things to examine the efficiency and competence of management. The reviews are also important as a means of obtaining information which is needed to make national economic policy, and can be used to further that policy. Given that the nationalized industries now derive most of their funds for investment from the Exchequer the reviews have also become the means of committing a sizeable amount of government expenditure.

The Select Committee believed that it was in the working of the investment reviews that the boards were most critical both of the extent of ministerial control over detailed aspects of management and of the lack of clarity of purpose in government policy. However, although it would be wrong to generalize, there have in the past been notorious cases where the standards applied by boards in passing new investment have not been those of financial return or the state of the market. The Select Committee pointed this out quite clearly in its report on ministerial control (and this was by no means the first time it had done so). For example, it quoted the Director General of Economic Planning in the Ministry of Transport as saying of British Rail:

> 'One certainly had a suspicion that investment is made here on general grounds that the service must go on where, on strict economic and commercial grounds, this should not be done.'[15]

The approval of new investment has been developed in a very similar way to the control of price changes. In other words the Treasury has for some years tried to develop a means of control which is systematic and which does not require ministers to take decisions on particular projects. As we saw in an earlier chapter, the principle that has been recommended by the Treasury (and now largely adopted by the boards) is that projects submitted for ministers' approval must be expressed in present values by the use of a *test rate of discount*. The rate used is selected by the government to represent 'the minimum rate of return to be expected on a marginal low-risk project undertaken for commercial reasons'.[16] The same rate has been applied in all the industries. In 1967 the White Paper, Cmnd. 3437, announced that a rate of eight per cent had been adopted (this was later increased to ten per cent). This figure was designed to measure the opportunity-cost of investment in nationalized industries in terms of alternative investment in the private sector.[17]

In selecting a standard test rate of discount the government is purportedly trying to make investment in the nationalized industries conform to an optimum allocation of resources in the economy as a whole. However, it is questionable whether a test rate derived in the same way as was recommended in 1967 will serve this purpose. Some economists argue that the basis for accepting marginal investment in public enterprise should not be the value of similar investment in privately-owned industry, but some other criterion such as the value of other forms of public investment or some special measure of social costs and benefits devised by the government. There is no particular magic in a figure measuring opportunity-cost in terms of private-sector investment, for the government might wish to control the latter too, and invariably does, although by much less precise means.

Even assuming that a widely-accepted test of marginal investment in public enterprise could be found and readily applied in conformity with an optimum allocation of resources, there is not much in any particular standard test rate of discount as a measure of a board's managerial efficiency and financial performance. Would it be sufficient simply to provide finance for all investment which passed the prevailing standard rate of discount? For one thing, there are numerous decisions to spend capital which boards are reluctant to subject to such a standard, such as projects designed to increase the safety or amenity of consumers. More important is the question of risk, which can be, and is, quantified as much as possible but which ultimately remains a matter for discretion. In some circumstances the standard rate will be much lower than the one which is normally applied to commercial investments. This is particularly true in the coal industry where by the very nature of the activity of mining the risks of investment are great. The government departments concerned have attempted, in conjunction with the boards, to work out methods of measuring risk but it is unlikely that quantitative standards can be widely applied.[18]

Closely related is the problem of forecasting demand, which is crucial, for example, in deciding how much capacity to provide in the electricity supply industry. The Select Committee devoted a lot of attention to the procedures for reviewing investment in this industry in its report on ministerial control. It showed how the Treasury and DEA had recently twice intervened to secure reductions to a programme already recommended by the Ministry of Power.[19] The interest shown by the Treasury (and for a time by the DEA) in the investment programme of the electricity supply industry arose mainly because of the importance of national economic growth as a determinant of the future demand in the industry. It was because these departments felt better qualified on this subject than the Ministry of Power or the Electricity Council that they brought about these cuts in 1965 and 1966.

This seemed to be reasonable ground for acting, but predicting national economic growth is only part of the picture when it comes to deciding reasonable estimates of future demand for electricity (or for that matter of any fuel). Why is the Treasury not equally concerned with investment in oil or any other large supplier of goods or services, the demand for which is closely related to the rate of growth of GNP? Perhaps it is, and some attempt is made in the pre-Budget Economic Statements to provide industry in general with relevant information regarding the official view of future demand. But the nationalized industries are much more closely tied to the government because of the statutory and financial powers of ministers. The real reason for any government's special anxiety in the case of forecasting in the nationalized industries is undoubtedly that it actually supplies the bulk of their long-term capital. We do not mean to suggest that crucial differences between the Treasury and the Electricity Council about the likely growth of demand are common or that the industry has regularly felt frustrated by financial restraint imposed by the government acting as 'banker'. Indeed, in the case of the investment programmes of 1965 and 1966 the evidence collected by the Select Committee shows that the Electricity Council would have made the cuts recommended by the Treasury and DEA on its own initiative. The question is whether the right people are concerned with the right decisions at the right levels. The government's role in making economic policy has been easily confused with its roles as 'banker' and 'shareholder' to the nationalized industries, but should the second simply be subsumed under the first?

This confusion can lead to misunderstanding and suspicion as it did for a time in the case of the coal industry.[20] The Coal Board have repeatedly complained that, in spite of the intentions expressed in the 1967 White Paper and elsewhere about leaving discretion to the boards, their own investment programme, which forms a minute percentage of GDP compared with that of the electricity supply industry seemed to be subjected to the same amount of scrutiny. The Board have argued that this cannot be justified by the importance of national economic trends to their own investment or vice versa.

Indeed the Treasury and the sponsoring Ministry have not justified it on these grounds but by pointing to the financial difficulties in which the Board has found itself in the past.

The fact is that in the past some boards have simply failed to run their undertakings as financially viable concerns. This has in some respects been the fault of the boards or their employees, in others the fault of ministers, and in others an unavoidable consequence of the condition the industries were in at the time of nationalization. The two largest undertakings affected in this way are commonly regarded as being the National Coal Board and British Railways. For a long time British Railways was hardly treated by governments as a commercial enterprise at all, so great was its accumulated deficit and its continued borrowing from the exchequer.

This meant among other things that attention paid by the Ministry of Transport to investment in the railways was far in excess of that shown in the normal relationship between sponsoring department and nationalized industry. The Select Committee in 1968 described the railways investment review as follows:

> 'The emphasis appears to have been on the *ad hoc* examination, often by formal questionnaires and correspondence, of the merits of a wide range of separate projects. Inevitably this had led the Ministry deep into the areas of management. The Ministry officials are now attempting to examine projects in almost as much detail, and with much the same material before them and with the same questions in mind, as the industrial managers themselves. And indeed the Ministry now wish to have exactly the same detailed case for projects submitted to them as is submitted to the Boards.'[21]

The Committee showed how a board like this, apparently in perpetual receipt of deficit grants from the government, was practically unable to face the future with any certainty and even so could not be subjected to effective parliamentary or ministerial control.[22]

If these circumstances had persisted it would probably have been best to transfer responsibility for the railways to the Ministry of Transport and to turn the Board itself into an agency exercising authority delegated from the Minister. As it happens, the decision was made to make a break with the past, to write off the Railways Board's existing debt, and to set it up on what was hoped would be a commercially viable basis. The impression we found in both Ministry and Board was that the relationship described by the Select Committee was – or should be – a thing of the past. The history of the coal industry is hardly as dramatic (and none of the fuel industries is subject to detailed scrutiny of individual projects under normal circumstances). Here too, however, a substantial financial reconstruction took place, past mistakes were admitted and a supposedly viable commercial entity was given its chance.

The experience of undertakings like coal and railways suggests that the role of ministers in controlling investment (and in other respects) depends a great deal on the financial results of the undertaking concerned. This does not seem unreasonable – shareholders would presumably be expected to ask more awkward questions in a year when results are bad than in one when they were good. The system of financial objectives introduced in 1961 was meant to provide some means of assessing the performance of individual undertakings in financial terms while taking account of different circumstances. But should ministers treat each undertaking's plans for investment differently? From the point of view of an efficient allocation of resources clearly they should not, because profitability is no measure of economic efficiency in this case. That is one major reason why the system of financial objectives was found to be inadequate as a basis for control, in that ministers still worried about the prices charged and the capital invested.

As we have seen, what is in some ways a more precise approach to investment has now been adopted by departments, one which is prepared to approve capital expenditure which passes a test of its opportunity-cost in the private sector. Some people both inside and outside government would like financial objectives to be deduced from the projected consequences of marginal-cost pricing and using DCF at the approved test rate (after taking account of other social and economic obligations and foreseeable demand and costs). This is inadequate in another way, however, because if followed rigorously it would not guarantee financial viability for individual undertakings. It would certainly provide some upper limit to capital expenditure in any one year, but only on the basis of a generalized view of what return should be expected on new investment. In so far as a board could not apply marginal-cost pricing, felt that the test rate adopted cut off some essential projects making a special contribution to expansion or development, or disagreed with the government's assessment of risk or market opportunity, then it would be a clumsy maximum to say the least. On the other hand it would not provide a universal minimum and particular 'problem' boards would still need individual attention. The dilemma is that the test discount rate is too clumsy because it pays too little attention to individual circumstances while the 1961 financial objectives were too clumsy because they paid too much. In other words, governments have two very different responsibilities for investment in nationalized industries: promoting an efficient allocation of resources and ensuring financial viability. That division might be the same as the division of responsibilities between the Treasury, on the one hand, and the sponsoring departments, on the other. How far such a separation would be feasible or adequate is a subject to which we shall return. Certainly some institutional solution seems to be essential since it is unlikely that any rule of decision-making could be found to ensure in all cases both economic efficiency and adequate financial viability at once unless, that is, financial viability is simply not considered important.

Is it conceivable that financial results could be replaced by something else as a yardstick of a competent and efficient undertaking? Apart from the psychological and other imponderables involved in that train of thought, there is one good reason why the financial aspects of investment are likely to continue to be important. This is that governments, although they do not like to admit it, want the means to control capital expenditure in these industries in a very exact way. We are now approaching the real reason why (rightly or wrongly) it was felt necessary to adopt some principle for controlling investment. Governments also control investment in the nationalized industries as part of their tactics for managing the economy in the short term. In our view this motive has been the most influential in justifying ministerial control. The government's tactics for managing economic activity in the short term have in most years normally meant restraining demand at home and 'releasing resources for export' in the interests of the balance of payments. According to some views – official and otherwise – the nationalized industries should not be singled out for special treatment in this respect. However, there is no doubt that they have been specially treated in recent crises. In fact the test discount rate is not very practical as a tool in this respect. The Treasury accepted that in the short term it was not effective simply to raise the test rate in the hopes of cutting investment in the nationalized industries. Control for this purpose actually took the form of 'administrative decision' when cuts were made for short-term economic reasons in 1966 and 1967. (In fact, the Treasury did not use the expression 'cuts' and regarded such interventions as a process of 're-phasing'.) The result was that certain marginal projects were postponed or cancelled by the boards concerned.[23]

This procedure can involve government departments, including sometimes the Treasury, in the details of the industries' investment programmes. The Select Committee wished that some means could be found of giving the boards of the industries some broad total, based on a system of rationing, and leaving it to them to make specific cuts. On the other hand, it is surely reasonable that the officials who have to reduce the amount of investment in response to the demands of economic policy should know what the effects of their action are likely to be and thus should try to ensure that its secondary effects will be taken into account? There is what the Select Committee itself called an 'educative value' in officials in the Treasury and elsewhere scrutinizing some individual investment projects. It is clearly better if officials responsible for economic policy can get some impression of the costs and benefits of different kinds of investment before deciding that investment in public enterprise should be restrained generally in the interests of capital expenditure elsewhere. This is always assuming that the government of the day is determined to use direct control over investment in the nationalized industries as a tool for managing the economy. An alternative would be to treat the public sector in the same way as the private sector by employing indirect methods. Apparently the departments concerned have not believed that this is possible. Is this because they positively want to use the wider opportunities of controlling nationalized industries' investment, or is it because they feel obligated as the trustees of public funds invested in the industries?

The implications of treating investment in the nationalized industries as a special instrument of national economic policy are possibly better grasped if one thinks of the opposite case, where government economists believe that economic activity needs an impulsion from new investment. What if the argument were that investment in the nationalized industries should be increased above the programmes approved by the boards as a deliberate measure of national economic policy? Indeed, to some extent control of nationalized industries' investment has been used by the government as a means of furthering specific social and economic objectives, for example, giving approval for new power stations in the electricity supply industry.

We have already seen that ministers are concerned here with the wider economic effects of an investment programme forming a very large percentage of GNP as well as with ensuring an adequate financial return on such a large commitment of public money. They are also responsible for taking account of the wider social consequences of this investment and, increasingly in recent years, for ensuring that the investment adds in the long term to the nation's resources of technologically advanced equipment and skills. These last two objects are presumably uppermost when the government gives approval for the construction of new power stations. The statutory basis for this approval is to ensure that general effects on amenity are considered in siting power stations. However, one element in the decision to approve a new power station has invariably been the social cost of unemployment in the coal industry. A closely related one has sometimes been the cost to the balance of payments and to the security of fuel supply of relying on oil imported from overseas. In recent years another kind of consideration has grown in importance, for example, the likely benefit from a prosperous electrical engineering industry manufacturing nuclear-generating equipment. This industry in turn has depended on a substantial regular demand for new nuclear power stations. At the same time, the government has been concerned that adequate supplies of cheap fuel should be made available to benefit British industry as a whole. This has not necessarily meant that oil and nuclear power should always be preferred, for a modernized and rationalized coal industry might provide cheaper primary fuel for electricity generation, other things being equal, than either of these competitors. The control of investment clearly takes on special importance if a government does intend to use investment in state enterprise as a weapon of its own social and economic policies. and it should be remembered that the aim might not always be to restrain demand but sometimes to place emphasis on economic growth and technological development. In the case of Italian public enterprise the latter has been the prevailing emphasis and we shall discuss later some of the problems which arise when investment in public enterprise is directed in that way.[24]

To make the techniques for measuring the financial return on investment the basis of an ideal role for ministers is therefore to treat the whole subject too narrowly. The existence of a test rate of discount for new investment in nationalized industries is clearly of only limited value to decision-makers in government departments in so far as the latter are really concerned with pursuing special social and economic policies. What such officials really need to know are things like the economic and technological consequences of particular investments and their social costs and benefits. The real question for us is whether it is wise or even possible for governments to control investment in this way. Why, if social and economic management is the real object of controlling nationalized industries' investment, have these particular industries been chosen for the purpose? Why should direct control be needed for steel, electricity, railways and telecommunications while indirect control is sufficient for chemicals, oil, shipping and computers? If it is only the size (and not the quality) of the investment which counts, then why do whole industries need to be controlled rather than a number of parts of different industries? These questions never seem to have been satisfactorily answered. Nor does anyone seem to have assessed what the cost is in terms of excessive centralization of investment and pricing decisions. We have already shown in this section that centralization of decisions makes it difficult to assess the performance of individual undertakings – even with the aid of discounted cash-flow techniques – and this is a question to which we shall return.

PROVISION OF SOCIAL SERVICES – THE CASE OF RAILWAYS

Deciding what services to provide at what prices cannot be based in a nationalized industry simply on judgements about what consumers are willing to pay and costs of production. Some account has to be taken of social obligations to provide certain types of service in particular ways, whether or not the costs of doing so can be recovered from those who benefit directly.

In the course of this century there has been a general increase in the British public's expectations of economic activity in both the public and the private sectors. Economic efficiency is inadequate as an end in itself and people seem to demand certain concrete results such as full employment, equality of incomes both among classes and among regions, stable prices, and so on. They expect both that undesirable effects of change will be avoided and that adequate provision will be made for a future beyond the scope of most ordinary commercial activity. Economists have spent more and more time trying to find means of taking rational and even quantitative account of such things in commercial activity. Few economists would now deny the need to consider the *secondary effects* or *social costs and benefits* of economic decisions.

There has been growing pressure on governments to restrict or to influence economic activity to help bring about the concrete results demanded. Indeed some political scientists suggest that in post war Britain there has emerged a 'Collectivist Era' in politics, when elections are won largely by a party's promise or ability to provide economic welfare.[25] In some ways political activity itself has become a kind of commercial process in which different suppliers compete to provide goods and services demanded by consumers. Modern governments are expected to provide the services required whenever ordinary economic activity seems unlikely to do so. Nationalization was partly a result of this unmistakable trend in politics.

On the other hand it has never been clear how far ministers are responsible for the social obligations of nationalized industries. In fact one reason why the industries were vested in public corporations and not in ministers was a fear that governments might be tempted to use the industries to bargain with interest groups which happen to have access to ministers. For example would not Labour Ministers feel obliged to run the coal industry in the interests of the National Union of Mineworkers, and would not Conservatives restrict the activities of the air corporations to help private operators in competition, and so on? It was also feared that ministers would be torn between voters' conflicting demands as taxpayers on the one hand and consumers on the other. Whether these fears were reasonable or not, it was probably absurd to suppose that a mere legal device such as vesting responsibility in public corporations would make all that much difference. Moreover, as we have seen, very little can be gained by trying to understand the motives of nationalization, since there were no articulate or consistent motives. In any event the statutory powers given to ministers to appoint the boards, make general and other directions, to approve investment programmes, and so on, were obviously intended to give them means to promote the public interest in all its different and conflicting meanings.

In fact it is now well known that ministers have been preoccupied with the provision of social services by nationalized industries. Sometimes the dominant concern has been how to react to financial losses said to result from providing a social service. At other times it has been how to react to public complaints that some service has not been provided or has been inadequate. Whatever was intended by nationalization, ministers have not been free from the temptation to get nationalized industries to provide social services. At the same time some boards have found themselves engaged in activities which, by their very nature or because of the history of their industries, cannot be carried on profitably (coal and railways are good examples). Attempting to transform these activities into financially viable undertakings itself raises wide-ranging social and political problems. Whatever the source of the obligation, the provision of social services invariably leads individual boards into financial difficulties, with which ministers are asked to help. The question then arises whether losses are caused by inefficiency and incompetence or by unavoidable economic circumstance. Moreover once financial viability is removed as a criterion of success, new means have to be found of assessing performance.

There have therefore been continuing and growing pressures on ministers to take responsibility for the provision of social services in nationalized industries. Ministers have responded to these pressures but have not always been wiillng to admit responsibility, seeking rather to convey pressure to boards themselves by trying to influence their decisions informally. This has in the past been a major cause of confusion in the minds of boards about the purposes of government policy. It has also made it extremely difficult, if not impossible, to assess the performance of individual undertakings.

The Select Committee on Nationalised Industries has always maintained that social services provided by the boards of nationalised industries should be accounted for separately and made the sole responsibility of ministers. This argument did get some support inside government in the early 1960s, but under the Labour Governments of the second half of that decade it began to exert real influence on policy. After about 1965 particular emphasis was placed in government on the use of social cost/benefit analysis as a means of quantifying the secondary effects of the industries' commercial activities. The principal object was to take separate account of the social obligations of boards, so that the rest of their activities could be treated as ordinary commercial activities judged in terms of a financial return. At the same time there was increasing willingness to give ministers responsibility for deciding that social services should be provided. The views of the Select Committee, therefore, are worthy of special attention, in particular those set out in its report on ministerial control published in 1968.[26] If the details are overlooked, what the Committee prescribed there was more or less adopted as the Government's own policy.

The Committee said that, although the initiative for providing a social service might come from a board or a sponsoring minister, 'the responsibility for selecting and defining social obligations should rest on ministers'. The selection and definition would follow a 'commercial' assessment of the value of the service, that is, an assessment based on the current test rate of discount for investment and prices equal to long-run marginal costs. Any service which failed this assessment would have to be 'precisely defined' by use where possible of social cost/benefit analysis, quantifying the secondary effects in monetary terms. This definition would have to be the responsibility of a government department, for only departments had access to relevant statistics, were sufficiently impartial and were qualified to dispense public money for social ends. Indeed once a service was selected by ministers as one which should be provided on social grounds, the boards should be compensated by the ministers concerned for the financial losses involved.

In the same report the Committee gave a useful list of social services provided by boards up to 1968 and showed how the procedures it recommended had been adopted to a greater or lesser extent in particular cases. We have not attempted in our own research to find out how fully or widely these procedures need to be or have been applied. However, we shall illustrate the problems arising from ministerial control of social services by describing aspects of one important recent case, that of grant-aided railway services.

British Rail have been, of all nationalized undertakings, probably the most seriously affected both by a heritage of past mistakes and by a burden of current social obligations. The financial performance of the railways has reflected this dual responsibility for practically the whole of the time since nationalization. Various attempts have been made to get them on to a sounder footing. During the period when Dr Beeching was Chairman of the Railways Board it seemed as if the intention was to dispense altogether with a system of railways as we have known it in Britain. However the 'Beeching axe' never actually fell. Following the election of a Labour Government in 1964 the Minister of Transport announced that he would not give his necessary approval for the closure of any more lines until a thorough review of the nation's whole transport needs could be undertaken. This review was then carried out and the resulting re-organization of transport, undoubtedly the most extensive since the 1947 nationalization, provided among other things a new financial and physical structure for the railways.

In the course of the review a system was worked out for separating those railway services justified mainly on grounds of social need from those which were thought to form the basis of a viable business enterprise capable of at least breaking even over a period of years. The 'social sector' of the railways was separately costed and was to be paid for out of public funds. The Railways Board was at the same time reconstructed financially. This whole procedure was worked out by a relatively new form of administrative device, a Steering Group under the Chairmanship of a Joint Parliamentary Secretary to the Ministry of Transport and including members from both the Railways Board and government departments, together with two independent industrialists and a railwayman. The terms of reference of the Group ranged from the subjects already mentioned (separation of social services and financial reconstruction) to the Board's management structure and organization, and pricing and investment policies. Two reports were received in the course of 1967 from the Joint Steering Group, one containing proposals for the 'scope and form of grants for unremunerative, but socially necessary, railway passenger services' and the other examining, 'what further steps would be necessary to put the Board's finances on a sound footing'. The Group's proposals were accepted by the Government and published in 1967.[27] The Group also produced unpublished reports on other parts of its terms of reference.

The proposals made, and broadly accepted, for dealing with unremunerative passenger services deserve detailed attention. The basic principle they expressed was that ministers should take responsibility for deciding to provide and pay for social services. The most important way this principle was to be applied was by identifying and costing separately all non-paying passenger services provided by the Board and deciding whether the social benefit justified the cost of keeping them.

> 'The decision in each case will have to be made by the Minister (not by the Railways Board) and in reaching that decision the Minister will weigh the cost of retaining the service – in terms of the amount of grant which will have to be paid – against the social and economic benefits which it will bring.'[28]

The Steering Group estimated that the grants paid out would cost £55 million per annum in 1969 and £50 million in 1974 (including interest assessed at present asset values). (Another way in which the same principle was to be applied was in assessing the cost of rationalizing existing track and signalling capacity. Since the Board itself could not be held responsible for modernizing this transport 'infrastructure', built mainly in the Victorian era, the Minister would contribute a grant amounting to no more than £50 million between 1969 and 1974.)

The Transport Act of 1968 empowered the Minister of Transport with the approval of the Treasury to make grants towards the maintenance of unremunerative passenger services for periods of not more than three years at a time. Grants should be calculated to make up the difference between expenditure on the service and the revenue received from it. This difference must be determined by the Minister after consulting the Board. The Act required the Board to include a separate statement of the financial results of these services in its Annual Report and Accounts.

The procedures adopted for executing the Act in the case of the passenger services was clearly influenced by the Treasury's reluctance to adopt a system of direct 'open-ended' subsidy for social services.[29] The relationship between Minister and Board was to be like that between the parties to an ordinary commercial transaction. The Government had clearly been impressed by the Select Committee's earlier argument that, in this way, 'no more and no less checking would be required than is normal in government contracts with other monopoly producers of goods and services'.[30] This criterion is not, however, so simple or so effective as it might seem. For one thing, the 'normal' checking in government contracts with commercial suppliers is often said to be inadequate. For another, there are several ways in which the railway passenger services concerned simply cannot be treated as ordinary commercial services provided at government request.

To encourage the Board to keep down the costs incurred in running a grant-aided service, grants were to be based on forward rather than past estimates of net losses incurred in running it. This might, however, lead the Board to bargain for as high an estimate as possible in negotiating for a grant. It would place a great responsibility on the Ministry to ensure accurate forecasting and estimating on their own part, in order to keep down the cost to the taxpayer. It will be especially difficult to decide how to treat changes in costs during the period of validity of a grant. The Steering Group had recommended that:

> '. . the Minister must have control over the frequency and standard of service, and the maximum fares, on any grant-aided service. The Board should be entitled to ask for a review of the grant if there is any increase in the deficit on any service as a direct result of the exercise of the Minister's control.'[31]

The Minister has indeed acquired a vital responsibility, not only for deciding which services to maintain (where possible by means of social cost/benefit analysis), but also for determining the quality and efficiency of the services provided.

However the division of responsibility between Minister and Board remains unclear. The Minister was only one of those made responsible for suggesting that a new grant-aided service should be provided, or that an existing one should be improved or extended. Where commuter services were concerned the 1968 Act created a new kind of body, the Local Passenger Transport Authority, representing local authorities within an area fixed by the Minister. These new Authorities were to work through Executives, which were in turn required to provide adequate passenger transport (by road or rail) in their areas and to break even in doing so. The Executives were empowered to pay grants out of the local rates to the British Railways Board to provide passenger railway services in their areas. In the event of disagreement between an Executive and the Board over the size and nature of this payment, appeal lay to the Minister, who could give a directive to the Board to settle the matter. Under the 1968 Act, therefore, the initiative for providing a grant-aided railway passenger service can come from a variety of sources: the Minister, a Local Passenger Transport Executive or Authority, or the Railways Board itself. Indeed in our own interviews in the Railways Board we found at the time that the Board considered itself to be in an excellent position to recommend new services or suggest improvements to existing ones, because they were well placed to see the needs of passengers on all kinds of service. As for the Ministry, although they are responsible for approving capital investment in all services for which a grant is provided, they gave the impression at the same time that they regarded it as the Board's responsibility to provide an adequate and efficient service and to make all proposals necessary to that end. The Ministry had no intention of 'playing trains'.

The Board must thus recognize on its own initiative the need for new grant-aided services or for improvements to existing ones. Presumably it will not be intended to earn a surplus on these services. The Board argues that in spite of this there are a number of reasons why it should wish to maintain the services and improve their quality. First, although the Minister will probably be a less fickle customer than the general public, on most grant-aided services passengers will continue to have to pay a substantial proportion of the costs. Moreover, the Board does not regard these services as 'social' in contrast to others which are 'commercial'. The Minister of Transport is simply the largest single customer on certain kinds of service. The grant-aided sector is worth maintaining at a high standard because it feeds other parts of the railway system and passengers will, to some extent, judge the railways as a whole by the performance of these services. Above all the Board will seek to make the services profitable in the longer term by attracting custom to them so that one day a surplus can be earned by running them without a grant.

There is still a problem in deciding what services to maintain. We cannot provide here any assessment of the adequacy of social cost/benefit analysis as a means of measuring the demand for a social service, but clearly much will depend on the relevance and accuracy of this technique used by the Ministry. Will the use of such techniques really replace political judgement based on electoral advantage, party ideology, patronage or bargaining as a criterion of need? If ministers are responsible for defining a social demand, what measure of consumer preference are they so particularly qualified to understand – electoral votes, Parliamentary feeling, the views of economists, pressure from interest groups, or what? At the same time the department will surely have to find out why a service is making a loss in the first place. There could be a number of reasons, apart from 'unavoidable' economic circumstances. For example, the board concerned might be inefficient or incompetent. When that is so, will it be sufficient reason in itself for making the service grant-aided or would the department rather try to ensure that the board improve its performance?

This leads to a related group of problems in deciding why to pay grants for the services selected. Will a grant be paid only when no other means of providing a 'socially necessary' service can be found? Already there have been complaints from British Rail that they have not been free to charge consumers what they would like for certain services, on account of ministerial control of prices. What indeed if there is disagreement between ministry and board about the elasticity of demand for a service: whose judgement is to be taken as best in predicting the relationship between price and demand? What if a service does not pay simply because of the government's policy for nationalized industries' prices? Generally, what are the grounds for making a service grant-aided? How far and how long will a board be allowed to try to make a financial proposition of a service before the government intervenes?

On the other hand, would the case for a grant stand if British Rail, say, were able to make a large annual surplus on its other activities, such as inter-city rail services, hotels and shipping? Would the Ministry of Transport and the Treasury then be inclined to encourage some 'cross-subsidization' from profitable to unprofitable activities? Or would they prefer to go on paying grants for social services while the Board's profits were ploughed back into these other things or perhaps paid to the Exchequer or even used to allow the Board to expand its activities in competition with the private sector? Clearly the separation of responsibility for social services cannot really absolve ministers from some responsibility for the operations of an undertaking as a whole.

There is another important reason for this which arises from the existence of a third series of problems. These are how to ensure that grant-aided services are efficient and adequate. Indeed the possibility of shelving responsibility for difficult services on to a minister might tempt a board to shift resources and interest to more promising business. Everything depends on how the board concerned interpret their responsibilities towards their operations as a whole. As we have seen the Railways Board maintain that they will not take advantage of the new arrangements to get difficult services off their back and argue that it would not be in their interest to do so. To some extent, however, this implies that they will temper their entrepreneurial zeal and commercial ambitions with professional pride and a sense for the longer term by providing some efficient and adequate services from which no immediate financial gain can be expected. It is interesting perhaps that the very things this Board were most criticized for in the past were showing too much professional pride and for failing to pay enough attention to immediate financial return. The real trouble is that ministers still do not know what to expect from a nationalized undertaking. If, in this particular example, they expect British Rail to maximize profits in the short term, they could be saddled with possibly permanent expenditure from taxation on certain unprofitable services and with the need to maintain elaborate machinery of inspection and control of these services to ensure efficiency. On the other hand, if they expect the Board to view the provision of the services as a special duty to the public or as a prudent safeguard of future profits, then the taxpayer's immediate financial burden might be less but at the expense of the Ministry's and Treasury's obligations as bankers and shareholders. Separating responsibility for social services does not make the job of setting financial objectives any less important or any less difficult.

In the case of British Rail we found these problems being studied in the relevant departments and answers to them were going to be provided in the Board's new corporate plan which was forthcoming. They are of general interest, however, and would arise wherever similar arrangements were made for providing social services in a nationalized industry. We shall return to them later. Two immediate conclusions are evident. First, giving a sponsoring minister responsibility for social services in a nationalized industry might increase and change the functions of his department. This may seem an obvious remark, but one aim of vesting nationalized industries in public corporations was purportedly to avoid doing this. The problems we have mentioned, some of which arise whenever governments pay for a social service and some of which were even envisaged at the time of nationalization, were not meant to be laid at the door of ministers, because the social services were meant to be 'hived off' to a public corporation. Since this did not work satisfactorily, it may be necessary among other things now to reform the central administration (by means other than 'hiving off'). It may even be necessary to re-consider the role of Parliament and of elections in articulating demands for goods and services. Secondly, separating social services from others does not reduce the minister's overall responsibility for an undertaking. The main reason for this is that the minister remains 'banker' and 'shareholder' to it. His duties in that capacity may even conflict with his interest in social welfare. At least they do not seem to make it easier for him to promote this interest.

PLANNING FOR A SECTOR – THE CASE OF FUEL POLICY

As well as ensuring that essential social services are provided, a government may seek to promote a general social and economic policy for a nationalized industry or group of industries. It often falls to sponsoring ministers to promote such things as adequacy of supply, full employment, and efficiency in their sector of industry. For example the Ministry of Fuel and Power Act of 1945 charges the minister sponsoring the fuel industries with 'the general duty of securing the effective and co-ordinated development of coal, petroleum and other . . . sources of fuel and power in Great Britain . . . and of promoting economy and efficiency in the supply, distribution, use and consumption of fuel and power, whether produced in Great Britain or not.'

The Ministry of Power (now absorbed in the Ministry of Trade and Industry) always maintained regular contacts with each nationalized industry and also with the private oil industry to carry out these responsibilities. The Minister and the Chairmen of the National Coal Board, Electricity Council and Gas Council met regularly together on a 'Co-ordinating Committee'. In January 1965 an 'Energy Advisory Council' was set up composed of leaders of the nationalized fuel industries and of the oil industry, representatives of industry in general and the trade unions, along with representatives of government departments. The Council considered the basis of long-term policy in this sector and discussed among other things estimates of energy requirements in the nation as a whole and the nuclear power programmes. In an important statement of policy for the fuel industries in 1967, the Government described its own responsibilities as follows:

> 'The Government's aim is to see that our growing energy requirements are supplied in the way which yields the greatest benefit to the country. . . In particular, that national considerations which individual consumers do not take into account in choosing between competing fuels are given their due weight among the factors determining the pattern of fuel supply and demand. Such national considerations include security of supply, the efficient use of resources, the balance of payments, and the economic, social and human consequences of changes in the supply pattern.'[32]

This role of sponsoring departments is something which is not peculiar to nationalized industries. Indeed in the fuel sector (as in others) it is performed for a nationalized industry often by means other than those provided in the nationalization statutes. We do not intend to provide here any general description of how the role is performed in the fuel sector, nor to assess the general value of government intervention of this type. Our main aim will be to illustrate how this aspect of a sponsoring minister's work can conflict with others and also require substantial involvement in a board's affairs by concentrating on one particular recent example: the relationship between the then Ministry of Power and the National Coal Board during the years 1965 to 1969.

A major problem of fuel policy has been providing a future for the coal industry which makes sense to workers and managers within it, while at the same time taking advantage of new and apparently cheap sources of primary fuel, in particular oil, natural gas and nuclear energy. The problem arises most acutely and most frequently in choosing fuel for generating electricity. For a variety of reasons the Minister of Power has been responsible for approving decisions to build new power stations.[33] The domestic coal industry is protected by a more or less complete ban on the import of coal and by a duty on imported oil. In addition the Central Electricity Generating Board has given priority to coal in consuming primary fuel, a policy which in that Board's view has sometimes kept its costs artificially high. Since 1965 the Government has made grants to the Coal Board to help it give benefits to miners made redundant by pit closures (not to exceed a total of £45 million between 1967–8 and 1970–1). In 1967 these grants were extended and also the Government decided to use public funds to pay the Central Electricity Generating Board and the gas industry for the cost of giving preference to coal. Earlier in 1965 rather less than half of the Coal Board's existing capital debt at the Exchequer had been written off and again in 1967 provision for financing the Board's deficit was increased from £30 million to £50 million.[34]

The main purpose of the support given to coal in 1965 was 'to improve (the industry's) competitive strength by supporting its reorganization and concentration on the most efficient collieries'.[35] In fact the demand for coal then declined at a rate faster than was envisaged and the new measures taken in 1967 had to take account of that. The general aim of the Government's fuel policy as expressed in 1967 was to ensure adequate supplies of cheap fuel for British industry and to take full advantage of technological innovation (including not just natural gas and nuclear power but also modernization in the coal industry). The Government had taken account of the likely social consequences of the coal industry's contraction. But it did not decide that these warranted, then at any rate, giving any extra support to the industry. Indeed there were unmistakeable signs in the 1967 policy statement that the social consequences of closing pits would be treated more and more 'in the context of the formulation of central and regional economic policy' rather than as a special concern of the Ministry itself or the Board.[36] At the same time the Government announced that the choice of fuel in new power stations should in future be based 'on an economic assessment of the method of generation which will enable [the electricity boards] to supply electricity at the lowest system cost consistent with security of supply and load balancing'.[37]

However, although it emphasized the 'continuing trend in consumer preference' and wished to avoid 'a mis-allocation of manpower and capital', the Government did not make economic efficiency a priority. It believed that the Coal Board would require 'continuing assistance' in order 'to secure an orderly transition'. The Board would have to maintain undistributed stocks of coal 'above the level necessary to ensure proper distribution and security of supply' and would need to be assisted in financing its modernization programme.[38] In this the Government had taken the advice of the Coal Board about the rate of contraction which was 'manageable', if the morale of the industry was to be maintained and the modernization programme made feasible.

On the other hand the Minister of Power did not claim to be preoccupied with social problems in the industry. Indeed during this time he was responsible, not just for the welfare of the coal industry, but also for developing new types of fuel and thereby fostering economic growth in the nation as a whole. For example, in approving the choice of fuel used in new power stations, the Minister would have met pressure from the oil industry and the manufacturers of nuclear equipment as well as having to take account of the needs of British industry as a whole for the cheapest possible supplies of secondary fuel. In reaching a decision he did of course have the help of the Generating Board who in theory as a public corporation might be qualified to choose the best primary fuel for generating electricity. However the Minister was obliged to 'ensure that the nationalized fuel industries use the resources they employ as efficiently and economically as possible', in view of their huge capital investment (about £1,000 million a year).[39] Meanwhile, the manufacturers of nuclear power argued that they needed a constant flow of orders for plant from the Generating Board if they were to maintain capacity sufficiently to compete in world markets. So it would be absurd to describe the role of a sponsoring minister like this as being simply to tell the Generating Board to make a 'commercial' decision, to promote economic efficiency or to provide for specific social services. He has a responsibility to British industry as a whole as well as to different parts of it. He has to weigh the demands of the different parts, as well as to take the advice of economists about what is desirable for the whole (and has moreover to compare what the economists say with the aggregate demands of industrial representatives themselves). Above all, in listening to the demands of industry, he is concerned with more than 'social welfare' and has to take account of the technical and commercial viability of different proposals. In this latter respect he is presumably forced to rely on the judgement of those directly responsible for the industrial undertakings concerned, whether public or private. But how passive should he be in taking their advice? A minister like this is – or should be – steeped in business with all its technical uncertainties and all its competing wills and interests.

The resulting confusion about the role of the minister can lead to a lot of unnecessary disagreement and even ill-feeling. Sometimes, for example, the relationship between the Ministry of Power and the National Coal Board was particularly strained, as is shown strikingly by the evidence given by the Board to the Select Committee on Nationalized Industries in the last few years. One source of disagreement, which did not perhaps turn out to be very important in itself, illustrates conveniently the problems involved. In its 1967 policy statement the Ministry of Power published an estimate of demand for coal in 1975 (120 million tons). The Coal Board told the Select Committee in 1969 that they had disagreed with this estimate and complained that they had not been properly consulted about it before it was announced. (In their own view a better estimate would have been 135 million tons.) They felt that the Ministry had underestimated the future competitiveness of the coal industry while also overestimating the growth in demand for natural gas and nuclear power. They believed that they would be able to offer coal from 'pits which by any normal standards are reasonably efficient pits producing coal reasonably cheaply'. What they feared was that no market would be available to take advantage of this. The Board has also complained about the failure to use coal in power stations built in areas where 'cheap' local supplies of coal could have been made available.[40] In so far as the Board were here challenging the Ministry's right to decide the relative commercial advantages of one product and another and the relative technical advantages of different methods of production, they might have been justified. Had not the boards of the nationalized industries been told that they were responsible for the management of their undertakings: for their commercial policies, their technical development and their labour relations? Were the Ministry of Power meant to judge these commercial and technical matters?

There is at least one good reason for a sponsoring ministry to judge commercial and technical performance of a nationalized undertaking. This is that the minister appoints the members of the board, supplies the capital, and in the absence of shareholders represents the nation's owning interest. However, in our present example the Minister did not claim to be so anxious about the financial results of the Board as about the wider advantages to be gained from greater productivity. Indeed in each year from 1965 to 1969 the Board failed to achieve its financial objective, but the Minister had apparently not considered this to be a mark of the success or failure of its management. The Select Committee has described the new financial objective of the Board set in 1969 as telling 'the industry to do what it is doing already'.[41]

The National Coal Board themselves certainly seemed at this time to be placing more emphasis on producing coal 'cheaply' than on finding people to buy it.[42] Or rather they seemed to approach the business of finding markets for their product by criticizing the Ministry's assessment of its social and economic value.

> 'The Board agree, and indeed have for many years urged, that a fuel policy is necessary. Such a policy must, however, be the outcome of a "total sum" calculation of all relevant factors. These factors must include among other things, all measurable economic costs, both social and commercial; effects on the balance of payments; strategic considerations; regional policies for industrial development; and wider social implications.'[43]

The Board also told the Select Committee in 1967 that, while the Ministry's task should be to give them 'business objectives', these should be qualified by reference to the 'total sum'. In assessing this the Ministry should take account of the Board's view of how different objectives would affect costs to the consumer and raise social problems of closing pits.[44]

In a way one cannot blame the Board for arguing in this way for a larger share of the market, even if it would require some protection and subsidy from the Government. In doing so were they not simply behaving as a good business concern would, that is, seeking to preserve (or expand) their viability as an organization? It so happened that in this case gaining a larger share of the market was partly a job of convincing ministers that more coal should be consumed. If the board of a nationalized industry are not meant to behave like this, then what are they there for?

However, we are not concerned here to discern the Coal Board's motives in arguing a particular case at that time, or with knowing whose estimate was the right one. This dialogue between Minister and Board was about many other things apart from the estimate for 1975. The interesting thing is the Minister's problem in deciding whose judgement to accept – the Board's or his own. It is clear that the Minister relied a great deal during this time on the Board's judgement about the technical and commercial possibilities of the industry (as all sponsoring ministers rely on the judgement of the boards of the nationalized undertakings under their tutelage). Was the only reason for the Board's existence to provide the Minister with objective and accurate information and then to pursue the financial objective set by the Minister on the basis of that? If so, then perhaps a board like the Coal Board at that time was unsuitable. Instead of Lord Robens – a dynamic and controversial figure, perhaps some more subservient individual should have been Chairman, say, a technician or accountant. For that matter perhaps the coal industry should have been made the direct responsibility of the Minister of Power and instead of the Board, civil servants should have taken charge of its management. As we know, that would have been widely regarded as out of the question and it was in fact deliberate policy to appoint energetic people like Lord Robens to the chairmanship of the boards.

The Ministry of Power and the Coal Board did finally settle most of their differences about the forecasts for fuel in 1975. In any event, it seems that the Ministry's figure was not intended to be a target for the Board or to be a criterion in approving its investment programme in the immediate future.[45] Changing circumstances anyway later made a coal shortage more likely than a surplus. Relations between the Ministry and the Board were in the summer of 1970 described by the Ministry as greatly improved. But what matters is not the cordiality of relations between minister and board.[46] The question is whether the sponsoring minister and the Treasury are able to apply the necessary means of control in the public interest. It was far from clear what the public interest was meant to be in this particular example and it was also unclear who was meant to represent it. It was not possible to say that the Minister was concerned purely with social and economic objectives. Nor could the Minister's objectives be described as purely strategic, confined to laying down general rules about pricing and investment policy and making calculations about likely social cost and benefits. The Minister also needed to know what would be the effects of different policies on the commercial and technical performance of individual undertakings. This raises a number of questions about the adequacy of the minister–board relationship in the nationalized industries.

First, are government departments equipped to perform this role?

Recruiting advisers competent in making decisions about future demand, the circumstances of technical innovation and social costs and benefits may not seem so impossible a task. Indeed many people have already suggested that the civil service needs to be reformed in this way, as we shall see. A greater problem is whether the factors which go into a sector policy like this are really quantifiable and can really be treated objectively by a minister. Is not such a policy in fact made up of the conflicting commercial demands of interest groups – the miners, the electrical engineering industry, the oil industry, and so on? These problems are not of course peculiar to making sector policy for nationalized industries, and are too general to be studied in depth here. However, vesting nationalized industries in public corporations was meant to avoid involving the civil service and Parliament in commercial matters.

That remark leads to a second question which is: how is nationalization meant to have assisted the making of plans for a sector like fuel and power? Some people believe nationalization is essential for this purpose.[47] If so, then why in the case of fuel policy do not the oil industry and the manufacturers of equipment for nuclear power stations have to be nationalized as well as gas, electricity and coal? Might not fuel policy otherwise tend to reflect the interests of these private undertakings rather than the interests of the nationalized part of the fuel sector? This is assuming that the government *does* have less control over the private undertakings. If it does not, and it has the same control over both public and private, then what sort of control does it exercise?

Thirdly, then, what indeed is the role of the board of a nationalized fuel industry? Some would say it is to behave like the board of a private firm so that the government's fuel policy should apply to private and public undertakings in the same way. The first question which springs to mind on that assumption is whether public ownership in the form required by nationalization has any purpose at all. It might well make the government's task more difficult in so far as nationalization creates or preserves certain crucial conditions of monopoly. These may exist in the private undertakings too, but, if so, what is it that is so desirable about the attitude of the board of a private concern that sets it up as a model for a nationalized industry? We have already seen that behaving in an 'entrepreneurial' way in a sector like this is not just finding what prices consumers are willing to pay for fuel, but convincing the government that more of one's particular fuel should be consumed. On the other hand, if a board is not meant to behave like a private firm, then there is need for much more clarification. For one thing, if the men on the boards of the nationalized industries are not business-men, how are the qualities of enterprise, initiative and competent industrial management meant to be provided?

Finally, therefore, what has happened to the minister's role as 'banker' and 'shareholder' to a nationalized industry? We have already seen that it was not meant to be a primary aim of policy for individual boards to break even financially. It is difficult to see how this could be a *primary* aim while the government is financially responsible for not just one undertaking but most of them in this sector. In other words, although the Coal Board could presumably be given a financial surplus by getting the Generating Board to buy more coal or to pay more for the coal it gets already, this would probably not help the financial position of the Generating Board, and would not further the Ministry's general duty of seeing that the undertakings under its tutelage were financially viable. It would be different if what the sponsoring department was seeking to do was to break even or achieve a surplus itself on the fuel sector *as a whole*. Indeed, one witness before the Select Committee on Nationalized Industries appropriately described the Ministry of Power as being 'the largest holding company in the world'. That is an interesting thought to which we shall return.

Must the financial results of an undertaking like the Coal Board always be left to 'come out in the wash'? Of course it could be possible for the Coal Board to conform to the government's policy and be financially viable at the same time. But what would that signify about its ability to provide primary fuel at the right quantities and of the right qualities for the benefit of the whole economy? And if it failed to break even, would the Board be justified in blaming the government for failing to provide a market for coal? Should it then run up a deficit, and eventually ask for its debts to public funds to be cancelled?

When a minister acquires responsibility for making policy for a sector as has been the case with the nationalized fuel industries he should also take responsibility for the performance of an individual undertaking as a business. Setting business objectives for each undertaking in terms of a financial return does not on its own seem to be an adequate way of carrying out that responsibility.

ENSURING EFFICIENCY

Ministers have to some extent already responded to the challenge to find means of assessing the performance of the boards of the nationalized industries as individual undertakings. First, of course, there is the system of financial objectives and we have already studied in detail the weaknesses of that approach.[48] In addition, however, they have made efforts – particularly in more recent years – to measure the efficiency of undertakings. To a government department 'efficiency' can mean not only overall economic efficiency (that is, an optimum allocation of resources in the economy as a whole), but also the 'technical' efficiency with which a single undertaking meets demand at given prices. This presumably can only mean the ratio of useful work performed to the amount of energy directly expended, or some similar measurable relationship. It is argued almost everywhere that the crucial decisions in bringing success or failure in a business are decisions about pricing, investment, forecasting, labour relations and so on. Clearly therefore the measurement of technical efficiency cannot tell one very much about the general competence of the board, or for that matter of the management. It cannot take the place of some sort of business objective.

The measurement of technical efficiency has been developed largely in applied studies of business management and is one of the functions of a management consultant. It is doubtful whether useful judgements of the performance of an undertaking can be made on this basis unless meaningful comparisons with other undertakings can be drawn. This is of course not always possible in the case of the nationalized industries. However, techniques have been developed for making 'inter-firm comparisons' based on measurements of technical performance in comparable undertakings, such as the concepts, *passenger load factor*, *aircraft utilization*, and *operating cost per c.t.m.*, used in measuring the technical efficiency of international airlines.[49]

It is very important for a board to find means of measuring the technical efficiency of its own undertaking. The boards of the nationalized industries do employ the kind of techniques we have mentioned and also make use of outside management consultants (although it is not our business here to inquire how adequately they do so). For a long time ministers seem to have treated efficiency in this sense as 'essentially a function of management',[50] but under the last Government the Treasury and the sponsoring departments showed a great deal of interest in it. This interest grew partly from the Labour Government's general enthusiasm for structural reform in British industry and for intervening more widely in all sectors to foster technological innovation and increase productivity. At the same time it was discovered that economic rules for pricing and investment were not sufficient means of making 'the best use of resources' and that:

'Continuous and critical attention has to be paid to costs themselves in order that an industry may play a full part in bringing about a more efficient and faster growing economy.'[51]

Many people in both government departments and boards told us that this recent interest in the efficiency of nationalized industry was a response to short-term political necessity. In fact the department's magniloquence on this topic dated from a statement made from 10 Downing Street on 7 September 1967. This was mainly concerned with announcing that in future all proposals for 'major price increases' in the nationalized industries would be referred to the National Board for Prices and Incomes. It also announced that the NBPI would be empowered to inquire into the efficiency of a nationalized industry in the course of examining a proposed price increase. Many believed that the Government's statement did not emerge directly from the review of the industries' financial and economic obligations which was then taking place (and the results of which were reported in the 1967 White Paper, Cmnd. 3437). It came as a surprise to many of those directly concerned with the Government's continuing policy for the nationalized industries. In fact it seems to have been intended mainly as a reaction to parliamentary and press criticism of increased electricity tariffs approved by the Government in the summer of 1967. The primary aim was to preserve the prices and incomes policy in the face of criticism that the policy applied to the private sector more stringently than it did to the public sector.

Thus, although the White Paper referred to a 'continuing' concern with technical efficiency on the part of the sponsoring departments, it envisaged an expansion of the role of ministers. To supplement the new functions of the NBPI the sponsoring departments would now be expected:

> 'to develop in consultation with the industries, indicators of performance which will provide regular and systematic information about each industry's success in controlling its costs, increasing efficiency and economizing in the use of manpower and capital resources.'[52]

The discussions which took place during the annual investment reviews were now to be used as an opportunity for this. The sponsoring departments had already used these reviews from time to time as a means of checking the procedures employed by boards to forecast costs and revenue, and to review the results of past projects. Indeed the Select Committee on Nationalized Industries, on the basis of evidence collected both before and after the 7 September statement, found:

> 'much scrutiny which goes so far in pursuit of efficiency within the industries that it ceases to be effective in achieving this purpose. . .'[53]

This complaint seems to have been based mainly on the experience of boards in marked financial difficulty, such as British Rail and London Transport during certain years. However, most board chairmen giving evidence to the Committee complained about the amount of work and time involved in the annual investment review and reported that the civil servants concerned seemed over-enthusiastic on occasions.

It is our impression that sponsoring departments have been frequently tempted to use the annual investment reviews as a means of inquiring into the general performance of management at various levels within an industry. This does not seem to have led to much more than simply asking questions. The boards we asked seemed to feel that they normally had the answers already available. However, any intensification of that questioning—as proposed by the September Statement and the White Paper of 1967—would probably lower the morale of the boards of the industries and worsen the complexity of the relationship between ministers and boards. In fact, it is far from clear what the White Paper's 'indicators of performance' were meant to indicate. (We spoke to some officials in 1969 and 1970 who had not even heard of the expression and asked us where we had come across it.) In the Treasury's own view the phrase referred to the sort of statistical information collected for making 'inter-firm comparisons'.

It is obviously part of the government's financial responsibility for the nationalized industries to ensure that the boards do employ these and other techniques of appraisal of internal management and also that they are generally competent as the bodies responsible for these huge undertakings. We doubt whether this also means that ministers should be concerned with applying these techniques themselves, and it is pretty obvious that they do not have the staff or the opportunity to do so. Moreover, ensuring technical efficiency is only part of the duty of the board of a large commercial undertaking. We shall postpone until the next chapter any general comments about whether the boards are justified in complaining at being questioned about management during the investment review or elsewhere. The main problem is to find some general notion showing what is and what is not worthwhile interference in this respect, particularly in view of the fact that the boards do not answer to shareholders or even, to any significant degree, to lenders of capital, other than the government of the day. Before saying any more about the competence of government departments in this respect, we should examine the role of independent public boards of investigation, such as the National Board for Prices and Incomes.

There has certainly been a concerted attempt, particularly in the last five or six years, to find more systematic and precise means of control by ministers while at the same time making ministerial control strategic rather than tactical. However, ministerial control is not based on any clear distinction between politics and business, and it is certainly difficult to see how it could be with the form of organization adopted in nationalization. It may even be that business and politics are inextricably mixed anyway, not because of nationalization, but because of the nature of the policies of modern governments. There are some important problems, however, which seem to arise especially in the case of nationalized industries.

The role of ministers in dealing with the nationalized industries is so complicated that it is impossible to communicate the public interest to the boards in a clear and consistent strategy. There is first the problem of weighing economic efficiency against other general social and economic policies.[54] Moreover, it does not seem possible that social and economic objectives can be practically translated into a meaningful and acceptable business objective, however necessary certain policies make that task. In fact general economic principles and techniques are of very limited value as an aid to ministers in reviewing the performance of the boards. Without a doubt the boards themselves feel that in some circumstances there is a conflict between these principles and their own duty to break even financially. Financial objectives have been developed as a means of giving greater coherence and articulation to that duty. However, the way these objectives are agreed is something of a mystery and there is little agreement about the criteria upon which they should be based. Too rigid an acceptance of economic rules for pricing and investment, and even taking account of social costs and benefits, could make it altogether absurd to assess the performance of an undertaking in terms of its financial viability. It would certainly help if there were a simple measure of the efficiency and competence of a commercial undertaking which could replace financial criteria such as return on assets, surplus on current account, and so on. Government departments, select committees and economists have not made much progress towards finding one. On the other hand, perhaps the problem is not so much the state of economic analysis as the very complexity and incongruity of the tasks assigned to ministers.

REFERENCES

1. See pp. 22–23 above.
2. See Select Committee on Nationalized Industries, Session 1967–8, *Ministerial Control of the Nationalized Industries*, HC 371, vol. III, Memorandum from Mr David Coombes, pp. 243–4.
3. *Ibid.*, vol. I, paras. 90–5.
4. It was too early to say when writing this book what would be the effects of the re-organization which took place in September 1969 absorbing the Ministry of Power into the Ministry of Technology and transferring to the latter also most of the functions of the former DEA. It might mean that – in the case of the fuel industries at least – long-term economic policy, efficiency, general sponsorship functions and economic growth could all be combined in the same department. See also below, pp. 233–34.
5. *Ministerial Control, op. cit.*, vol. I, paras, 384–93.
6. *Ibid.*, vol. I, para. 383. One board member told us that ministerial interference with prices had made nonsense of his board's financial objective. See also, *Ibid.*, vol. III, Memorandum from the National Coal Board, pp. 226–8.
7. Nationalized Industries: A Review of Economic and Financial Objectives, November 1967, Cmnd. 3437, para. 24.
8. See pp. 44–50 above.
9. *Ministerial Control, op. cit.*, vol. I, paras. 280–2, 406–8.
10. The Treasury offer some guidance on the application of marginal-cost pricing to individual circumstances in their evidence to the Select Committee on Nationalized Industries, *op. cit.*, vol. II, pp. 7–8, qq. 2091–3. See also Nationalized Industries, *op. cit.*, paras. 18–22.
11. *Ministerial Control, op. cit.*, vol. III, Memorandum from the National Coal Board, pp. 226–8; Report from the Select Committee on Nationalized Industries, Session 1968–9, *National Coal Board*, HC 471, vol. II, pp. 61–5.
12. *National Coal Board, op. cit., loc. cit.* The possibility of conflict between a board's financial objective and the principle of marginal-cost pricing has been emphasized many times by the National Board for Prices and Incomes, whose reports are a major source of evidence on this problem. See below pp. 128–35.
13. *Ministerial Control, op. cit.*, vol. I, paras. 508–10
14. *Ibid.*, vol. I, Appendix, pp. 205–22.
15. *Ibid.*, vol. I paras. 435–42.
16. See pp. 44–50 above, and *Nationalized Industries, op. cit.*, paras. 6–9.
17. Techniques employing discounted cash flow analysis and even a test rate of discount of eight per cent had already been in use in the Electricity Supply Industry before 1967. British Rail and the National Coal Board have been making a point of getting both applied where

they are relevant and practical (see *Ministerial Control*, *op. cit.*, vol. III, Memorandum from British Railways Board pp. 184–8; *National Coal Board*, *op. cit.*, vol. II, Minutes of Evidence, qq. 650–3). A senior officer in the Coal Board headquarters in London had been touring the Divisions and Areas lecturing to managers on the use of these and other modern accounting techniques.

18. *Ministerial Control*, *op. cit.*, vol. II, q. 1806.
19. *Ibid.*, vol. I, pp. 227–32. The decision in one case was partly influenced by the change in economic prospects announced in July 1966.
20. See pp. 110–18 below.
21. *Ministerial Control*, *op. cit.*, vol. I, para. 564. See also, *ibid.*, paras. 543–5 and 565–6.
22. *Ibid.*, paras. 472–7.
23. *Ibid.*, paras. 272–4.
24. See pp. 196–203 below.
25. See, for example, S. H. Beer, *Modern British Politics*, Faber and Faber, London, 1965, pp. 318–58.
26. *Ministerial Control*, vol. I, paras. 711–52.
27. Ministry of Transport, *Railway Policy*, November 1967, Cmnd. 3439.
28. *Ibid.*, para. 8.
29. See pp. 37–40 above.
30. *Ministerial Control*, *op. cit.*, vol. I, para. 752.
31. Railway Policy, *op. cit.*, p. 27.
32. Ministry of Power, *Fuel Policy*, November 1967, Cmnd. 3438.
33. Sec. 2 of the Electric Lighting Act 1909, and the Ministry of Fuel and Power Act 1945.
34. At the same time the Coal Board have undertaken a number of social obligations of varying importance: for example, the Board has sometimes refrained from mining open-cast coal in the interests of amenity; many of the costs of benefits and compensation to redundant miners have been paid by the Board itself; and they have from time to time delayed the closure of pits in response to the needs of the seasonal employment situation.
35. *Fuel Policy*, *op. cit.*, para. 54.
36. *Ibid.*, para. 71 and *passim.*
37. *Ibid.*, para. 98.
38. *Ibid.*, paras. 89–92, 102–10.
39. *Ibid.*, para. 81.
40. *National Coal Board*, *op. cit.*, vol. II, Memorandum from the National Coal Board, pp. 53–8, Evidence from Mr Derek Ezra MBE, q. 334 and *passim.*
41. *Ibid.*, vol. I, paras. VII, 35–8, 58–60.
42. *Ibid.*, vol. II, Evidence from Lord Robens, q. 647–8.
43. *Ministerial Control*, *op. cit.*, vol. II, Evidence from Lord Robens, q. 477.

44. *National Coal Board*, *op. cit.*, vol. I, paras. IX, 12–22.
45. *Ibid.*
46. *Ibid.*
47. Ministry and Board have always stressed that their day-to-day relations are good, in that they have found each other perfectly approachable and have been able to understand each other's difficulties.
48. See pp. 59–65 above.
49. See, for example, Report from the Select Committee on Nationalized Industries, *The Air Corporations*, May 1959, HC 213, paras. 125–77.
50. *Ministerial Control*, *op. cit.*, vol. II, Memorandum from H.M. Treasury, p. 6.
51. *The Nationalized Industries*, *op. cit.*, para. 27.
52. *Ibid.*, para. 32.
53. *Ministerial Control*, *op. cit.*, vol. I, para. 521.
54. However economists have done a lot to make this task an easier one. Even so the problems of application are enormous. See in particular, P. Henderson, Investment Criteria for Public Enterprise, in R. Turvey, ed., *Public Enterprise*, London 1968, pp. 127–8; and W. G. Shepherd, *Economic Performance under Public Ownership: British Fuel and Power*, New Haven and London, 1965, pp. 142–3.

Chapter 7

THE NATIONAL BOARD FOR PRICES AND INCOMES

One reason why the nationalized industries have been subject to political control is that in some ways they are monopolies outside the monopolies legislation covering the private sector. At the same time the boards of the industries are expected to observe certain economic rules for pricing and investment. In the absence of any other control, there is probably a need to check also the internal efficiency with which a given output is produced. However, as we have seen, ministers are only partly concerned with seeing that these obligations are fulfilled. Ministers are interested in the prices, costs and investment decisions of nationalized undertakings for other reasons, in particular in order to further wider social and economic objectives. In spite of the government's attempt to evolve general rules of decision-making, it has been impossible to avoid considering a large number of cases individually on their merits. Anyway people cannot agree which set of rules is 'desirable' economically. There is also the problem of whether government departments are equipped to decide highly technical matters such as the relationship of costs to prices, and so on. Would it be possible to find some means of promoting efficiency in the public sector which would relieve ministers of this responsibility?

The National Board for Prices and Incomes, as is now well known, was set up as a tool of the short-term economic policy of the Labour Government in 1965 and was meant chiefly to help to slow down rises in prices and incomes. So it may be surprising that we think of it in this context and even devote a whole chapter to it. Moreover the Board was abolished after the General Election of 1970 and was anyway about to lose its identity in a new body called the 'Commission for Industry and Manpower'. The aim here was to merge the Board with the Monopolies Commission, and then to 'develop' the work carried out before by the two bodies separately. The new body would have been concerned with both private and public sectors of industry; 'productivity, prices and incomes policy, and "competition" policy will no longer be treated as if they were entirely separate strands of our economic strategy'.[1] In many ways this change would have followed naturally from the development of the NBPI. It is important to be aware of this in understanding its role in relation to the nationalised industries.

Naturally we shall not provide here a full account of the Board's work. We shall be unable to do justice to what has been a major part of its activity, namely, inquiring into proposed wage increases and examining productivity and prices in the private sector. We shall not even presume to assess its single recommendations for the nationalized industries. However we can briefly trace the general development of the Board.

The principal function of the Board to begin with was defined in a Joint Statement of Intent signed by representatives of the Government, the employers' organizations and the Trades Union Congress:

> 'To examine particular cases in order to advise whether or not the behaviour of prices or of wages, salaries or other money incomes is in the national interest as defined by the Government after consultation with management and unions.'[2]

Cases were submitted to the Board by the minister responsible for the prices and incomes policy (that is, up to 1968 the Secretary of State for Economic Affairs and after that date the Secretary of State for Employment and Productivity) either alone or jointly with other ministers. The criteria used by the Board in dealing with these cases were set out in a series of White Papers on prices and incomes policy. In the first place the Secretary of State was notified of proposals to raise prices or incomes largely on a voluntary basis, but the Prices and Incomes Act of 1966 gave the Secretary of State power to impose a statutory 'freeze' on price and wage increases which lasted more or less until June 1967. From then until 1970 the Secretary of State had power to defer a proposed pay or price increase for varying periods following a recommendation from the Board. Although the Board seemed in view of this to be linked closely with a special aspect of short-term economic policy, it had in practice come to be concerned more and more with the longer-term implications of rises in prices and incomes and with the effects of rises in costs on the productivity of single professions, services or business undertakings. Indeed a White Paper in 1966 described the Board's duties as not just to examine proposals referred to it for 'detailed examination', but also

> 'To examine reference made to it from time to time by the Government on matters of longer-term significance in the field of productivity, prices and incomes.'[3]

For its own part the Board had been very interested in longer-term questions and it preferred to think of itself as not depending on statutory backing for its influence but rather as an expert body useful to industry and trade as a whole. Indeed the Board, which consisted of representatives of both sides of industry and of specialists in law, accountancy and economics, did not act as a quasi-judicial body or as an industrial court of arbitration. Its proceedings were held in private and avoided formality in procedure. Its inquiries were based, less on the taking of *ex parte* evidence than on an independent and specialized investigation into the cases submitted to it. For this purpose the Board had built up a staff of experts in the relevant fields, and considered as an essential ingredient in its work the production of otherwise unobtainable statistical information on costs, profit-margins, rates of return on investment and so on. Also special was the speed with which it sought to complete its inquiries. The NBPI was an important innovation, the role of which extended beyond the prices and incomes policy of the Labour Government. Among other things it was given special responsibilities for dealing with the nationalized industries.[4]

THE ROLE OF THE BOARD IN RELATION TO THE NATIONALIZED INDUSTRIES

We remarked in an earlier chapter that proposed price increases in some nationalized industries were referred to the Board as a normal part of the Government's prices and incomes policy but that the boards felt that the policy had borne more heavily on them than on the private sector. We said it was uncertain whether nationalization was seen as an opportunity to help short-term economic policy by controlling an industry's prices and investment. One consequence of using industries like that can be – and often has been – to stop boards achieving the financial results expected of them.[5] In fact the NBPI has said that there are special advantages in applying the prices and incomes policy in the public sector, because 'the impact on the public mind of price increases in the public sector might be greater than price increases taking place in the private sector'.[6]

However, the Board seemed (like many others involved) to be taken a little by surprise when in September 1967 it was, as we have seen, required to review in future all 'major' price increases in nationalized industries as well as to take on the job of examining efficiency.[7] The White Paper, Cmnd. 3437, in 1967, explained that:

'This decision is intended to show clearly that prices and incomes policy criteria apply equally to price increases in both the public and private sectors.'[8]

Nevertheless the boards of the industries were put out by the fact that only selective price increases in the private sector were referred to the NBPI and they felt sure that they were in for harsher treatment. Moreover there was the problem of how the recommendations of the Board would affect the financial objectives the boards had already agreed with ministers, and how they would relate to the rules of economic efficiency for pricing and investment laid down in the 1967 White Paper. The Statement from 10 Downing Street said that:

> 'It is within the context of the Government's overall financial policy for these industries that the reference to the prices and incomes board will be made. These references will be directed to the need to determine whether proposed increases are justified having regard to the industries' financial objectives, to their efficiency, to pricing policy and to other relevant considerations.'[9]

On the other hand it is difficult to see how the Board could make useful recommendations about prices while taking the financial objectives as given. In examining cases the Board has frequently remarked on the different, often incongruous, elements of government policy for the nationalized industries, rather in the same way as we have in earlier chapters here. And it has paid special attention to side-effects of price rises in the public sector, such as the economic effects of nationalized industries' prices, 'the greater element of monopoly inherent in nationalization', and social costs and benefits.[10]

The Board has, all the same, undoubtedly felt restricted by the requirement in its terms of reference to take a board's financial objective as given. Six months after the September 1967 Statement it reported on a number of proposed price increases in nationalized industries, in all of which there was conflict between the financial objective and other aspects of policy. One way the Board has approached this problem is to treat prices primarily from the point of view of the financial objective as long as this did not give a price which diverged 'unduly' from the 'long-term trend' in costs.[11] It felt obliged to weigh the different variables according to the circumstances of each case. For example, granting a price increase to let a board reach its financial objective might be less inflationary than withholding an increase and forcing a board into a financial situation where government borrowing or taxation would need to be increased in order to assist it.[12]

However the Board has clearly sought to do more than to see whether prices are related to costs and to weigh inflationary consequences. Reporting first on gas tariffs and then on the Central Electricity Generating Board's *bulk supply tariff* it made some general criticisms of the financial objectives in both industries. The Board showed on the one hand that the objectives conflicted with the Government's published fuel policy. On the other hand, it felt that there might not have been as much self-financing in the Generating Board's financial objective as would have been needed by a private undertaking in similar circumstances.[13] The objectives of some Gas Boards might also have been too low in its opinion.[14] However in neither of these examples did the Board feel qualified to suggest that the objectives should be made higher and it was in any case unwilling to recommend the full price increases proposed. Its main grounds for not accepting the full increase in the bulk supply tariff were that the financial objectives of the Generating Board and the Area Electricity Boards conflicted since the Area Boards would have to pay for the increase. This was also bad because the Generating Board would not feel the effects of a tariff rise on demand.[15] In other words, the NBPI's problems were almost the same as the government's. Rather than concentrate on one of the many aspects of the elusive public interest, the Board sought to reconcile them all.

It reacted in a similar way two months later to a proposal for rises in fares by British Rail. Here the Board paid fuller attention to the Government's optimal 'pricing policy' for nationalized industries (the famous 1967 White Paper and its formula for long-run marginal-cost pricing).[16] Again, however, its approach was essentially pragmatic. It emphasized the difficulty of allocating long-run marginal costs to different forms of service of British Rail. To guide the Railways Board in their general pricing on passenger services it introduced the idea of 'avoidable costs', that is the costs of accepting an additional consignment. The level of these costs was that 'below which no fares or charges should fall unless for quite exceptional reasons'. However the Railways Board also had to meet overheads and needed to earn net revenue to meet its financial objective. To do this it should aim to maximize the margin between 'avoidable costs', as defined, and the 'price of competing forms of transport'. Meanwhile the NBPI recognized that on some passenger routes prices could be reduced to increase business and therefore revenue. It concluded that 'setting prices within the upper and lower limits is then a matter of commercial judgement in balancing the changes in revenue against changes in costs'.[17]

Having suggested so aptly how economic efficiency might be mixed with financial gain in this instance, the Board went on not to support the full proposals of the Railways Board. This was mainly because it thought the Board's marketing efforts had been inadequate. The Report went on to criticize various aspects of the Railways Board's organization and commercial policy. It seems therefore that the NBPI did feel qualified to judge an undertaking's financial performance. It was evidently keen to assess the competence of the Railways Board as directors of their undertaking, including their ability to ensure the efficiency of its management. The assumption was perhaps that competition did not exist in this sector, or was inadequate to ensure efficiency. Perhaps the NBPI was advising the Minister of Transport in connection with his statutory duty to appoint the Railways Board.

For the nationalized industries the NBPI was obviously intended to pay heed to more than what price increases meant for short-term management of the economy. It had been given the duty to carry out 'efficiency audits' (in the language of the September Statement) or 'efficiency studies' (in that of a later Memorandum sent to the Board by the DEA).[18] The difference in wording could be important. Some people would understand by 'efficiency audit', something much more regular, direct and formal than an 'efficiency study', which implies something discontinuous, and indefinite in its form and consequences. Above all the word 'audit' clearly suggests a judgement on the past resulting in some action or settlement. 'Study' includes the future, is more vague and does not suggest authority over the subject. In fact it is 'efficiency studies' with which the NBPI has been concerned. The main subjects of its inquiries were meant to be an undertaking's productivity, and operational planning and control by the boards, or, as the 1967 White Paper put it: 'the industries' machinery for keeping down costs including the appropriate forecasting and decision-making techniques'.[19] The Board said that the likely subject-matter of its inquiries was: 'manpower budgeting, the extent of work study, information flows, the scope for operational research, management control systems, and methods of investment appraisal.'[20]

In spite of this, in the one example we have been able to study the Board interpreted 'efficiency' in a very wide sense. In its study of the 'use of modern techniques in planning and investment appraisal' in the gas industry it dealt with the problem of setting a future strategy for the industry. It said that the gas undertakings should not seek to 'maximize net revenue' but rather to 'minimize costs', meeting all demand resulting from the 'appropriate' pricing policy. The Board recommended that the industry should not adopt a pricing policy 'inconsistent with the rapid absorption of natural gas'.[21] In stating this objective the Board was acting in conformity with the Government's own fuel policy. It went on to discuss some of the detailed problems of forecasting demand in the industry and of applying investment appraisal based on a test rate of discount.

On pricing policy itself the Board again gave practical guidance to a nationalized industry faced with conflicting obligations to conform to a sector policy, meet financial objectives and obey rules of economic efficiency. The first problem was the Gas Council's bulk supply tariff. The consumption of natural gas would not for some time require a lot of additional capital expenditure by the Board, but when 'peak demand' began to take up the capacity of the existing system, costs would rise and, if prices were equal to marginal costs, the tariff would rise sharply and consumers would be 'aggrieved'. The Board recommended charging prices higher than marginal costs which would also help the industry to cover its 'accounting costs'. This was anyway required by the 1967 White Paper along with observance of the marginal-cost pricing rule.[22] As for the Gas Boards' retail tariffs there was an even greater likelihood of boards not breaking even if the White Paper's famous rule were followed. (This was mainly because prices based on the rule would not provide for the cost of past expenditure on the old town gas system.) On top of this was the fuel policy:

> 'It is not easy, if indeed possible, to compare the economic consequences of increased taxing or borrowing by the Treasury as against those of a slower exploitation of North Sea gas than might otherwise be possible.'

The Board decided to plump for the fuel policy: 'What is clear is that the obligation to meet a financial target should not unduly retard the exploitation of North Sea gas'. The White Paper's rule was not in fact much help. The Board made two suggestions. The natural gas industry, as it might be called, should be separated commercially as far as possible from the old town gas industry. The natural gas section should then be given freedom to price above marginal costs in order to cover accounting costs but should not seek to maximize net revenue. But it might be released from its statutory obligation not to show 'undue preference' to enable it to compete more effectively with the oil industry.[23]

We have no criticism to make here of these proposals and are concerned simply with what they indicate about the role of 'efficiency studies'. They suggest among other things that these studies involve finding how nationalized undertakings can be financially viable and not just with assessing efficiency at a given level of output. It might be supposed that in order to do this effectively the studies would have to deal with actual financial results in relation to actual prices and costs. In the case we have examined the NBPI did not do this. It was more concerned with the setting of objectives than with their realization or with their inflationary effects in real circumstances. Nor did the Board seek to provide an 'efficiency audit' designed to show in the absence of competition or shareholders or other potential checks that an undertaking is performing efficiently. Indeed the Board showed a marked interest here as in other inquiries in whether boards were able to compete effectively in order to make an adequate financial return.

There were other 'efficiency studies' in the inquiry into gas which we have been considering but the Board did not set out to make 'a comprehensive examination' of the industry's efficiency, thinking this impracticable.[24] These other studies were of labour efficiency, certain aspects of consumer services (on which it had a number of criticisms to make of the boards) and proposals for joint meter reading by the gas and electricity supply industries. The Board's staff were clearly rather proud of these studies; the boards of the industries themselves seemed more sceptical. The general response from boards to such inquiries is that they themselves can – and do – employ management consultants for the same purpose. However it is significant that in the case of gas this opportunity had not already been used to reveal the deficiencies found by the NBPI's staff. What matters for us is that the Board has not been any kind of substitute for financial or commercial restraint serving to promote competence and efficiency in the boards.

On the contrary it has supplemented political control of the boards rather than compensated for it. It has advised ministers how to combine their financial interest in the boards and their economic policies. It has not been the dispassionate advocate of economic efficiency (a kind of extension of monopolies legislation to the nationalized industries) which many hoped for. One can see no way in which its existence has made it possible to limit ministerial intervention in order to give the boards of the industries more initiative and enterprise. Nor has it made the functions of the boards noticeably clearer or more definite.

The Board's most controversial report on a nationalized industry was that on *Steel Prices* published in May 1969. Among other things the Board recommended that increases in selling prices proposed by the British Steel Corporation should be cut by 25 per cent. This was partly because it felt that the Corporation had not taken sufficient account of the scope for reductions in costs (a priority of the prices and incomes policy) but also 'because of the direct and indirect consequences for the balance of payments of a rise in steel prices'.[25] On the other hand, the Board had already remarked that the proposed selling prices were below long-run marginal costs as the Corporation defined them. The 1967 White Paper's rule was, it said, too difficult to apply in this case.[26] Having made this recommendation, based partly on a commercial judgement different from the Corporation's own and partly on a view of what the balance of payments needed, the Board then went on to suggest that its recommended cuts should be applied only to that group of individual products for which it thought the Corporation enjoyed 'market power'.[27] The Corporation itself, with widespread support in the financial press and elsewhere, objected to this further recommendation as an interference with its 'commercial freedom'. While it was prepared to accept the cuts proposed by the Board it wanted to use its own commercial judgement in applying them. In the end the Minister upheld the Corporation's view and the reduction in the total price increase was made 'across-the-board'.

Whatever the rights and wrongs of this case, one is bound to suspect that boards of nationalized industries were confused about the purpose of the NBPI. Was it an instrument of short-term economic policy, and, if so, did it apply to public and private sectors alike? We have already seen that the Board believed that there was a special reason for prices and incomes policy in the public sector and also thought that special factors ought to be considered in reviewing nationalized industries' proposals, including not only a board's financial objective but also its duty to the government's social and economic objectives. Yet the boards had been led to understand elsewhere that they were not to be used as special instruments in short-term economic policy, that they were not to be demoralized, and that they could encourage their managers and men by proving that nationalized industry was a business just like any other. The NBPI pointed out quite rightly in response to criticism of its report on steel prices that 'in the absence of external scrutiny the Corporation would have a privileged position enjoyed by no private undertaking, since it is a nationalized industry exempt from the legislation on monopolies...'[28] However, it was news to some boards that the NBPI was concerned with monopoly or market power and not with other matters altogether.

On the other hand if the Board did not seem to be mainly concerned with monopoly or cost-saving in the nationalized industries, this could be because it had been instructed to act within existing government policies for the industries. In many ways this had been rather like asking a silly question without much caring about the silly answer as long as one did not have to be the first one to say it in public oneself. The Government had not laid down financial objectives for private firms and had not stated economic rules for their pricing and investment decisions. It was fairly obvious that the Board did not like its duty to take financial obligations as given whenever it reviewed nationalized industries' prices. The Board welcomed the 'more flexible approach' towards these objectives of the 1967 White Paper and pointed out that there were a number of means of 'bridging' a shortfall in a financial objective. It would clearly have liked a greater opportunity to discuss what boards' financial objectives should be.[29]

Assuming the Board discussed such things (and as we have seen it did generally have a lot to say about the nature of financial objectives as well as the financial performance of boards in general) what would this have meant for the Board's role and for the boards of the nationalized industries? Evaluating the role of the NBPI from the point of view of nationalized industries may now be of mainly historical interest. It does, however, raise a number of topics which are central to our main argument.

THE VALUE OF THE BOARD IN RELATION TO THE NATIONALIZED INDUSTRIES

It was not very clear from its reports just what the NBPI did reckon to be its actual or ideal role where nationalized industries were concerned. It could have been four things: a tool of the prices and incomes policy of the Labour Government; an extension into the public sector of machinery for controlling monopoly; a special body for advising ministers how to reconcile conflicting objectives for the nationalized industries; and, finally, a substitute for those forces of competition and financial restraint which are meant to promote efficiency in private firms.

If it was mainly the first of these things, then it was somewhat disqualified from acting as the others, because in the other roles it would presumably need a measure of independence from government and also a certain breadth of interest. However the Board's part in the prices and incomes policy (later called the policy for '*productivity*, prices and incomes') clearly overlapped with what was in fact a kind of control of monopoly or 'market power':

'A prices and incomes policy . . . is intended to deal with two problems: the problem of a consensus of views over wage and price actions or expectations, and the problem of market power – that is, a power to influence, indeed, to set prices and earnings at will.'[30]

The crucial difference between prices and incomes policy and other weapons of short-term economic policy, therefore, is that the former is micro-economic whereas the latter are primarily macro-economic. We are not (mainly for reasons of space) concerned here with the Board's work on incomes, but one could say that in both main aspects of its work – which cannot therefore really be separated – it sought to avoid identification with a particular government or with temporary or emergency measures: in the case of incomes, the subject of its inquiries ought to be described as productivity; and in the case of prices, it was interested mainly in the internal efficiency and competence of individual undertakings.

This means for one thing that the work of the NBPI overlapped with that of other public bodies concerned with inspecting monopoly and with promoting efficiency in trade and industry. (The Government did recognize this by proposing to merge the Board into a new body with broader functions, the 'Commission for Industry and Manpower'.) We have already seen that one of the main grounds for political control of the nationalized industries is that the undertakings concerned are in many ways considered to be monopolies and that, not just for this reason but for others, ministers feel obliged to look into their efficiency. We have also seen that these obligations confuse and sometimes conflict with others. The thought that the NBPI might be the model of an independent public board to see how nationalized industries' prices are affected by 'market power' raises the possibility that control by ministers might be reduced or made simpler. Such a body would thus naturally have special relevance in the public sector.

In practice the Board's approach to the nationalized industries did not have this effect on ministerial control. On the contrary the boards of the industries themselves seemed to feel that its existence fortified rather than diminished the incidence of political control on their policies and actions.[31] One reason for this might, as we have seen, be the terms of reference of the Board, instructing it to take financial objectives and other government policies as immutable premises of an investigation. The main problem here was that the Government had a policy of its own designed to promote efficiency in nationalized undertakings and to control their pricing and other decisions in the interests of wider social and economic objectives. This policy was not meant to undermine the financial viability of boards or 'interfere' unduly with their commercial policies. We have seen that this was an extremely difficult aim and that the Labour Government did not succeed in it. The reports of the NBPI have done much to illustrate this and they may in fact have given invaluable guidance on mixing the different ends of policy. Yet it was never clear exactly on what grounds the Board gave one particular aspect of policy the priority over others. Was the Board meant to be strictly independent and was its advice needed for that reason? If so, then on what grounds did it decide, for example, that the rapid exploitation of natural gas was more important than the Steel Corporation's commercial policies? The Board was not elected in any way to represent the people any better than the government of the day. Perhaps it took instruction on these matters from a minister. But how was it, then, independent? The fact was that ministers still had to decide such matters and had to decide them on their own (and Parliament's) view of the public interest.

Or would it be argued that the Board's value was in its skill? Perhaps ministers sought its advice because their own departments were not equipped with staff who could take stock of the technical problems involved. The Board certainly seemed to us to see their function partly as applying rational methods to solve problems of allocating resources. Would they—or ministers—have maintained that the stage had been reached where government decisions should be deduced from such 'expertise'? If not, then the role of ministers in weighing different variables on the basis of political compromise, intuition and even doctrine had to continue.

The fact is that there is as yet no commonly agreed, readily applied formula in business decisions for seeking economic efficiency, social welfare or both. The NBPI has been absolutely justified in treating each case brought before it on its merits. The famous rule of long-run marginal-cost pricing stated by the Labour Government in its 1967 White Paper is of very limited value in application. The Board has tended to argue that marginal costs should be seen as a minimum below which prices should not fall and otherwise to treat prices on pragmatic grounds. It is not clear, however, whether in doing so it has been guided by the ruling of the White Paper or by its own judgement. Certainly many people would disagree with the yardstick of marginal costs even as a minimum. And what about social objectives?

Doubtless the Board's reports would have been more convincing as independent, expert views if they could have been distinguished more clearly from the Government's own policy. One obstacle there was the Government's financial responsibility for the nationalized undertakings. Since the Government had already made financial objectives for these undertakings (or should have done) then it was difficult for the Board to reach some different conclusion without making the boards of the industries even more uncertain who was responsible for directing their undertakings. But what was it that these financial objectives represented? If they were a guide to commercial decisions in the nationalized industries based on a desirable mix of the different objectives of government policy (including efficiency), there would have been little point in asking the Board's advice on what the Government had already decided. However, if the objectives did not represent this, but rather some sort of speculative financial return which the Government would consider desirable from its own point of view as 'banker' to the industries, then the NBPI should have been allowed to look into them. There would have been less confusion if ministers were not directly interested in the financial performance of the nationalized undertakings. As long as they were it was bound to be difficult to discern the NBPI's motives in recommending some commercial policy for a nationalized undertaking. It had no financial interest in any nationalized undertaking itself. While it might be seen as advising the Government on the inflationary implications of different financial results, it did not presumably share the Treasury's necessary concern for financial probity and caution with the taxpayer's money. Nor was it responsible for appointing the boards of the industries and thus for deciding whether the latter were competent and efficient. It could have approached financial objectives in the way the Select Committee on Nationalized Industries had recommended, namely, by deducing them from 'desirable' social and economic policies. But, if it had done, why on earth should the Board's view of what was socially and economically desirable be worth knowing compared with that of ministers or MPs or, for that matter, financial journalists or the man in the street?

We seem to have come some way from extending to the public sector control of monopoly in the private sector. But have we? If we consider again the NBPI simply as a means of doing this, and try to leave government policy out of it, we still meet a number of intricacies which prevent a clear separation of political from other forms of control.

The first knot to untie is the relationship between prices and financial results. Discussion of a reasonable price is properly discussion of a reasonable relationship between prices and costs, and, in the existence of 'market power' of a reasonable margin between the two. Thus in looking into proposed price increases in the private sector the NBPI has evaluated profit margins, self-financed investment programmes and other aspects of business which depend on the final relationship between prices and costs.[32] Now it is beyond our present task to say whether or not the NBPI was equipped to reach valid conclusions on topics like this. It is enough for us to record that (as we have seen at least in its reports on nationalized industries) the Board sought to be more than a substitute for the Monopolies Commission and consciously tried to take in a range of likely consequences of changes in prices and incomes.

It would not, for example, confine itself to pointing out the existence of 'market power'. It would not act simply as a kind of policeman who detected and arrested those who broke the law; it wanted to be a probation officer and a prison governor as well, and even so had a rare scepticism about the ordinary citizen's respect for the law:

> 'The policy for prices and incomes applies both to products where competitive conditions prevail and to those where conditions are uncompetitive. It is, however, more pertinent where uncompetitive conditions obtain; indeed it could be said that it is designed to act as a substitute for competition where this cannot be brought about.'[33]

In other words, the Board undoubtedly interpreted its role as a positive, and not a negative, one.

Thus, not only was the Board bound to consider prices in relation to financial results, it was also required to go into the question of costs. The Board was clearly to be congratulated on having refused to accept any vague 'blanket' definition of efficiency (such as that presented in the 1967 White Paper on nationalized industries). But this honesty itself implied a certain conceit on its part. It brings us to its interest in 'efficiency studies'. Now attention to internal efficiency—(perhaps to the general competence of the directors)—may well be needed when financial results no longer reflect adequate restraints or incentives. This applies to nationalized undertakings, as we have seen, because for various reasons there are good grounds for thinking that the boards of these industries are not subject to the same checks and influences as private firms in competition. So it was probably not such a controversial thing in itself that the NBPI should be asked to carry out 'efficiency studies' of these industries. Indeed the Board has maintained that its inquiries into both prices and efficiency in the nationalized industries were 'a natural extension of the work we have already carried out on private sector prices'.[34] The staff concerned with efficiency studies in nationalized industries were not different from those who dealt with references from the private sector.[35] But the question is not whether inquiries into internal efficiency by the NBPI were an unreasonable interference with the public sector. If 'efficiency studies' were expected to 'substitute for competition' were they anything like enough?

If some means of substituting for competition really could be found, then many people would be able to retire earlier at night. Among other things some of the worst problems of political control of nationalized industries would be solved. But the sort of inquiries conducted by the NBPI could hardly be considered an adequate substitute. For one thing it is clear from what we have already shown that the Board did not interpret 'efficiency studies' in order to mean any kind of general assessment of the performance of an undertaking. As we have seen the Board often criticised failure to take enough advantage of commercial opportunities. But the reports have been mainly concerned with the objectives which boards should pursue rather than with how well they have pursued them.

Indeed, finding a suitable 'substitute for competition' is in itself a tendentious occupation and might be read as putting too much store by the standards and behaviour of the market. If the Board was truly trying to do that, and doing so especially for the nationalized industries, it could be that someone was pleading a special case and, as some suspected, did not like nationalized industries. Was not the Board's real job promoting cost-saving and productivity in industry as a whole?

Now in fact the NBPI had justified its interest in efficiency mainly from this latter point of view. It said of its efficiency studies into nationalized industries: 'The distinction between an efficiency study and a study of cost-saving opportunities is one not of kind but of time'. The Board also went on to suggest that:

> 'The case for references of this kind applies not only to the nationalized but also to the private sector, especially where competition is limited by the dominance of a single company or a small group of companies.'

The Board admitted that not all nationalized undertakings could be described as being 'in a monopolistic position'.[36]

If the Board had it in mind to provide a substitute for competition in the private sector, too, then its already extraordinary task was enormous. Moreover the Board had re-emphasized that the problem of monopoly required more than simply restoring competition. Sometimes the element of monopoly might be unavoidable or necessary.[37] What, then, was an 'efficiency study', the means recommended by the Board for dealing with such circumstances:

> 'The point of an efficiency study is not to review individual decisions

by managements so much as to examine the processes by which decisions are reached and in this way to help undertakings to improve the quality of their decisions and hence their performance. An efficiency study can bring under examination the "totality" of the managerial function: the management of labour, that is to say, can be looked at together with the management of other inputs or factors or production, so that wages and prices are seen together, not in isolation. There is in our view a sound long-term case for this "total" look at the operations of an undertaking or industry.'[38]

How, then, are good decisions made, and what is good performance? Should undertakings be expected to break even over a period of years as required by the nationalization statutes, or to maximize profits, and, if the latter, over what period of time? We have already remarked that much of the Board's advice about the 'efficiency' of nationalized undertakings actually concerned their ability to take advantage of commercial opportunities and to improve on their financial returns: (for example, its criticisms of British Rail's commercial management and its suggestions about competition between gas and oil).[39] This is the sort of performance which shareholders are supposed to care about and which should presumably interest the Treasury as 'banker'. Scrutiny from outside by a body of experts might be a sensible way of compensating for the lack of shareholders in nationalized industries and helping the Treasury in this rather peculiar aspect of its work. What is envisaged here, however, seems to be a long way from control of monopoly. A policeman does not usually try to promote the general prosperity of suspected felons (although he might just conceivably do so if his local inspector were keen on crime prevention).

On the other hand attempts to give bodies inspecting monopoly and promoting industrial efficiency some kind of judicial status or role have a disappointing history. They tend either to confuse those responsible for the undertakings concerned or to produce irrelevant or meaningless findings. This has invariably been the experience with regulatory commissions in the United States. Their quasi-judicial character has also been said to be one of the main weaknesses of previous bodies dealing with restrictive practices and monopolies in the UK. Intervention in business activity on behalf of the public interest is today generally thought to require a more or less positive approach. Something more than just conciliation or arbitration is usually thought necessary, for example, some means of compensating the parties for losses, some attempt to 'upgrade' the parties to a new and 'more favourable' position. (The analogy of 'crime prevention' is not all that remote, therefore. Moreover, a dispute is not always considered necessary before action in the public interest may be taken.) If this trend away from a judicial approach to a 'welfare' one does indeed exist, the NBPI was evidently in the forefront of it. But what should be the status and role of bodies carrying out such policies? In so far as government policy can be expressed in general and agreed rules of behaviour which can be readily applied to individual cases, then bodies independent of the central government are to be preferred. In so far as the discretion to be exercised in applying the policy is using scientific principles, then a specialist and 'expert' body is necessary. A body staffed and organized rather like the NBPI would, therefore, seem to fit the bill.

The real problem, however, is that government policy for preventing abuse of monopoly and promoting efficiency may not be expressed in general or agreed rules and perhaps it cannot be. This seems to be so at least where nationalized industries are concerned. There is, above all, the need to decide which kind of performance one wants from business and how one is most likely to get it.

We cannot get away from the fact that it is pointless trying to make conclusions about efficiency without having first a clear idea of the *purpose* of a business undertaking. We know that many people thought nationalized undertakings should have special purposes, different from those of private firms. We do not know more than this, but it seems that financial viability (beyond the equivocal 'breaking even') was probably not meant to override economic efficiency or social welfare or a mixture of the two. The trouble is that easy criteria do not exist for translating these 'wider' (indeed, macro-economic) objectives into standards for a single undertaking. In view of this, perhaps the solution lies in some institution, endowed with the wisdom, flexibility and authority to show when financial results should be less important and to take their place in measuring internal competence and efficiency. If so, then perhaps the NBPI provided the embryo of such an institution. However, it should be remembered that the existence of a body like this cannot take from ministers the responsibility for deciding individual cases, at least where general rules do not exist and where many social and economic objectives bear at once. It is perhaps worth mentioning at this point that economists are sometimes over-confident of the impartiality and generality of their views.

Indeed the NBPI itself has admitted that there is no solution in a simple distinction between monopoly and competition. Had it not done so, then it would certainly be necessary for the supporters of nationalization to point this out. One argument for nationalization is that competition is inadequate or altogether undesirable in certain circumstances. By the same token the new standards adopted under nationalization should apply wherever similar industrial conditions could be found, and not just in existing nationalized industries. Perhaps the aim of institutions like the NBPI should be to apply these standards through 'efficiency studies' to the private sector as well. We suggested earlier that the development of independent bodies promoting efficiency and inspecting monopoly might be to remove some peculiar features of nationalized industries and thus to make some forms of political control less necessary. We now see that it may on the contrary be to extend political control even further and to increase it in the private sector as well.

We are not saying that the Labour Government or the NBPI committed themselves to one or other approach to evaluating business performance. Indeed, the main problem was that they did not make up their minds. Therefore it was inevitable that the NBPI was viewed with suspicion, at least by the boards of the nationalized industries, and that the Government's proposals for a 'Commission for Industry and Manpower' were viewed just as unfavourably. In many ways these proposals were readily defensible, both as a logical step from what had already happened and as a recognition of some important lessons of the past. It was of course reasonable that the new body should deal with 'structure as well as behaviour', with uncompetitive behaviour as well as inflationary consequences and should cover both public and private sectors. The Government was no doubt justified in arguing that the conventional notion of monopoly (as employed by the Monopolies Commission) might no longer be adequate and that 'the growth of large industrial units has weakened competitive forces' so that machinery was needed to deal with 'all situations of imperfect competition'. Accordingly it was intended to refer to the Commission cases arising from 'all major firms (defined as those with capital employed of more than £10 million) as well as those in a monopoly position'.[40] The powers of the Commission would have been a fairly straightforward amalgam of the former powers of the NBPI and the Monopolies Commission.

It is not within the scope of this book to discuss the desirability of these proposals in detail either for the private sector or the nationalized industries. In any event the return of a Conservative Government has led to their abandonment. However, most of the same limitations which we have found in the work of the NBPI (either actual or potential) would have applied also to the new Commission. Above all there were still inarticulate assumptions about the way different kinds of business performance should be valued.

It may well be that the boards of the nationalized industries have benefited in many ways from the NBPI's inquiries (for example, learning things, not always published in reports, but discussed with the Board's staff during an inquiry). It is also probably true that it is often better for boards to get criticisms into the open and have them discussed by an independent body of this kind, whether the latter says good or bad things about an undertaking. Apart from this the NBPI clearly added to the confusion of nationalized boards about their own role. It did not make any substantial contribution to solving the problems of political control, or (what would have been really helpful) to making this sort of control any less necessary. Its experience and our speculations how it might have worked with different powers and scope tend to throw doubt on the general value of independent boards of this type as a means of controlling nationalized industries in the public interest. However, we have not explored all possibilities and we shall return to this topic later. It is for the time being one tentative conclusion to be drawn from our study of the NBPI. Another more certain one – and one that it is becoming increasingly apparent from our argument in this book – is that the relationship between nationalized industries and politics cannot really be separated from that between politics and industry in general.

REFERENCES

1. Department of Employment and Productivity, Commission for Industry and Manpower, January 1970, para. 4.
2. Joint Statement of Intent on Productivity, Prices and Incomes, 16 December 1964.
3. Department of Economic Affairs, *Prices and Incomes Standstill*, Cmnd. 3073, 29 July 1966.
4. See National Board for Prices and Incomes, Report No. 122, *Fourth General Report*, July 1969, Cmnd. 4130, paras. 82–6.
5. See pp. 89–93 above.
6. Select Committee on Nationalized Industries, *Ministerial Control of the Nationalized Industries*, HC 371, vol. II, Memorandum submitted by the Rt Hon. Aubrey Jones, p. 677.
7. See pp. 120–22 above. See also *ibid.*, vol. II, p. 678.
8. *The Nationalized Industries: A Review of Economic and Financial Objectives*, November 1967, Cmnd. 3437, para. 1.
9. Text of a Government Announcement Issued from 10 Downing Street on 7 September 1967.
10. *Ministerial Control*, *op. cit.*, vol. II, p. 678.

11. National Board for Prices and Incomes, Report No. 59, *The Bulk Supply Tariff of the Central Electricity Generating Board*, March 1968, Cmnd. 3575, para. 7.
12. National Board for Prices and Incomes, Report No. 56, *Proposals by the London Transport Board and British Railways Board for fare increases in the London Area*, March 1968, Cmnd. 3561.
13. National Board for Prices and Incomes, *Bulk Supply Tariff, op. cit.*, para. 55.
14. National Board for Prices and Incomes, Report No. 57, *Gas Prices*, March 1968, Cmnd. 3567, para. 44.
15. *Bulk Supply Tariff, op. cit.*, para. 49.
16. See pp. 89–93 above.
17. National Board for Prices and Incomes, Report No. 72, *Proposed increases by the British Railways Board in certain Country-wide fares and charges*, May 1968, Cmnd. 3656, paras. 57–8.
18. *Ministerial Control, op. cit.*, vol. II, pp. 679–80.
19. *Nationalized Industries, op. cit.*, para. 32.
20. *Ministerial Control, op. cit.*, vol. II, pp. 678.
21. National Board for Prices and Incomes, Report No. 102, *Gas Prices*, February 1969, Cmnd. 3942, paras. 19–20.
22. *Ibid.*, paras. 56–60.
23. *Ibid.*, paras. 63–5.
24. *Ibid.*, para. 4.
25. National Board for Prices and Incomes, Report No. 111, *Steel Prices*, May 1969, Cmnd. 4033, paras. 55–61.
26. *Ibid.*, paras. 24–6.
27. *Ibid.*, paras. 62–7.
28. National Board for Prices and Incomes, *Fourth General Report, op. cit.*, para. 53.
29. See, for example, National Board for Prices and Incomes, Report no. 77, *Third General Report*, July 1968, Cmnd. 3715. paras. 22–3.
30. *Fourth General Report, op. cit.*, para. 25.
31. See pp. 43–44 above.
32. For a summary of cases see *Fourth General Report, op. cit.*, paras. 46–7.
33. National Board for Prices and Incomes, Report No. 80, *Distributors' Margins on Paint, Children's Clothing, Household Textiles and Proprietary Medicine*, August 1968 Cmnd. 3737; see also *Ministerial Control, op. cit.*, vol. II, Evidence from Rt Hon. Aubrey Jones, q. 2251.
34. *Ministerial Control, op. cit.*, vol. III, p. 678.
35. Its staff had to be expanded to take account of its new responsibilities for the nationalized industries after September 1967. A group of about a dozen or so members was built up in the first instance including mainly management consultants, business economists and accountants, as well as experts in operational research and work

study. However the Board continued to rely a great deal on the use of outside consultants working on a temporary basis.

36. *Fourth General Report*, *op. cit.*, paras. 49–51.
37. *Ibid.*, para. 52.
38. *Ibid.*, para. 50.
39. See pp. 130, 132 above.
40. Commission on Industry and Manpower, *op. cit.*, para. 316.

Chapter 8

JOINT CONSULTATION WITH WORKERS AND CONSUMERS

The role of employees of nationalized industry and the role of consumers' representatives of course merit whole books to themselves. The boards of the nationalized industries are all in their various ways required to follow formal procedures for consulting both workers and consumers on a wide range of problems. In this respect the nationalized undertakings are different (at least in degree) from their counterparts in the private sector. This needs to be recognized when the two sectors are compared (and thus when policies are formulated on the assumption that the two should be treated in the same way). Unfortunately we shall only be able to give a cursory examination to these questions here.

Labour relations have been a vital aspect of the management of all the nationalized undertakings, and in some cases they have been of absolutely overriding importance. This fact is probably not always given the weight it deserves by government departments or select committees although it is a problem stressed by the boards, particularly those (such as the Coal Board and the Railways Board) which have had to bring about large and painful changes in their industries. This is not directly related to the fact that these industries are nationalized. It is a result of the physical nature of the industries and of the state they were in at the time of nationalization. Moreover, most large private firms today regard labour relations as crucial.

There is a tendency among most commentators to confuse the nationalized industries with the boards themselves, and to overlook the fact that the industries can include many different organizations, various levels of authority and a great range of occupational and professional interests. Not only is it legally wrong to make this confusion (for the statutes do not give authority to 'industries' but to 'boards'), it is also misleading for policy-makers. It could be one reason for the failure to pay sufficient attention in appraising the boards' results to business management and the standards of its performance compared with economic principles on the one hand and financial accountability on the other. We return to this argument in a later part of this book.

Unfortunately little is known about the effects of joint consultation on the performance of the boards of the nationalized industries – for example, whether it is an essential aid to making difficult changes, or whether it is an unnecessary constraint on management. We have not carried out any research on this aspect of the nationalized industries and must therefore confine ourselves to suggesting that a full study is greatly overdue.[1] The procedures for joint consultation employed in the nationalized industries need to be evaluated in their own right and also compared with similar procedures in the private sector. This would be valuable, not only from the point of view of industrial relations, but also in formulating government policy for the industries and especially in deciding their future organization and role.

As for the role of consumers, it is again difficult to decide just how far the existence of formal procedures for consultation affects the management of a nationalized industry. It is fairly safe to make a generalization and to say that the role of consumers' organizations in the nationalized industries is essentially consultative – in that consumers' representatives have the right to make complaints and suggestions of their own and at the same time the boards are obliged in most cases to hear those representatives on a range of subjects directly affecting the consumer. Special consumers' organizations exist for each nationalized undertaking and this has led to a close relationship between management and consumers' representatives.[2] The latter do not, however, exercise any executive powers, although sometimes their influence can be decisive, especially in cases where ministers are obliged to take their views into account in approving decisions of the boards (for example, in railway closures). In general the subjects on which consultation takes place most often are price changes, the quality of goods and services, and other changes in the way a service is provided.

A number of problems have arisen in the consumers' organizations in the nationalized industries. A recent inquiry by the Consumer Council found that their structure had not been adapted to keep step with the many changes in structure and organization of the nationalized industries themselves. The same inquiry found that in four industries studied 'only a relatively marginal impact has as yet been made by the consultative organizations . . . on the awareness of the consuming public in general'.[3]

Many of these problems can be explained by the general ambiguity of the consumer's role in society. Perhaps the concept 'consumer', like the concepts 'worker', 'voter', 'shareholder', 'manager', is hardly meaningful as a description of collectivities of people with identifiable interests, views and needs. How far consumers' representatives represent 'consumers' rather than the other collectivities just mentioned is sometimes uncertain. Consumers cannot easily be organized into tightly-knit bodies like trade unions. Nor can their interests easily be expressed by voting for representatives who in turn deliberate on the consumers' interest. Conventionally, consumers assert themselves in the market place; their right to vote is their right to withdraw their custom. Much depends, therefore, on whether the nationalized industries are considered competitive. Indeed special consumer representation in the nationalized industries seems to have been justified mainly because the boards are monopolies liable to exploit their consumers.[4]

In so far as consumers' organizations in the nationalized industries are responsible to the boards of the industries and consulted on matters affecting price and quality of service, then they are probably best seen as a logical extension of the boards' own marketing and public relations. They are something more than this at the present time. In essence they seem to be machinery created by Parliament (and appointed for the most part by ministers) to prevent the boards 'exploiting' the users of their products and services by charging monopolistic prices. In this respect the existing consultative bodies are almost certainly quite inadequate unless supplemented by ministerial control and by autonomous boards like the NBPI and Monopolies Commission. Indeed it is probably safe to suppose (without, that is, having carried out any research on the role of consumers' representatives) that control of monopoly is mainly exercised at the centre either by ministers or by independent bodies of the kind discussed in the previous chapter. In whatever ways ministers might decide to provide representation of 'consumers' in the exercise of such control the same principles could presumably be observed for all kinds of commercial activity where monopoly is thought to exist.

So far therefore representation of workers and consumers has not been used in nationalized industries as a means of substituting for political control. Its role in nationalized undertakings is different only as a matter of degree from that in other business concerns of the same size and importance.

REFERENCES

1. But see W. A. Robson, *Nationalized Industry and Public Ownership*, London, 1962, pp. 319–60.
2. *Consumer Consultative Machinery in the Nationalized Industries*, A Consumer Council Study, HMSO, London, 1968, *passim*.
3. *Ibid.*, p. 8.
4. *Ibid.*, pp. 59–64.

Chapter 9

SOME PROPOSALS FOR REFORM

We have seen that the only effective kind of political control over the nationalized industries so far has been control by ministers. We have also seen, however, that ministerial control has raised three particular problems. First, it seems to have produced a division of responsibility between minister and board which gives too many commercial decisions to civil servants and too little scope in commercial matters to boards. Departments do not seem to want to get involved in the industries' affairs more than is politically necessary or commercially harmless, but many people believe that they do get involved to that extent. Not only is the division of responsibility unclear and inconsistent but the criteria for weighing up the performance of the boards are doubtful. The extent of ministerial control and its ambivalence make it difficult to decide when boards are successful and when they are not. Finally, from the point of view of government itself, the degree and nature of ministerial control of nationalized industries has produced an irrational allocation of functions among departments and placed new demands on the personnel and procedures of central administration.

For some time now these criticisms have been acknowledged in government and, as we have noticed, efforts have been made to respond to them with changes. Some distinguished observers – including the Select Committee on Nationalized Industries – have suggested that reform has not gone far enough. We shall consider now some proposals for further reform. All of these were mentioned in some way during the Select Committee's recent inquiry into ministerial control,[1] although not all of them were supported by the Committee itself. Some of them are relatively new, even for the Select Committee; others have been around for some time. Nevertheless, the proposals do go together – particularly the first four of them. In fact, as we shall see, some are really alternatives to others, but many writers make them at the same time. The last one is a good deal more radical than the rest but none of them (at least as recorded here) envisages an end to public ownership. And all accept the existing method of capital financing.

MANAGEMENT BY ECONOMIC PRINCIPLES

We have seen that some reforms have already been made (mainly at the initiative of the Treasury) to economic decision-making in government about the nationalized industries. We are not concerned so much with those reforms here[2] as with the proposal of the Select Committee on Nationalized Industries that certain economic principles should be made the basis of 'standard' policies for the nationalized industries.

One difficulty with this proposal is that some economists would argue that following the principles recommended (long-run marginal-cost pricing and the application of a standard test rate of discount) would not lead to the ends desired, namely, an optimum allocation of resources. This must surely reduce the value of these principles as sources of *standard* policies for the nationalized industries. Indeed the Select Committee did not give nearly so much attention to the views of economists who disagreed with the principles as they did those of their own adviser who was very strongly in favour of them.

Even if widely accepted economic principles could be found it would still be absurd to employ them as operational criteria of efficient – or for that matter successful – management. In fact the Select Committee would not have done this and devoted some time in its Report to explaining how the boards of the industries should still be set financial objectives. However, the Committee felt that the financial objectives should in future be literally deduced from the government's 'standard' economic policies for the nationalized industries.[3] It is true that it would not go all the way to treating them as standard, for it would qualify them with 'publicly stated requirements and by social and other public interest obligations imposed on the industry by ministers'. We have already shown, however, that financial objectives derived in this way would deprive the boards of that freedom in pricing and investment policy which they themselves have argued is basic to commercial and industrial enterprise. Those financial objectives might provide a yardstick of the internal efficiency of an undertaking but it is doubtful whether that is an adequate measure of the competence of the boards. The question is: who is responsible for directing the undertakings, ministers or boards?

Now we have seen in our own analysis of ministerial control of the nationalized industries that there is an important obligation on ministers to ensure that the nationalized undertakings are managed efficiently. Not only are ministers given clear statutory duty of appointing the boards, but it stands to reason that some person or body has to take the place of shareholders. Moreover, ministers now lend vast sums of money to the boards and, whatever one feels about the value of competition in the private sector, the nationalized undertakings are clearly not subject to the same forces of restraint and incentive which are ideally supposed to exist in private industry. Indeed we have hinted that, in view of all these things, ministerial control might well have been inadequate up to now especially since the boards of the industries are not generally pursuing their own pricing and investment policies.

When considering the Select Committee's proposal for deriving financial objectives from government economic policies, therefore, one thing we should ask is whether this proposal is likely to make ministerial control more adequate. In fact the Committee seems to have been concerned less with the problems of ensuring efficiency than with ensuring that government economic policy would be carried out. Moreover, it had a fairly partial and individual notion of what economic principles should govern that policy. One of the Committee's chief aims was to make ministers more clearly accountable to Parliament for their responsibilities for the nationalized industries. In the past it has usually tried to avoid getting into an argument about what the functions of ministers should actually be. In this particular inquiry it had clearly either given up that convention or failed to maintain it.[4] The result was that it got on to ground where the bi-partisan nature of its inquiries was a hindrance rather than a help. The proposals in the 1968 Report on *Ministerial Control* were consequently based on elusive and inarticulate premises. That on its own need not concern us. What matters is that the Committee's inquiry acted in this case as a kind of focal point for a partial attitude towards nationalized industries of some importance.

If the Committee really meant that the performance of the boards should be evaluated according to their success in carrying out the government's social and economic policies, then it was suggesting a rather different approach to nationalized industries than the one normally assumed by the boards themselves. For the most part the latter seem to believe it to be at least part of their duty to run their undertakings as successful business concerns. Now we know already that that is in itself a vague and elusive object, but the Select Committee did nothing to make it any clearer or to show how it fitted with social and economic obligations. We have seen that it can be argued that the nationalized industries should be used as special instruments of social and economic policy, their own interests as commercial enterprises taking second place, if taking any place at all. Some people seem to think that this was the main purpose of nationalization. If the Select Committee was truly taking the same approach, then it was going further than most governments, which have always maintained that commercial interests (whatever they were interpreted to be) should not take second place, but should simply be *combined* with social and economic obligations, the order of priority being indifferent or unknown. What interests us particularly is that, the more the Select Committee did want to relegate commercial interests, the more it needed to find some alternative to provide aims and standards for management. We shall inspect its other proposals to see whether any such alternatives emerge there.

But the full weight of what the Select Committee might have been proposing (if it really wanted financial objectives derived from economic principles) should be emphasized. The Committee made great play of its idea that its proposal would actually reduce the need for ministerial control of decisions by the boards, that ministers could henceforth be confined to strategy and the boards left to tactics. We have already shown in previous chapters why this would not be the result of its proposal. First, ministers would still need to control the boards in order to ensure efficiency; indeed, they would need to do so all the more in so far as the economic principles adopted override the commercial policies of the boards. Secondly, since the Committee was over-confident about the general applicability of its economic principles, in practice most decisions would continue to be pragmatic and the different social, economic and financial obligations of boards be weighed up in each case. Consequently the Committee's formula would seem to place an awful lot of trust in the discretion of decision-makers in central government. Perhaps it is necessary to do so, but the costs of such a degree of political control need to be carefully examined and prepared for.

A CLEARER DIVISION OF RESPONSIBILITIES

One cost of political control is the amount of power it gives to the executive branch of government. Some people would perhaps not consider that a very great cost, if cost at all, but the Select Committee has normally been most anxious to find means of ensuring that ministers can be held accountable to Parliament for their responsibilities for the nationalized industries in the normal way and that nationalization should not entail a reduction in the power of Parliament relative to the executive. This, after all, is probably the most important political question raised by the idea of public ownership in a liberal democracy. Another related cost of political control is that it tends to confuse responsibility between minister and board so that

Parliament (or the people) cannot know whom to blame when things go wrong. Perhaps this sounds rather pessimistic and puritanical. But surely it is again a very important question in a democracy where the government and its agencies are meant to answer to the people for the political power they exercise. The Select Committee has certainly not been alone in pressing the question (and anxiety about it was instrumental in getting the Committee set up in the first place).

The solution usually proposed by the Select Committee and by others has been to provide a clearer division of responsibility between minister and boards by revising the statutes. In its 1968 Report it brought together some earlier proposals to this end. At the same time it noted that much had already been done by various governments to provide a clearer division of responsibilities. The system of financial objectives had itself been an improvement. But the Committee wanted ministers to be given explicit statutory authority to use 'the main instruments of strategic control' over pricing and investment policy.[5] It believed that the scope of ministers' powers to make general directions 'in the national interest' should be broadened by removing the statutory phrase, directions 'of a general character', which had been a legal inhibition to ministers in cases where they might have used it but did not.[6] The Committee also argued as a general rule that:

> 'Where extra social or wider public interest obligations are imposed on or undertaken by the industries, they should be publicly identified, quantified and appropriately financed by the Ministers concerned.'[7]

The same procedure should be followed to take account of departures from the 'standard' pricing and investment policies recommended by ministers. The aim was to ensure that the House of Commons could be kept informed of how ministers carried out their responsibilities and could hold ministers to account through Parliamentary Questions and other means. Among other things the Committee recommended that a White Paper should be published periodically for each industry. This 'should set out the anticipated financial and productive performances of the industry for the forthcoming year, together with some information about pricing proposals, technical and other developments, the quality of service aimed at, etc.' The White Paper would also set out the sector policies for the industry, the pricing and investment policies required by the minister and the social obligations of the boards.[8]

As for separately identifying and paying for social obligations, we have already seen that recent governments have been favourable to the Committee's point of view, and measures introduced for the railways and for the coal industry go a long way to adopt the sort of arrangements recommended.[9] It has in fact been far from easy to decide how much should be paid to boards in compensation for providing social services. The main justification is that, although it is difficult to set up, at least the Committee's arrangement enables Parliament to decide how much should be spent on social services which benefit particular groups of people (such as coal-miners or commuters) or conform to some intangible national interest (such as prestige abroad or regional development at home). It is said to be better to entrust Parliament with this task than simply to raise the the money from consumers in the form of higher prices for a nationalized industry's products or services.

The implication is that Parliament would be able to decide whether or not to provide uneconomic railway services, rural electricity, and so on and to decide how much these services should cost. Yet parliamentary control of public expenditure is a problem in its own right. Many people question the effectiveness of Parliament in controlling expenditure on such services as hospitals, university education and defence, where departments do already carry the expenditure on their own votes. Why should Parliament be any more effective in controlling expenditure by departments on services provided by nationalized industries? What parliamentary control of expenditure normally means in practice is departmental control with periodic general parliamentary approval. The benefits of separating social obligations and subsidizing them should not therefore be exaggerated by implying that it would increase participation in these matters by the public or their parliamentary representatives. That would beg a number of difficult questions.

In general giving ministers more precise statutory authority to intervene in nationalized industries in the public interest would probably not do much to preserve the rights of Parliament. For one thing, it should be remembered that parliamentary time is already inadequate and it is far from clear where additional time could be found to hold ministers accountable for new powers. Moreover, as we have seen, the public interest is almost impossible to define with any consistency or clarity. Indeed, while ministers are responsible for the boards' financial performance as well as for their social and economic obligations, then it would be wrong to restrict ministers to 'social' matters leaving 'commercial' questions outside their scope. The problem is not the lack of clarity or formality with which functions have been allocated so much as the nature of the functions themselves.

Yet as long as ministers exercise these functions it would probably be best to admit the fact by explaining in legislation what it is they are expected to do. By this means the real consequences of nationalization for public expenditure and ministers' powers could be made more apparent. It would, for example, be clearer that vesting nationalized industries in public corporations had not relieved the civil service of the need to participate in important business decisions.[10]

REFORM OF THE CIVIL SERVICE

Another cost of political control is the effect on the functions of civil servants in the departments exercising it. Indeed this was one of the assumptions on which the Fulton Committee based its proposals for reform of the British home civil service.[11] However, most criticism of civil servants concerned with the nationalized industries has been very unfair. In the first place these civil servants have on the whole reacted soberly and intelligently to modern techniques of economic analysis and intellectually speaking cannot be reproached. As in so much recent criticism of the civil service, far too much emphasis has been placed on the learning of specialist skills, particularly those associated with economics. The real disability of the civil service in this (as in some other) sectors is one for which it cannot be held responsible and which is in fact in other respects its main virtue. The general disposition of the British higher civil service is to support a system of Parliamentary Government based on the convention of ministerial responsibility. Now some commentators would argue that this is a poor system and would consequently prefer a different type of civil servant. When their argument is expressed respectably, however, it makes an explicit demand for change in the system of government. The Fulton Committee made no such demand nor have the typical critics of those civil servants who deal with nationalized industry.

The main complaint made by members of boards of nationalized industries, the Select Committee, and others has been that officials in the sponsoring departments and the Public Enterprises Division of the Treasury were too 'generalist' in their professional experience, training and outlook. A common remark has been that, in the words of the Select Committee, 'few people seem to spend more than four or five years in any one post'.[12] Another is that the officials concerned generally have no industrial experience and thus cannot fully appreciate the problems at second hand. Finally, it has been said that there are insufficient people in the relevant government departments with the requisite specialist qualifications. These criticisms are of course similar to those made by the Fulton Committee and by many of the witnesses who gave evidence to it. It is also significant, we suggest, that the chief critics among the industries themselves seem to have been British Rail and the National Coal Board (two 'problem boards') whereas the electricity supply industry seemed to be far less conscious of the same inadequacies. Our own impression is that critics have sometimes taken advantage of the prevailing mood of cynicism about the British civil service to put up some diversive action on their own behalf.

It cannot be denied that the officials concerned have been overwhelmingly 'generalist' in the sense that they have usually been members of the administrative class. There were remarkably few of them, whatever their background, and clearly there was a shortage of those with training in specialist techniques. Administrative class officials have now and then been seconded to an industry to broaden their experience, but there have been limitations to this practice. (The Select Committee reported in 1968 that in the Ministry of Power six out of thirty-four senior staff concerned had served at some time in a nationalized fuel industry.[13]) One vital function which the Ministry of Transport has now acquired is auditing the social services provided by British Rail. The Department at the time of our inquiry had a Directorate General of Economic Planning, which consisted of about forty economists, but only one division of this (a 'handful' of economists was a term we heard) was concerned with the Railways. The task of auditing the management of the passenger services receiving grants from the Ministry was in fact expected to fall largely to officers of the executive class. These officers would be generally similar in experience and type to the officers working in the department of the Comptroller and Auditor General.

Indeed, the Select Committee believed that its own recommendations would create a need for far more specialist staff in the relevant government departments, if not as permanent officials then at least as 'advisers':

> 'Now that the industries are being required to use more sophisticated pricing and investment criteria, it is important that more use should be made by the ministries, in developing and checking these criteria, of the specialist talents of economists, accountants, business methods, specialists and statisticians.'[14]

One former chairman of a board recommended that an 'Industrial Civil Service' should be created and made quite separate from the rest of the civil service, in recognition of the special aptitudes and qualifications required in dealing with nationalized industry.[15] Indeed, already statements of government policy for the nationalized industries have reflected increased dependence on specialist economic advice. The Fulton Committee was quite right to point out that the expanding and deepening responsibilities acquired in sectors such as this are bound to place unbearable strain on the 'generalist' administrator. Intellectual effort and a willingness to learn new ways can only do so much, and a new approach to recruiting, training and employing senior officials might have to be instituted.

We cannot go here into the general question of reforming the civil service. However, we shall make four particular observations, bearing in mind that the Fulton Committee itself did not see changes in personnel as a sufficient answer to the challenge of modern government, and called for more attention to structure and machinery, among other things supporting devolution to autonomous boards on the model of the nationalized industries! First, most recommendations to recruit more specialist advice are just as glib as the one we quoted above from the Select Committee. They do not answer the pertinent question of where people with the necessary qualifications and experience can be found. All they do is to set up the civil service to compete, for example, with the boards of the industries for staff with requisite industrial experience, and with firms of management consultants and bodies like the NBPI for scarce manpower appropriately qualified in economics and other suitable subjects. Secondly, even assuming that supplies of such people were readily available to work in government departments, they could only be as useful as their particular backgrounds or disciplines allow. In fact economic principles and even the techniques of the management scientist are of limited value in ensuring that nationalized industries serve the public interest. It would be taking too narrow a view of the function of ministers towards the nationalized industries to see the cost of political control being reduced very much by taking more specialist advice. Even when national economic policy and social costs and benefits are being weighed there is a danger of 'technocracy'. If this is considered desirable, then it ought to be justified in its own right in terms of its effects on the political system as a whole.

Thirdly, and of more immediate concern to us, is the fact that the government's roles as 'banker' and 'shareholder' to the industries call not for the application of intellectual techniques of analysis but rather the adoption of certain attitudes and norms of behaviour which may simply be incompatible with the other functions of civil servants in parliamentary government. We refer here mainly to ministers' responsibility for the financial performance of the boards of the industries. In this respect particularly it may not be the subjects studied by civil servants at university or their professional experience which are wanting. Their constitutional position as the advisers of ministers imbues them with a respect for traditional parliamentary financial control and an anxiety to do what is politically safe and expedient which is just as necessary in government as it is out of place in business.

Finally, therefore, is it not rather absurd to argue for an 'Industrial Civil Service' to provide special skills and attitudes when public corporations have been set up to do that very thing? If vesting the nationalized industries in public corporations has not obviated the need to change the conventional orientation and aptitude of the civil service, then surely it has proved rather pointless? (By the same token, the argument for wider devolution to autonomous public boards also fails.)

Some recent reforms in the training and employment of civil servants may well have been desirable and, however well the system of public corporations worked, it might still be desirable for officials in the government departments concerned to have wider training and experience than was customary before the Fulton Report. The point is that reform of the civil service is no solution to the problems of political control of nationalized industries. Indeed it would be ironic if the Fulton Committee recommended more devolution to public corporations as a means of adapting government to its modern responsibilities, if one consequence of such devolution was to make reform of the civil service even more urgent than before! The Fulton Committee may itself be a victim of this irony. But by careful study of the subject it can be avoided; we repeat that it is the nature of the functions devolved which is crucial.

A MINISTRY OF NATIONALIZED INDUSTRIES

The proposal for a new government department with this title was another item in the report of the Select Committee on Nationalized Industries and was very closely related to the Committee's other proposals. (However, it is possible to support any or all of the three proposals already considered without believing that such a department should be created.) The proposal has been criticized for being as irrelevant as some of the other proposals we have been discussing here. On the other hand careful scrutiny reveals that there is actually more to the idea than appears at first sight.

The main objects of the proposal were, first, to separate the two functions of representing the public interest and acting as spokesman of the industries now combined in the sponsoring departments and, secondly, as a partial consequence of this, to provide for greater specialization and consistency in ministerial control.[16] It was not entirely clear what the Committee meant by 'the public interest'; in fact, the phrase seemed to refer to any 'wider' social and economic factor, such as the secondary costs and benefits of commercial policy, short-term economic policy, and policy for national economic growth and development. The new department was not intended to concern itself with these matters, but to take over from the existing sponsoring departments all responsibilities 'that are chiefly directed at overseeing and seeking to ensure the efficiency of any of the nationalized industries'. It would be responsible for the 'commercial interests' of the industries and their consumers; this is what the Committee seemed to understand as being the function of acting as an industry's 'spokesman'. This included laying down the 'standard' economic principles which would, in the Committee's scheme of things, determine the financial objectives of the industries. But essentially the Ministry would take over what the Committee saw as the government's functions as owner of the industries:

> '. . . the interest of the state as owners of the industries in their efficiency would be separated from sector policy in just the same way as the interest of the owners of private enterprise companies are separate from the responsibility for policy of their sponsoring minister. In this respect the nationalized industries would be put into the same relationship towards the sponsoring minister as are private enterprise companies.'[17]

The Committee envisaged the new department: taking responsibility for appointing members of the boards; laying down the 'standard' pricing and investment policies adopted for the industries by the government; agreeing with the boards at the same time their financial objectives (which would follow from these policies); reviewing investment programmes and 'overseeing' efficiency by means of 'efficiency studies'; and performing other miscellaneous statutory duties now belonging to sponsoring ministers affecting the industries' borrowing powers, research and training programmes, forms of accounts, and so on. Responsibility for all policies designed to secure 'wider public interests' would be vested in other departments, particularly the existing sponsoring departments such as the Ministry of Transport and the Board of Trade, but also all 'those whose interests would benefit from such policies', for example, the Department of Employment and Productivity where employment policy was concerned.[18] When the public interest in this sense dictated a decision leading to financial losses for a board, then the department concerned would pay compensation on its own vote.

One interesting idea contained in the Committee's proposal is that ministers' responsibility for the financial performance of the industries might be separated from their responsibilities for setting economic and social objectives. It is also noteworthy that the Committee sought to rationalize the existing departmental structure for dealing with the nationalized industries. The question is whether creating such a Ministry of Nationalized Industries would be the best means of achieving either of these ends. There are a number of snags in the proposal.

First, the relationship of the new department with the Treasury would be rather confused. It is far from clear just how many functions of the Public Enterprises Division of the Treasury would, in the Committee's view, be transferred to the new Ministry. According to its report, the Committee envisaged the Treasury giving only 'economic guidance' to the new Ministry, settling the test rate of discount, and reviewing investment programmes against an economic background.[19] However, while the state continued to provide such a substantial amount of the boards' capital it is doubtful whether the Treasury could cease to concern itself with the boards' financial results. As we have seen the fact the industries are publicly owned and financed means that it is very difficult in practice to separate financial from economic control.

The Committee seemed to be suggesting in fact that some wider economic responsibilities should be given to the new Ministry. In other words, it would agree suitable financial objectives with each board based on the 'standard' economic policies of the government. Secondly, then, if the financial obligations of the boards of the nationalized industries are wholly or partly derived from their social and economic obligations, it would be better to settle all these obligations together; indeed the sponsoring departments do take some responsibility now for co-ordinating these obligations. But one feature of a sponsoring department is that it deals with both private and public industry. (Thus the Ministry of Power has sponsored the privately-owned oil industry and the private steel sector as well as the nationalized fuel and power industries.) Again the sponsoring department is responsible for sector policy as well as for the efficiency and financial performance of the nationalized undertakings in its care. This is at least some guarantee that the demands of policy will be realistic and practicable. In other words, there are certain advantages in the dual economic and financial role of the sponsoring department. And what about the need to co-ordinate policy for the public and private sectors?

Thirdly, if some rationalization of departments concerned with industrial policy is considered desirable, then why not do this by amalgamating some existing departments rather than by creating new ones? The Government took a much more sensible step towards rationalization than that proposed by the Select Committee when in September 1969 the Ministry of Power was merged with the Ministry of Technology and the role of the latter was extended to include most of the industrial functions of the old Department of Economic Affairs. That helped to bring a slight reduction in the number of departments while retaining joint control of public and private parts of the sectors concerned, and keeping economic and financial control under the same roof.[20] The Select Committee's proposal would have increased the number of departments and created an odd sort of 'underlord' ministry in search of an 'overlord', which would hardly be a rationalization of functions at all.

Finally, therefore, whether all the members of the Committee intended it or not, these would be special arrangements for the nationalized industries compared with the private sector, and ministerial control would be increased. In fact the new Ministry would probably not have much influence in the making of economic policy. Sector policy would be determined elsewhere, and the Treasury would still be supreme in economic policy for the short term and would still have to ensure that the public received an adequate return on the capital invested in the nationalized industries. The new Ministry would doubtless be concerned mainly with efficiency studies and here the Committee saw it developing new techniques as much as carrying on work previously done by sponsoring departments. In other words, the proposal would increase intervention by ministers and mean an increase in the number of officials concerned with the nationalized industries.

The dual role of the sponsoring departments has disadvantages as well as advantages. For example, the Coal Board is sometimes confused by the difference between what the Minister of Power's Accountant General expects of the Coal Board in terms of a satisfactory return on investment, and what the same department's Chief Inspector of Mines demands in terms of safety precautions in the design and management of pits. However incongruous the various roles of the Government may seem, however, it is essential to provide effective co-ordination of them at some point and the creation of a new Ministry with rather limited and uncertain powers would probably make this even more difficult. As for separating responsibility for commercial results and financial viability, there are other ways of providing for this.

AN EFFICIENCY AUDIT COMMISSION

Professor Robson, who is one of the main advocates of an Efficiency Audit Commission, criticized the Select Committee's proposal for a Ministry of Nationalized Industries on the grounds that ministers have neither the statutory authority nor the practical ability to 'ensure efficiency' in the nationalized industries. This is not so far away from our own argument that the need to check that the industries are run competently and efficiently is probably the most difficult aspect of political control. Moreover, he complained as we have done that, although the Select Committee stressed the importance of efficiency, it did not say what this meant and simply recommended certain 'strategic' pricing and investment policies.

However, it is far from clear what would be the purpose of a body like Professor Robson's proposed Commission, which would take the basic organization of a nationalized industry and government policy as given, and examine the 'operating efficiency' of the board concerned:

> 'The Audit Commission would inquire into such matters as the character, quantity and quality of goods and services provided; price policy; efficiency of administration; personnel questions, including pay, recruitment, and methods of promotion; relations between the board and the consumer; capital expenditure, and the methods of financing it, and so forth . . . It would build up a skilled staff possessing an unrivalled insight into the problems of nationalized industry and an unequalled ability to compare methods adopted by the several boards for coping with them.'[21]

Certainly the agenda of subjects listed by Professor Robson seems to include most of the criteria which would determine whether a board was commercially successful or not. In other words, the word 'efficiency' seems to be used there (as in other contexts) catachrestically for 'successful performance' or 'effectiveness'.

The bodies in the best position to ensure efficiency are the boards in which the industries are vested. This was recognized in the nationalization statutes, although it has never been made absolutely clear. The idea was to provide as far as possible the same kind of control as is thought to exist in the most efficient parts of the private sector of industry. In other words, the boards would be required to meet their expenditure with their revenue, so that their performance could be judged by their commercial results over a period of time. In practice, of course, commercial results cannot be used as a criterion of performance, because they have been distorted by a variety of social, economic and financial obligations. It is significant, however, that in spite of this few people have proposed any change in the basic organization of the industries in order to provide some other yardstick. For example, the industries could be organized as government departments, so that Parliament and the Treasury would control their expenditure directly and they could be subjected to the same administrative discipline as ordinary public services. On the contrary most reforms have aimed to distinguish *more clearly* between the consequences of obligations imposed from outside and the consequences of the boards' own efforts, so that commercial results could be used as a criterion of performance as was originally intended.

This used to be the Select Committee's argument but, as we have seen, it has recently proposed that the financial objectives of the industries should now be derived from social and economic obligations decided by ministers. Under these circumstances the boards' financial performance would reflect their efficiency in pursuing government pricing and investment policies rather than the commercial judgement of the boards themselves. The proposal for a Ministry of Nationalized Industries can be seen as following directly from this approach in that it would provide an administrative alternative – that is, 'efficiency studies' – to replace commercial results as a measure of performance.

Professor Robson's own authoritative and comprehensive theory of nationalized industry has always been that the boards should themselves take responsibility for social and economic obligations in the public interest.[22] He is really in much the same position as the Select Committee, therefore, in that he also finds 'ordinary commercial criteria' of performance somewhat irrelevant.[23] His Efficiency Audit Commission would be designed to solve the same problems as the Select Committee's Ministry of Nationalized Industries, although it would set out to do so in a rather different way. What, then, is the argument for 'efficiency audits' in general and an Efficiency Audit Commission in particular?

One reason why commercial results may be an unreliable measure of performance of nationalized industries is that in many respects the boards of the industries are monopolies. Under these circumstances some external scrutiny of prices and costs is usually considered desirable. It is not clear how far the Efficiency Audit Commission would look at efficiency from this point of view. We have already shown that this kind of scrutiny has been provided in some ways by the NBPI and has also been provided in the private sector by the Monopolies Commission. Why create a special body to inspect monopoly in the nationalized industries? Monopoly and the economic inefficiency associated with it are general problems of modern industry, whether public or private, and are the objects of public inspection and regulation in most western democracies. The problem in Britain is that nationalized industries have been left out of the general arrangements for dealing with monopoly.

Another reason why some external examination of efficiency is thought to be necessary is that there are no shareholders to make the boards accountable. Again, the government lends money to the boards and most lenders of large sums of capital presumably ask questions before doing so about the competence and viability of the borrowers. Is the purpose of 'efficiency audits' to take up the responsibilities exercised in private firms by shareholders and bankers? Little enough is known about the role of either shareholders or lenders of capital in the private sector. The Select Committee on Nationalized Industries has never inquired into the controls exercised by merchant banks or large insurance companies over the business concerns which depend on their financial support to see whether similar arrangements should be made for nationalized undertakings.

However, Professor Robson for one would regard the private sector as a poor model for the kind of checks on performance needed in the public sector. His main reason for wanting some new means of 'ensuring efficiency' is that a nationalized industry's performance should be determined by various social and economic objectives rather than by commercial results. He finds the Select Committee's proposed economic criteria for pricing and investment inadequate because he believes they are based on what is expected in the private sector.[24] Yet both he and the Select Committee seek some means of administrative audit of performance in nationalized industry. Both have suggested bureaucratic devices, the one the creation of a new government department and the other that of an independent, public board. It is interesting that neither say that they would extend their proposed audits or studies to cover the private sector but this is probably not because they believe that firms in the private sector can be relied on to be efficient without any form of public inspection and regulation. Indeed many representatives of private industry have argued for reforms in the way shareholders and lenders of capital exercise their functions and it might be rewarding to compare their ideas with proposals for an Efficiency Audit Commission or greater ministerial control in the case of nationalized industry. The fact is, however, that the Select Committee and Professor Robson are not interested in the efficiency of industry in general, but in seeing that the nationalized industries are run according to special social and economic criteria which do not, by implication, apply in the private sector. They do not want the boards of the nationalized industries treated like private concerns. This implies that they have positive reasons for wanting public ownership and for wanting the nationalized industries used as instruments of government policy. The consequence of such an approach seems to be more political and administrative control of the industries.

The boards of the nationalized industries themselves seem to be unanimous in rejecting the idea of an Efficiency Audit Commission, not because they are dogmatic but because they prefer the system envisaged by the statutes. The Electricity Council told the Select Committee that in their view:

> 'It is proper that there should be regular, though not frequent, inquiries in order to discover whether the industries are conducting themselves in such a way as would lead to efficiency, whether they have available the right sort of expertise, and whether the way in which they tackle major problems appears to informed outsiders likely to produce the right decisions.'

They clearly felt that there were already adequate means of furthering the public interest in this respect. A more detailed and regulatory kind of review as seemed to be envisaged by the proposal for an Efficiency Audit Commission would in fact tend to make the boards less efficient. For one thing, 'the ability to describe actions rather than to execute them would be regarded as an increasingly valuable administrative skill'.[25] The civil service has often been criticized for revealing just such a tendency and it was partly to avoid it that the nationalized industries were vested in public corporations. In general, all the boards seemed to prefer hiring their own consultants when specialized advice was needed. In particular, they felt that, if they were made accountable to some external body of investigators over the whole range of administrative decision (which is what the proposal for an Efficiency Audit Commission seems to involve), then they would be unable to compete with the private sector for staff of the required outlook and calibre. Indeed, it is easy to see that under such circumstances the boards might be unable to compete effectively at all.

A very important objection to the proposal is that criteria simply do not exist for making such a general assessment of managerial performance from outside. Most groups of consultants or *ad hoc* official committees of experts are appointed to deal with special problems (such as a specific engineering project or work study) and not to reach conclusions about the general effectiveness of a firm or board. Yet, as the Gas Council pointed out to the Select Committee:

> 'The object of an audit of whatever kind, is to check on the conformity of administrative action to criteria laid down in advance; without criteria there can be no audit. More generally, systematic accountability of any kind depends on the existence of criteria, explicit or implicit.'[26]

The real danger in the type of body proposed is that it might set up criteria which were either meaningless or objectionable. The real problem of assessing the efficiency of management is the absence of clear and acceptable criteria. The absence of agreed criteria of performance naturally, as we have already emphasized more than once, makes the study of efficiency pointless. Indeed in recent years there has been a kind of Efficiency Audit Commission in the shape of the NBPI. Now, as we saw, that body did not at any time succeed in producing any kind of general judgement of an undertaking's overall performance or efficiency and was obliged to take criteria already laid down by government as given (however obscure and conflicting these criteria have been).[27]

The fact is that in most proposals for efficiency audits and studies, whether these are to be carried out by public agencies or government departments, the notion of 'efficiency' is a woolly substitute for 'success'. What the boards have been saying – with absolute justification – in criticism of such ideas is that they are not compatible with the statutes. It is difficult enough to know what the statutes intended. But it is fairly obvious that the performance of the boards as individual undertakings (including the efficiency with which they achieve a given performance) was meant to be measured by commercial results. That tells us (and the boards) far too little of course, but the implication is that these nationalized undertakings are not to be run according to standards administratively laid down (for example, ceilings on expenditure fixed by the Treasury). If the statutes were wrong in this implication then the onus of finding some alternative is on Professor Robson, the Select Committee and other opponents of 'commercial criteria'.

Paradoxically Professor Robson and the Select Committee do not wish to take a different approach and would probably be shocked to read this interpretation of their proposals. What they really want to mean by 'efficiency' is something far less than the general performance of an undertaking, but rather the technical efficiency with which it achieves a given output, its ability to take advantage of cost-saving opportunities, and so on. Undoubtedly what they are getting at are the promotion of technological innovation, the studies of productivity, the encouragement of better labour relations, the provision of better statistics, and so on, about which recent governments have been so busy, as part of a general transformation to a positive industrial policy for both public and private sectors. In this way it is difficult to see how the proposed Efficiency Audit Commission would fit in with other zealots for efficiency in nationalized industries such as the sponsoring departments, the Treasury, occasional *ad hoc* committees of inquiry, the Consumers' Consultative Councils, the NBPI or Commission for Industrial Management, management consultants hired by the boards of the industries themselves, the Select Committee on Nationalized Industries, and indeed the boards of the industries themselves. Of course it is not for an impecunious social scientist to complain about the proliferation of studies of organization and administration, which provide opportune supplements to university salaries. But at some stage the efficiency students will have to turn their attention on to themselves to analyse the costs and benefits of their own contribution.

Whenever the word 'efficiency' is found in the context of an argument about political control of nationalized industries, the reader should stop to ask a question. Does the writer mean by 'efficiency' the economy and skill with which certain results are achieved? In this case what he is writing about is primarily the responsibility of the directors or the board of the undertaking concerned (who will, it is hoped, take advice from 'experts' of the relevant kinds and who may be subjected to periodic examination from outside – often for their own good and at their own initiative). Or does he mean some substitute for commercial results as a measure and goal of the performance of the undertaking as a single enterprise? There he is referring to something by which indeed the directors of the enterprise will themselves be judged and on which their continuation in office may depend. Of course, a board may fail the second kind of test because they have already failed the first. But the first cannot be a substitute for the second. If the test of performance is not achieving commercial successes and financial gains, it is silly to employ businessmen on the boards of the nationalized industries: politicians, civil servants or 'efficiency experts' might be better (and cheaper).

HIGHER PAY AND STATUS FOR BOARD MEMBERS

In view of what has just been said it may seem extraordinary that some people have proposed paying members of the boards of the nationalized industries salaries nearer to those paid to the directors of large private companies at the same time as proposing the reforms we have considered so far. It is a fact which emphasizes that those who propose that degree of political control of the industries still want to treat nationalized undertakings as businesses and to promote efficiency and competence by the same means adopted in the private sector, for example, appointing able directors who command high salaries.

It is sometimes argued, along with the need for higher salaries, that the members of the boards of the nationalized industries are too dependent on ministers for their appointment. It has occasionally been advocated that board members should be appointed from within the industry, on the recommendation of the existing board, who should serve until retirement. The Select Committee on Nationalized Industries (while agreeing that higher salaries should be paid) opposed this argument on the grounds that, given the responsibilities of ministers in the public interest, it was essential that they should have power to appoint and dismiss members of boards.[28] It should not be forgotten, however, that the chairman of the board of a nationalized industry is, as a consequence of the minister's power of appointment, placed in a much weaker position *vis-à-vis* the minister than the chairman of the board of a private firm. He is even in a weaker position than the chairman of a private company before the shareholders at an annual general meeting, because there will probably be many shareholders and the meeting will probably be held in public. On the other hand, there would certainly be little point in strengthening the security of tenure of board members in nationalized industries, or in giving them higher salaries and status, if it was felt that control by ministers was inadequate.

In the last decade there has been a concerted attempt to appoint men to the boards with a more typically business background and to pay them higher salaries than in the first ten to fifteen years of nationalization. The most notable examples were the appointment of Dr Beeching to the Railways Board and of Sir Giles Guthrie to BOAC. Salaries in general still have a long way to go before they reach the level of equivalent private sector posts but members of nationalized boards certainly enjoy more status and independence than used to be the case.

However, the fact is that there is little point in trying to get successful businessmen on to the boards of nationalized industries, unless it is in the first instance thought desirable for the boards to be commercial undertakings and unless government policy in general is geared to that end.

HOLDING COMPANIES

Another idea which seems to be an alternative, at least to some of the proposals we have considered, but which has actually been recommended to supplement them, is that certain functions of ministers might be entrusted to new public corporations acting as holding companies for existing nationalized undertakings. This idea seems to be relevant for the existing nationalized industries from three points of view. First, a public holding company or companies would be expected to provide better co-ordination among different boards in the same sector than government departments are able to do. Secondly, they would offer a means of separating ministers' responsibility for financial results from the making of social and economic policy and would also ensure that this responsibility was exercised by people with a business rather than civil service background. In this respect it seems a good alternative to the proposals for an Industrial Civil Service or a Ministry of Nationalized Industries and probably to the idea of an Efficiency Audit Commission as well. Finally, as a consequence of these two features, it might be a means of making the boards more independent of ministers.

We have already seen that the sponsoring ministry for the nationalized fuel industries has itself become a sort of holding company. Not only is the minister responsible for producing a co-ordinated fuel policy intended to meet the country's fuel needs efficiently and cheaply, but he is also obliged to ensure that the individual nationalized fuel undertakings are financially viable and internally efficient. The sponsoring minister does not strictly speaking own the nationalized undertakings under his charge: the assets of the coal, gas and electricity supply industries are vested in the boards themselves. Nevertheless, the minister provides the boards with the bulk of their finance for capital investment, he appoints their members, he approves their programmes of capital investment, and represents 'the nation' as shareholder. We have seen in fact that the sponsoring ministers of nationalized industries do seem to exercise functions of ownership whether this was intended by the statutes or not. But these functions are exercised against the background of Treasury control and are not separated from the wider social and economic interests of government. Moreover, the officials in the sponsoring ministry are civil servants and the more the role of government departments in making policy for nationalized industries has been extended the less the intention of entrusting the industries to public corporations has been realized. The main obstacle to reducing political control in a sector like fuel, however, is that the policies of the individual undertakings are so interdependent. As we concluded before, it would probably be more sensible to seek a financial return on the whole sector (or at least that part of it which is nationalized) than to aim to make each individual part financially viable.[29]

Might it be, therefore, that the only public corporation which could be set up and run viably in the fuel sector, for example, would be an 'Energy Board' in which the assets of the present coal, gas and electricity supply undertakings were vested and which worked through divisional boards operating these individual undertakings? The Board would approve programmes of investment, appoint members to the boards of the individual undertakings, and set financial objectives for them.

A proposal of this kind has been made by Mr Aubrey Jones, Chairman of the NBPI. He thought that it would place the boards of the nationalized industries at a greater distance from 'political influence' and that the background of the boards and those responsible for supervising them would be made the same:

> '... for the board of a holding company would mirror the expertise on the boards of its own component divisions. The background of both holding board and divisional boards would be the same.'[30]

In other words, the proposal would aim to deal with many of the problems which have led to calls for reform of the civil service and a new Ministry of Nationalized Industries. It would also help to separate the making of social and economic policy from responsibility for the performance of individual undertakings. Mr Jones felt that government was simply not equipped to exercise this responsibility:

> '... the emergence of a considerable public sector operating in the commercial sphere means that the relevant part of government should either commercialize itself or transfer a considerable part of its functions to a more commercially orientated body.'

The Select Committee rejected this idea for three reasons. First, it thought that ministers would be less able than before to impose social and economic obligations on the industries. Secondly, it feared that ministers would be less accountable to Parliament for the boards than before. Finally, it argued that, while ministers were responsible for lending capital to the industries and 'overseeing' their efficiency, then they would be bound to review investment and scrutinize price changes, so that it would be difficult to see what holding companies could do.[31] Certainly the idea of holding companies for the nationalized industries would make sense only if the companies held all or some of the assets now vested in the individual boards and if the companies rather than the government supplied the substance of the industries' capital. However, the Committee probably meant by its objections that it considered social and economic obligations to be of overriding importance and thus really did not want to make the boards of the industries any more independent of ministers. The Committee's own proposals for a Ministry of Nationalized Industries thus clearly suited its own objectives much better than Mr Jones's idea.

The important thing to know is how the holding companies would raise their capital or to whom they would answer for their performance. To place an extra tier of this kind between minister and operating boards might well do what Mr Jones wanted: that is, to put the operating boards at a further remove from political control and to increase the role of businessmen and specialist managers in making policy for the industries. However, this in itself might simply make political control more difficult and more confused, which would be no gain at all. It all depends on the extent to which powers really can be given to a holding company. There is in fact nothing very new in the idea except perhaps in name. The British Transport Commission was a kind of holding company or board for the nationalized transport undertakings. The 1947 Act created six separate transport executives, organized virtually as distinct public corporations, each responsible for different transport services. The British Transport Commission was created to make general policy for these executives, and to co-ordinate and control their activities. In 1962 the Commission was abolished and its co-ordinating functions were for the most part transferred to the Minister of Transport. The remaining transport executives had their status increased and became independent Boards. One view was that the Commission had failed in its duties of co-ordination. It has also been argued, however, that the change in 1962 increased the power of ministers unnecessarily over the individual transport undertakings.[32]

The real problem, as with all the proposals we have been considering, is to decide how much political control one wants. There is no point in trying to reduce the role of ministers if one really believes that nationalized undertakings are largely political bodies and that their policies should be made on political grounds. Of the proposals we have considered here only the last two seem to be genuinely intended to reduce political control, and then only if certain other steps are taken and special circumstances prevail. For the most part people are conscious of the disadvantages of political control but have not really made up their minds about the alternative. Could nationalized undertakings be organized and run as business undertakings? What does it mean to treat a nationalized undertaking as a business? Is this compatible with nationalization? Is it compatible with the general aims sought by public ownership? If not, can any reliable means of reducing or eradicating the costs of political control be found? Before trying to conclude with an answer to these questions, we shall look briefly at the experience of two West European countries where state enterprises have been treated far more as businesses than in Britain.

REFERENCES

1. First Report from the Select Committee on Nationalized Industries, Session 1967–8, *Ministerial Control of the Nationalized Industries*, HC 371.
2. See pp. 89–102 above.
3. *Ibid.*, vol. 1, paras. 482–98.
4. Professor Robson agrees. See 'Ministerial Control of the Nationalized Industries', in *Political Quarterly*, vol. 40, No. 1, January–March 1969, p. 104.
5. *Ministerial Control, op. cit.*, vol. I, para. 417.
6. *Ibid.*, para. 664.
7. *Ibid.*, paras. 711, 716.
8. *Ibid.*, paras. 867–8.
9. See pp. 38–39 and 102–18 above.
10. See pp. 86–122 above.
11. *The Civil Service*, vol. I, Report of the Committee 1966–8, June 1968, Cmnd. 3638, HMSO London, paras. 7–9.
12. *Ministerial Control, op. cit.*, vol. I, para. 837.
13. *Ibid.*, vol. I, paras. 831–5.
14. *Ibid.*, para. 839.
15. *Ibid.*, vol. II, Evidence from Sir Stanley Raymond, pp. 575–80.
16. *Ibid.*, vol. I, paras. 884–90.
17. *Ibid.*, para. 925.
18. *Ibid.*, paras. 900–1.
19. *Ibid.*, paras. 902–10.
20. At the same time, responsibility for the air corporations remained with the Board of Trade, and for the nationalized inland transport undertakings with the Ministry of Transport. So the rationalization did not go all that far, see pp. 233–34 below.
21. W. A. Robson, *Public Enterprise*, London, 1937, pp. 79–81; See also Ministerial Control of the Nationalized Industries, *Political Quarterly*, *op. cit.*
22. W. A. Robson, *Nationalized Industry and Public Ownership*, George Allen & Unwin, London, 1962 (2nd edn), *passim.*
23. See also W. A. Robson, *Ministerial Control, op. cit.*
24. *Ibid.*
25. *Ministerial Control, op. cit.*, vol. III, Memorandum from the Electricity Council, p. 215; for similar remarks by other boards, see *ibid.*, Appendices 32, 33, 35, 38 and 40.

26. *Ibid.*, Memorandum from the Gas Council, p. 218.
27. Nor has the French *Commission de Verification des Comptes des Entreprises Publiques* provided general assessments of performance, although it is frequently quoted to support the case for an 'Efficiency Audit Commission'. See E. L. Normanton, *The Accountability and Audit of Governments*, Manchester University Press, 1965, pp. 335–54.
28. *Ministerial Control*, *op. cit.*, vol. I, para. 288.
29. See pp. 117–18 above. A former Minister of Power implied a broadly similar view to the Select Committee: *Ministerial Control*, *op. cit.*, vol. II, Evidence from Rt Hon. Richard Marsh, p. 1267.
30. *Ibid.*, vol. II, Evidence from Rt Hon. Aubrey Jones, p. 682.
31. *Ibid.*, vol. I, paras. 931–5.
32. For different views on the subject see W. A. Robson, *Nationalized Industry and Public Ownership*, *op. cit.*, pp. xi–xv, pp. 95–8; Ernest Davies, Reorganization of Nationalized Transport, *The Political Quarterly*, vol. 32, No. 2, April–June 1961, pp. 185–9.

    A proposal has recently been made for a National Air Holding Board to exercise financial and policy responsibility for BOAC and BEA: *British Air Transport in the Seventies*, Cmnd. 4018, 1969.

Part IV

INTERNATIONAL COMPARISONS AND CONCLUSIONS

Chapter 10

STATE ENTERPRISE IN SWEDEN

In spite of the degree of political control to which they are subject in practice, there is a widespread impression in Britain that individual nationalized undertakings should be run primarily as 'ordinary business concerns' and should be judged on that basis. Although these undertakings are expected to observe special social and economic obligations, and therefore may be required to qualify their 'business' objectives in important ways, nevertheless the function of the boards of the nationalized industries and the style of the management underneath them are meant to be broadly similar to those of directors and managers in any large firm engaged in producing some nationally important commodity or service. The Labour Government responsible for nationalization hoped to have 'the best of both worlds', to 'combine progressive modern business management with a proper degree of public accountability'.[1] Even the Conservatives, when returned to power, were able to live with the nationalized undertakings by seeking to make them more 'businesslike'. Thus they encouraged competition, for example, between private airlines and the public air corporations; they introduced the system of five-year financial objectives in 1961; and they appointed to boards members who were said to be more commercially minded and independent.

However, as we have seen, political control is such that the nationalized undertakings in Britain have hardly been business undertakings in any adequate sense of the term. They are engaged in commercial activity right enough, but rarely can anyone be satisfied with considering an individual board successful in commercial terms. Earning financial surpluses is not enough on its own, because of the monopolistic advantages enjoyed by most boards and because the boards do not raise their capital in competition with private firms. There are, moreover, no shareholders or other private suppliers of funds to which boards can be said to be accountable. For the same reasons expansion cannot automatically indicate success. Above all, a lot of people seem to have doubts whether either financial surplus or expansion are desirable objectives at all and use the term 'commercial' to refer to an optimum allocation of resources. Indeed it is widely assumed that desirable 'commercial' qualities can be ensured only by the attention of ministers and their officials or by that of independent public boards of inquiry. There is in fact a vicious circle of political control. The less the nationalized undertakings can be judged by ordinary business standards, the more political control of their performance is called for. Yet the more their performance is influenced by political control, the less are the boards capable of behaving as commercial bodies.

We have recognized that there is a view that nationalization was intended to replace commercial standards with political (or economic) ones, and sometimes those who hold such a view have had the consistency to propose extending the functions of government to accommodate that change. For those whose prime concern is restraining the growth of government however (not at the expense of social and economic objectives but in the interests of efficiency) the main question is how far can political control be reduced without harming the public interest. This is not an eccentric or unreasonable attitude, for we have seen that most ministers, civil servants and board members like to think of the nationalized undertakings as not placing excessive new burdens on the system of government. If we give the nationalization statutes the benefit of the doubt, then even they sought (by vesting the industries in public corporations) to avoid giving the civil service or Parliament unsuitable tasks to perform.

Quite apart from the costs to the political system of political control, there are disadvantages for the industries. Even in the Labour Party there have been complaints in the last twenty years about the degree of centralization in nationalized undertakings. Some commentators on the Right Wing of the Party won a lot of public attention and support in the late 1950s for their argument that the creation of state-owned monopolies like gas, electricity and coal had made it more difficult to ensure efficiency and exercise financial control, and had worsened labour relations and weakened the influence of consumers. In place of the form of organization adopted in the 1945–50 nationalization measures, various suggestions for 'competitive public enterprise' were put forward. Running through much of this debate was an idea that public ownership was limited as a tool of social and economic policy and should be used sparingly and precisely. The view that public ownership was positively desirable, being inherently superior to private ownership, was contested as doctrinaire and unrealistic. It was also argued that a government need not own or finance whole industries to realize social and economic objectives, but could often achieve the same ends by partial ownership of single firms or industries. In other words, there was a concerted attempt to convert the Labour Party to what we have called a *contingent* approach to state enterprise.[2] In practice, however, these arguments were rarely if ever turned into new proposals for the existing nationalized industries and had little effect on the Labour Party's official attitude towards these industries.

The model commended by many of these writers was that of state-owned enterprises in Sweden. In fact the approach to public ownership adopted in that country exemplifies a quite different kind of motivation and organization from the British and we shall now examine the relationship between government and state-owned enterprises in Sweden in recent years.

LEGAL BACKGROUND

State-owned enterprises in Sweden are divided legally into two main types. First, there are what are officially called 'public enterprises' (*affärsdrivande verk*), which are organized in effect as ordinary government departments. In 1969 there were seven of these: the State Forest Service, the National Defence Industries, the Airports Administration, the Post Office, the State Railways, the Board of Telecommunications and the State Power Board (supplying electricity generated mainly from water-power). Secondly, there are 'state companies' (*statliga aktiebolag*), which are independent legal entities subject to the regulations of the Companies Act and in which the state owns all or a majority of the shares. There are about fifty of these companies including some which the public enterprises themselves have set up as subsidiary companies. The activities in which state companies are engaged are various. The largest companies are those responsible for former, or continuing, state monopolies (such as wines and spirits, football pools and lotteries, and tobacco) and the LKAB, which exploits iron ore deposits in the north of Sweden. Following closely on these in size of turnover is the holding company which operates Sweden's share in the airline, SAS. The numerous smaller companies are engaged in activities such as hotel and catering services, research and development of atomic energy, manufacture of transport and mining equipment, engineering, shipbuilding, maintaining shipyards, iron-mining, printing and publishing and so on.[3] (There is also a third type of state enterprise – credit and finance institutions – but we shall not be concerned with it here.)

The public enterprises were set up on the same lines as conventional public services provided by the central government in Sweden.

In other words, they are basically similar in organization to the bodies responsible for police, education, regulation of industry, labour relations, and so on. The point is that most public services in Sweden are vested not in ministers but in public agencies or boards. Ministers and the tiny offices of civil servants which assist them are concerned only with policy-making, accountability to Parliament for policy, administrative appeals from private citizens, and conducting relations between parliament and the government, on the one hand, and the agencies or boards, on the other. The agencies or boards really constitute government departments in Sweden (although there is simply no equivalent there to the British ministerial department). In many ways they are like British public corporations, except that they are subject to extensive parliamentary and ministerial direction and control, unlike most British public corporations.

The Swedish public enterprises differ from the other public boards in some important respects and have far more discretion. Even so there are a number of restrictions on their activities which do not apply to British nationalized industries vested in public corporations. Above all, their assets and liabilities form part of the government's annual budget and all their long-term capital is drawn from the government. However, the government (that is, the King-in-Council) is formally responsible for the charges made by the enterprises, although in practice their prices are nearly always fixed in response to the market. The enterprises are also subject to the same kind of parliamentary scrutiny as other public boards and, in particular, are covered by the well-known Act on the Right to Obtain Access to Public Documents.[4]

The government is represented by a minister (or his civil servants) acting as a shareholder at the annual general meeting of every state company. This meeting appoints the board of the company and approves the previous board's annual report and accounts. The board itself appoints private auditors to audit its company's accounts. Formally speaking, therefore, the companies are completely different in their organization from the public enterprises and are not subject to ministerial or parliamentary control in the same way as normal public services. Parliament's main opportunity to control the activities of the companies arises when the government wishes to increase the subscription for shares and presents a bill before Parliament for this purpose. Companies are generally not subject to the same regular and direct parliamentary scrutiny as public enterprises.

Particular undertakings acquired one of these types of organization largely by historical accident. As might be expected the public enterprises were originally regarded as ordinary public services and some of them still are considered strictly as public utilities (railways and the postal service, for example). In many cases, however, public enterprises now face severe competition (in particular, the forests, electricity supply and the defence industries). The distinction between the two types of organization is now practically of no help, either in explaining the objectives of the undertaking concerned, or in indicating how much freedom it has from ministerial control. Most of the public enterprises have delegated commercial tasks to subsidiary companies in order to avoid direct government control of these. On the other hand, ministers can naturally exercise enormous influence over the boards of state companies by using their powers as shareholders. Even where minority shareholders still exist, these have in most cases ceased to exercise any important influence over policy. The ministries concerned (sometimes within certain legal requirements), settle with the boards the main objectives of the companies, and approve all significant changes in structure and organization.[5]

PUBLIC OWNERSHIP AS A CONTINGENCY

State enterprise in Sweden has interested foreigners by its distinctive style. In the first place Sweden has a much longer history of public ownership than most other European countries: state undertakings such as forests, railways and hydroelectricity date from the nineteenth century. Secondly the method of extending the state's interest by the purchase of shares in individual companies has been associated particularly with Sweden (although the practice is now fairly common elsewhere). One reason why Swedish state enterprise is thought to be unique, however, is that, in spite of the existence of a sizeable public sector, nationalization has never been a leading political issue there. In France and Britain nationalization of public utilities like railways and fuel and power, and even of other industrial activities like making steel or motor cars, usually took place as a direct consequence of electoral victories by socialist parties. In Sweden nationalization (in the sense of whole industries being taken into public ownership) has never really occurred and the Social Democratic Party, which has been in office almost continuously for nearly forty years now, has never made it part of its programme.[6]

These features of Swedish state enterprise (and particularly the last one) have attracted a lot of favourable attention from Right-wing supporters of the British Labour Party. Certainly it seems that Swedish governments have avoided many of the problems involved in running state-owned monopolies. There is no doubt that the state company has proved to have great advantages as a form of commercial organization and increasingly public enterprises have borrowed some features from it. The Swedish Social Democratic Party does not share the British Labour Party's well-known ambivalence about profit-making and ordinary business activity. It has also been far less centralist in its outlook in that it has never assumed that intervention by the central government is the only, or even the best, means of influencing economic activity in the public interest. These traits have enabled Swedish governments to use competition as means of promoting economic efficiency in state enterprises and to adopt readily in the public sector many of the same standards of performance as are used in efficient private enterprise.

Even in Britain we are not without examples of state enterprise where the state owns parts rather than the whole of a particular industry. However, the Labour Government of 1945 established a precedent of nationalizing whole industries or undertakings, which has been followed almost exactly in the case of steel and the Post Office in recent years. If British nationalization is seen as a post-war phenomenon, therefore, it was carried out for motives which were quite different from those which led to public ownership in Sweden. The main difference is that British nationalization was justified ideologically, whereas Swedish state enterprise has normally been justified on empirical grounds. As we have seen, one cause of the complexity, and sometimes the sheer incongruity, of the objectives of British nationalization, is the presence of this often inarticulate ideological element. In time it has found some expression as part of a policy of economic planning and 'positive government', according to which nationalization is regarded as a necessary means of attaining social and economic ends. On the other hand frequently underlying support for public ownership in Britain has been a dislike or rejection of the methods and standards associated with private enterprise.

In Sweden public ownership has generally been associated, neither with a policy for national economic planning which requires control of 'the commanding heights of the economy', nor with a doctrine of industrial organization which deliberately rejects ordinary business principles. The Swedish Minister of Industry was able to say in 1967 that the majority of government enterprises:

> 'have all been founded not because of the conception that the State has any superior ability as an entrepreneur but because these enterprises have been charged with certain tasks that differ from those that possibly could, or should be, carried out by private enterprise.'[7]

It is relatively easy in Sweden to justify every example of public ownership according to some specific social or economic policy of government. Some undertakings are treated unashamedly as public utilities, meaning that they are expected to follow publicly approved pricing and investment policies and must not be guided primarily by the market (for example, railways and the Post Office). Others exploit natural resources (such as iron ore and forests) in search of monetary profit, but profit which will accrue to the state rather than to private individuals. The official policy of temperance and prohibition has required that trading in alcohol be subject to close government supervision and control. In other cases there were fiscal reasons for public ownership (for example, in tobacco). Some activities affecting national security, such as some aspects of the production and manufacture of materials used in defence, cannot be left in private hands. The state has also become an entrepreneur in Sweden in order to preserve competition in particular sectors, especially those in which the state is a consumer. Finally, some undertakings have been kept in existence mainly to provide employment in problematic regions. We are not discussing here whether or not public ownership for these reasons was justified in Sweden. However, in general the motives for state enterprise (and therefore the objectives of it) seem to be much clearer when it is contingent as in Sweden than when it is positive as in Britain. Specific reasons (often similar to those just listed) are sometimes argued for public ownership of the British nationalized industries. They are invariably confused, however, by much more general and equivocal justifications, such as that the state is superior as an entrepreneur, or that there are inherent advantages in large-scale undertakings and unavoidable disadvantages in competition, or that the government needs control of 'the commanding heights of the economy' to achieve its social and economic goals.

Sweden is an exception among European countries, however, and for reasons other than the contingent style of her state enterprise or the political consensus about it. First, Sweden's industrial revolution took place a century later than Britain's so that there is not such a sharp division of politics based historically on economic interest as there is in Britain. Secondly Sweden was virtually an underdeveloped country in the nineteenth century so that public ownership was easily accepted by all classes and parties as a means of increasing the supply of capital and providing communications and employment in remote and desolate regions. The same fact can be explained in geographical terms in that, thirdly, Sweden's national expansion took the form not of external growth into territories overseas, but of internal growth into underdeveloped parts within her own national boundaries. Finally, some Swedish state enterprises have been subject to the effects of foreign competition (intense in the cases of forests and shipbuilding).

Above all, it should be remembered that, although similar as a proportion of national totals, the scale of public enterprise in Sweden is in aggregate terms small in comparison with Britain.[8] Thus in 1967 the total proportion of fixed investment by state-owned undertakings in Sweden was one-eighth of the British equivalent while the total of employees in public enterprise was one-tenth.

It is doubtful, therefore, whether the Swedish style of state ownership could ever have been practical in the British context. There was no parallel in Sweden to the problems which were faced in this country with public utilities in the fuel and power and transport sectors either before, or at the time of, nationalization. Would the Swedish style be more applicable in this country now perhaps? One sobering lesson is that extending public ownership by contingency has increasingly led to problems in Sweden similar to those already met in Britain and other countries. There have recently been three outstanding problems which we shall treat here in ascending order of current importance.

First, as in other countries where the state has acquired a financial interest in industrial and commercial activities, it has proved difficult in Sweden to provide financial control of an acceptable kind. This problem has been of far less public importance in Sweden than in Britain or France but that is largely because there seems to be less concern among Swedish politicians and administrators about the dangers of 'over-investment' in state enterprise. (As a result the methods of allocating a share of national resources to these enterprises and of controlling its use seem to be far less rigorous and elaborate than those now adopted in Britain.) However, while it has never become an important political issue, reform of the financial accountability of state enterprises has been frequently urged.[9] A familiar dilemma has been faced: whether to make state undertakings accountable primarily to the market and to measure their performance by financial results obtained by more or less unrestrained commercial activity, or to subject them to greater parliamentary and administrative control. Some politicians have expressed anxiety about parliament's relative lack of control over the government's financial stake in the state companies, which now constitute the normal type of organization adopted for new state undertakings in Sweden. In practice 'commercial freedom' seems to have won the day and more rigid parliamentary and administrative control to have been dismissed as retrograde.[10]

One aspect of financial performance has become particularly

important, however, and has not been solved by the device of the state company. We can consider it in fact a problem in its own right and we have met it before. It is deciding how to deal with social obligations, in this case mainly to provide regional employment as part of government policy. The three undertakings which most accept social obligations like this are the State Forests, the steel-works (*Norbotten Järnverk*), and the Uddevalla shipyard. The last two of these (which are state companies) have made losses on current account for a number of years, and the widely-accepted reason has been that the boards of these companies have felt obliged to adopt policies serving the interests of the government. The Minister of Industry has suggested that different means of furthering these interests might be found in future and has emphasized the contingent nature of this form of public ownership:

> 'A government enterprise that has been established in order to solve an immediate employment problem does not necessarily have to exist forever. As well as we are prepared to establish new government enterprises we must also be prepared to review the conditions and justifications of those already in existence.'[11]

However, as in Britain, the government in Sweden has had difficulties in evaluating the performance of enterprises with special social and economic responsibilities.

A third aspect of state enterprise which has been widely criticized in Sweden is the character of political control itself. Until quite recently sponsoring responsibility for the various undertakings was spread over no less than seven different ministries and this was thought to lead to too great a diffusion and confusion of responsibility. It has been argued that this was one reason why state companies were often at a disadvantage compared with private competitors in raising capital for development and in taking up opportunities for innovation and expansion. The individual ministries were too frequently distracted by their other, more central responsibilities and one effect was that the commercial undertakings under their sponsorship often became pawns in the general social and economic strategy of the ministry. Another reason for the same feeling of frustration was the pressure which we have already mentioned for more detailed and precise parliamentary and ministerial control of the financial affairs of the state companies. Raising new capital (for example by an increase in the value of the state's shareholding) has often been self-defeating in view of the amount of political scrutiny and control demanded in return; state companies argue that they cannot compete while ministers and the *Riksdag* are 'looking over their shoulders'.

Finally as in Britain it has been maintained that the ministries are not equipped to deal with questions of commercial and industrial management and that the allocation of responsibility between ministers and enterprises should therefore be made clearer.

While some answer to these problems of contingent state enterprise has been sought, another argument altogether has gained prominence. This is that the government should generally take a more positive approach to its various commercial and industrial interests. There has been growing pressure within the ruling Social Democratic Party for some years now for such a positive approach. This has been related to complaints that the party leadership and government policy have become too unadventurous and 'bi-partisan'. Special emphasis therefore is now placed on the need for the state to influence investment in ways favourable for economic growth. In fact there have recently been decisive steps in Sweden towards a more positive approach towards economic policy in general. On 1 January 1969 a new Ministry of Industry was established combining a former part of the Ministry of Finance (in which a separate Minister of Industry had recently been appointed) and some responsibilities of other ministries, including sponsorship of a number of state-owned enterprises. The new Ministry was set up for much the same reasons and with similar objectives as was the Department of Economic Affairs in Britain in 1964. The Swedish Ministry of Industry, however, has much wider and more concrete responsibilities than the DEA ever had in Britain and in terms of actual functions the Ministry of Technology in this country as set up in September 1969 is a much better comparison.

Meanwhile a Royal Commission was set up to inquire into the future of state-owned enterprises and this body produced an initial report in January 1969. This report, which is concerned mainly with problems of co-ordinating state undertakings at government level, is of interest to us for two main reasons. First, it contains proposals for reducing political control of the State's commercial interests which might be relevant to similar problems in Britain. Secondly, however, its arguments betray increasing support in Sweden for a positive as opposed to a contingent approach to public ownership. So we shall consider this report and its results at some length.[12]

THE STATE HOLDING COMPANY

The main recommendation in the Commission's report was the creation of a new state holding company as the basis of a general reorganization of the relationship between government and state-owned enterprises in Sweden, spread out over a number of years to come. In June 1969 a Bill was presented to Parliament for setting up the new holding company and followed closely the main objectives of the Commission, although it was left to the Company itself to set up its own organization once it was created. On 1 January 1970 the holding company was set up under the name of National Swedish Enterprises Ltd (*Statsforetag AB*) owning twenty-two companies wholly or in part (two more have been added since).

The ultimate objective of the Royal Commission was to simplify and unify ministerial responsibility for all (or nearly all) of the state's commercial and industrial interests. This was to be done partly by vesting the state's existing shares in the majority of existing state companies in the new holding company and partly by making the Ministry of Industry the normal sponsoring department for state-owned enterprises. *Statsforetag AB* is in fact placed under the tutelage of that Ministry and at the same time, following the Commission's recommendation, two of the public enterprises (the Forests and Defence Industries) have been transferred from other sponsoring ministries.[13] Since the public enterprises are organized on a different legal basis from the state companies, they could not be included in the new holding company. Moreover, some of them were still run largely as public utilities, their pricing and investment policies being greatly influenced by ministers and rarely being designed to promote commercial expansion or financial surplus. However, the Royal Commission produced an ingenious scheme for including the public enterprises in the new system so that eventually they might become an integral part of it. It recommended that a Public Enterprises Commission should be established to co-ordinate the activities of the public enterprises and to handle their relations with the holding company. Such a body has now been set up with largely advisory functions, although with the right to approve programmes of investment by public enterprises before these are passed on to ministers. The Commission is responsible not only for the three enterprises now under the sponsorship of the Ministry of Industry but also for the Post Office and the State Railways which for the time being remain under the Ministry of Communications. The Commission's membership consists of two representatives of that Ministry and the whole of the board of *Statsforetag AB* (which itself includes some representatives of the Ministry of Industry).[14] The intention clearly is that in time the public enterprises will become more and more like state companies in their organization and objectives and that the traditional legal differences in Swedish state enterprise will disappear or at least cease to have any practical meaning. There is a clear implication that, because of its essentially commercial character, the state company has been adopted as the standard model for state enterprise as opposed to the public agency or board.

The role of the holding company is based on an interesting distinction between the functions attached to ownership and those belonging to an enterprise itself. The Commission listed the following as being the main functions of ownership where state-owned undertakings were concerned:

1. To lay down the objectives of an undertaking;
2. To appoint the boards of directors of individual undertakings;
3. To ensure that necessary financial resources are made available;
4. To review the policies of an undertaking and to see that its objectives are fulfilled;
5. To take corrective measures in the event of objectives not being fulfilled.

The main functions of the enterprise itself were given as follows:

1. To provide co-ordination and planning so as to fulfil the objectives laid down;
2. To supply the owners with enough information to perform their own functions.[15]

It seems to be assumed in the new arrangements that *Statsforetag AB* becomes the owner, or majority owner, of the various companies underneath it, but that it exercises this right of ownership on behalf of the government. Therefore the goals of the holding company should be set up within the framework of government policy and representatives of the Ministry of Industry will sit on its board. The general duty of the company is stated vaguely enough as being to seek to expand so long as it is able to pay its way. After a transitional period the government will expect to receive dividends on its capital invested in the company that are at least as large as those it used to receive from the individual companies now made subsidiaries. The holding company will, however, receive the dividends of its subsidiaries and be able to raise loans on the open market.

The principal aim of the establishment of the holding company is clearly to place the functions of ownership for state-owned enterprises in the hands of a commercial rather than a political body. Although the government is still regarded as the ultimate owner, it will no longer have direct dealings with the boards of the operating companies (which will be appointed by, and accountable to, the holding company). It is hoped by this means to reduce political control of operating state enterprises and, by forcing the minister concerned to frame his policy in terms of a general policy for the parent company, to provide a working distinction between decisions which need to be taken by a politically responsible authority from those of a technical or commercial nature. It is indeed an ingenious and constructive means of dealing with this most difficult aspect of the relationship between government and state enterprises: namely, the state's position as owner or shareholder. Of course this difficulty is much easier to overcome in Sweden, not only because the units involved are small, but also because the right of ownership is represented in shareholdings which can be readily identified and not vested in some vague notion of 'the State'.

However, some critics of the Royal Commission's report have argued that the real purpose of the new holding company will be to expand the government's financial stake in commerce and industry at the expense of private enterprise and initiative. They fear that the proposal is intended to give governments greater influence for their social and economic policies rather than to strengthen the independence of state-owned undertakings. Certainly the Commission's report suggested, however guardedly, that one advantage of the new arrangements would be a more positive approach by governments to their commercial and industrial interests. Among other things the report complained that: 'It is not possible to direct the investment of the state-owned enterprises into the most desirable fields of activities and production'.[16] It was not clear what 'desirable' meant in this context and some commentators have suggested that it implied a need for more ministerial intervention. For one thing they pointed out that the companies assembled under the new holding Company were engaged in a great variety of activities, so that the need for co-ordination was difficult to understand, unless, that is, the aims were to increase the financial power of the state in the economy.

Nevertheless it would be wrong to see the recent changes as a fundamental shift of attitude in Sweden towards the role of state enterprise. Indeed, the managing director of the *Statsforetag AB* is a well-known industrialist and former Conservative member of the *Riksdag*, Mr Gunnar Svard, who could not be identified at all with Left-wing pressure in the ruling Social Democratic Party for a more positive, socialist approach to industry. In fact the new arrangements could just as well be seen as conforming exactly to the traditionally contingent approach to state enterprise in Sweden. Indeed they might well help to remove many of the disadvantages of the previous relationship between state undertakings and ministers.

Not only is much of the function of ownership transferred from ministers to the board of the holding company, itself organized on commercial lines, but it is hoped that a solution to the problem of social and economic objectives (mainly the maintenance of full employment) has been found. It is suggested that a variety of state companies are now under unified direction, so that social obligations need not bear on particular undertakings in financial difficulty or facing declining markets but can be spread around the subsidiary companies in a more rational way. The parent company will be able to know where surplus manpower is likely to be created and by reacting to this knowledge can serve both the commercial interests of its subsidiaries and the social policy of the government at the same time. It is suggested for example that the holding company should submit tenders to the government for carrying out special tasks of this type, thereby clarifying in its own mind the purpose of the various functions it undertakes and providing at the end of the day a more useful account of its performance in each of them. (For example, the company might offer, in return for payment from ministers, to undertake re-training schemes for unemployed workers and to set up an employment bureau.[17]) At the same time the company will be expected to take advantage of opportunities for rationalizing its holdings.

These proposals for a state-holding company in Sweden are pertinent to the general problem of trying to treat state-owned enterprises as businesses. In the first place the Swedes hope that their holding company will keep many functions of ownership out of the hands of ministers, at least where individual undertakings are concerned. As we have seen, it is exactly these functions which governments are so unsuited to perform. Secondly, in so far as there are wider social and economic reasons inhibiting the growth or financial viability of an individual state undertaking, the holding company is in a good position to reconcile the two needs (of commercial viability and social obligation) by taking advantage of the diversity of its subsidiary companies. Suppose at a theoretical level that state transport were vested in such a holding company: the social need for rural transport, now met uneconomically by railway services, could be met instead by road transport, without requiring planning or co-ordination by ministers, but simply as a result of a holding company following its own commercial interests. The possibilities for significant devolution of functions from central government are obvious. The need for 'co-ordination' and 'phased development' has often been put forward as a sufficient reason for nationalization in the British style, where whole industries or sectors are taken into public ownership. The new Swedish system illustrates a possible means of filling the same need without creating cumbersome and monopolistic entities like the

British nationalized industries and without raising the associated problem of political control.

On the other hand, the new arrangements might undermine some traditional features of contingent state enterprise. Almost by definition the new holding company will increase centralization and, just as it will probably reduce the influence of particular ministers on particular companies, it could increase the influence of the Minister of Industry on the whole set of companies which it now sponsors. That is, although the direct effect of ministers on commercial policy might be less, the indirect effect of a general economic policy might be even greater.

However, under previous arrangements individual companies were often subject to pressures of a social and economic kind from their sponsoring minister who also took responsibility for their commercial performance. Under such circumstances a financial surplus might be obtained simply as a result of a government subsidy and eventually cease to be treated as a meaningful yardstick of efficiency. If the minister concerned had had a wider set of commercial activities to influence, he might have been able to find some commercial interest with which his social policy was compatible. In Britain such a policy has invariably meant increasing the powers of ministers. In Sweden, as we have seen, rather than centralize control of related commercial activities by extending political control, an attempt has been made to achieve the same results by preserving as far as possible a commercial organization. Whereas in the case of British nationalized industries the functions of ownership seem to have slipped unintentionally into the hands of ministers, the Swedes, noticing such a trend in their own system, have tried to halt it by the timely creation of their holding company.

Another safeguard which, if preserved, should prevent pressures for greater centralization of control resulting in an amorphous and unaccountable organization, as British nationalized industries often seem to be, is the competitive nature of the individual state undertakings. It may be that the influence of the private shareholders in the state companies will be insufficient on its own to ensure that commercial opportunities are taken up or that an undertaking is managed efficiently. Indeed, ingenious proposals for parliamentary representation are provided for in the new arrangements. However, the important thing is that for the most part the operating companies face appreciable competition from privately-owned concerns both at home and abroad.

Much of the inspiration and a good deal of practical guidance for the recent reforms in Swedish state enterprise came from the experience of the famous Italian state holding companies, IRI and ENI. For a fuller understanding of the advantages – and the problems – of this approach to state enterprise, therefore, we shall now look at the main features of the relations between those bodies and their own government.

REFERENCES

1 See Select Committee on Nationalized Industries, Session 1967–8, *Ministerial Control of the Nationalized Industries*, HC 371, vol. II, Memorandum submitted by Mr D. N. Chester, pp. 522–5.
2. See pp. 24–25 above. See C. A. R. Crosland, *The Future of Socialism*, London, 1956, pp. 332–40.
3. For a full list, see 'State-owned enterprises in Sweden', Appendix I to *Statliga Foretag 1968*, Ministry of Finance, Stockholm. December 1968 (mimeograph), pp. 23–8.
4. *Ibid.*, pp. 6–8. The Act mentioned requires that most of the files of administrative offices are open to the press and public. In fact certain business documents of the public enterprises are normally classified as confidential and are excluded from the scope of the Act.
5. For a fuller account of the development of the system, see D. Verney, *State Enterprise in Sweden*, University of Liverpool Press, 1963, pp. 30–57. Our own impression is that Verney underestimates the extent to which the two types of institution have become similar in practice. His attempt to defend the 'integrity' of the state company is justified, but not for the reasons he gives, as we shall see below.
6 *Ibid.*, pp. 7–15.
7. Appendix 1 to *Statliga Foretag 1967*, Ministry of Finance, Stockholm, December 1967, p. 12 (official translation).
8. State-owned enterprises were responsible for 7 per cent of Swedish Gross National Product in 1967 (compared with the nationalized industries' share of 10 per cent in the UK in the same year), and they employed 6·5 per cent of the economically active population (compared with the British nationalized industries' 7 per cent). Figures for Sweden from *Statliga Foretag 1968*, *op. cit.*
9. Verney, *op. cit.*, pp. 18–123.
10. *Ibid.*, but see note 5 above.
11. *Statliga Foretag 1967*, *op. cit.*, p. 12 (official translation).
12. 'The Delegation on State-owned Enterprises: Recommendations concerning co-ordination of the state-owned enterprises', Ministry of Industry, Stockholm, June 1969 (mimeograph). Bodies of this type are especially important in the Swedish system of government, although in many respects they perform a similar role to our own Royal Commissions. Whenever a measure involving substantial reform is envisaged an ad hoc commission of this type is appointed

by the Government and consists of representatives of the major political parties, relevant experts and representatives of all interested private and other bodies. The secretariat of the present Delegation or Royal Commission (as is normal) was provided by civil servants from the relevant ministries. Also following normal practice, the Commission's report was circulated among public agencies and private organizations for comment.

13. Some state companies will also be transferred from the tutelage of other ministries to that of the Ministry of Industry. The State Power Board was already under that Ministry's tutelage.
14. The official translation reads 'Delegation of Public Enterprises' but to avoid confusion we have preferred the anglicized expression used here. See *State-owned Enterprises in Sweden*, Ministry of Industry, Stockholm, March 1970, pp. 13–20.
15. 'Delegation on State-owned Enterprises', *op. cit.*, pp. 14–15.
16. *Ibid.*, p. 9 (official translation).
17 Among its subsidiaries is a corporation specifically designed to create new jobs by establishing new industries or expanding existing ones, whether as state-owned concerns or in conjunction with private or municipal bodies.

Chapter 11

THE STATE HOLDING COMPANY IN ITALY

The two large Italian state holding companies, IRI and ENI, are already quite well known in Britain, both in their own right as important commercial enterprises and as a foremost example of a special style of state enterprise. In fact there are other state-owned industrial undertakings in Italy which are organized on more familiar lines (such as the railways, postal services and electricity supply), as well as some smaller bodies on the same lines as IRI and ENI; but we are concerned here, like most other foreign students of Italian state enterprise, with the special contribution of IRI and ENI. That contribution has been referred to in a lot of recent English writing on the role of state enterprise in general and it is that which has prompted us to look further into the relationship between the Italian holding companies and the government in search of lessons for our main theme.[1]

IRI (*Istituto per la Ricostruzione Industriale*) now controls about 130 firms engaged in activities such as banking, mining, shipbuilding, merchant shipping, chemical, telephone services, airlines, radio and television services, civil engineering, and the manufacture of a variety of products such as motor vehicles, industrial equipment, and so on. ENI (*Ente Nazionale Idrocarburi*) is mainly concerned with the exploitation, production and distribution of oil and natural gas, and also has interests in the transportation, refining and marketing of petroleum products. As off-shoots of its basic activities it has now developed interests in nuclear energy, chemicals, textiles and engineering.

IRI and ENI are known in the Italian system of public administration as *enti di gestione*, literally 'administrative bodies', but this tells us little or nothing about their actual structure or means of working.[2] The various operating subsidiaries are organized as ordinary joint-stock companies, usually with a substantial amount of private equity capital. In the case of IRI these companies are divided into sectors each headed by a subsidiary financial holding company, answerable in turn to the Institute itself, which owns a majority interest in their equity. ENI also acts through subsidiary companies in which it owns a majority of the equity and these have in many cases also become holding companies, having created their own operating subsidiaries, but they are each engaged in a variety of activities cutting across sectors. IRI and ENI themselves are really holding companies but are subject to public law (rather than private company law) and do not issue equity shares, although they do raise capital on the open market by the issue of debentures. They are answerable to the state (since 1956 in the form of a Minister of State Holdings) for their own activities, and their rights and duties are set out in statutes.

IRI and ENI could not be described in any sense as 'state monopolies' like the British nationalized industries. The undertakings which they control are vested in operating companies which compete with other firms in the same industry and which themselves rely for a substantial amount of their capital on the open market. They are also free from many of the statutory restrictions imposed on the British nationalized industries and in practice enjoy a great deal of freedom to diversify their activities. The statutory objectives of the two corporations are extremely loosely stated. IRI is instructed simply to 'manage the participations and capital assets it owns', although the Council of Ministers is given the power to determine the Institute's general policy 'in the public interest'. ENI is obliged among other things 'to manage and carry out initiatives of national interest in the field of hydrocarbons and natural gases'. The only real statutory guidance the IRI and ENI are given about the way their responsibilities should be carried out is that they should 'operate according to economic criteria'. Their independence from government in practice is explained by IRI and ENI themselves mainly as a consequence of their access to the open capital market. There are in fact various means by which capital for the groups of holdings is raised (including self-financing as well as borrowing from outside) and they are too complicated to consider here. One recent study estimates the state's share of the sources of finance for all *enti di gestione* to have been 7.4 per cent on average between 1953 and 1962.[3] In return for the interest-free state endowments which they receive IRI and ENI are obliged to pay 65 per cent of their net profits to the state, but since there is no readily agreed definition of profit, this requirement has limited practical importance.

It is well known that IRI and ENI now have a wide-ranging role in the Italian economy, which was not entirely foreseen when they were established. IRI came into being as a result of an operation to save certain important banks from ruin in the years of world financial crisis between the two world wars. ENI was established in 1953 mainly to develop domestic resources of natural gas and to keep them under state control. However, their main function has become increasingly to give the government wide influence in the national economy. Indeed it is now agreed, although with reservations by some commentators, that IRI and ENI contributed a great deal on their own to Italy's post-war economic recovery. This contribution was made quite consciously and deliberately and the nature and scope of the undertakings have frequently been justified in terms of a national strategy for economic growth and development. As a result of this IRI and ENI have been enthusiastically studied by would-be economic planners in other countries. In Britain supporters of *positive* state enterprise have contrasted the behaviour of these undertakings with that of our own nationalized industries.

There are other reasons why people in this country have looked to IRI and ENI for guidance. As we have seen one of the main reasons why ministers need to control British nationalized industries is that the minister is responsible for many of the functions of ownership. A system of holding companies on the Italian model exercising the state's responsibilities as 'owner' and 'banker' for the British nationalized industries might give a sufficient degree of co-ordination with a greater degree of commercial independence. Although the undertakings controlled by IRI and ENI are rather different from the typical British nationalized industries, nevertheless the value of a comparison is obvious. This is all the more so in that the two Italian Institutes have been celebrated perhaps most of all for their ability to mix the entrepreneurial zeal valued in the private sector (and sought, some would say, in the Morrisonian public corporation) with observance of social and economic obligations.

THE NOTION OF 'PUBLIC ENTREPRENEURSHIP'

The role of IRI, and with some variations that of ENI as well, is justified by what is nothing less than a doctrine which the organizations have articulated and which teaches both ideas of expansion and adventure associated with the private entrepreneur, and those of social service linked with public administration. The 'entrepreneurial' part of the doctrine is intended to provide two kinds of incentive: first, a willingness to take risks which it is said would be avoided in Italy both by private investors on their own and by government agencies; secondly, a watchfulness for waste and inefficiency, sustained partly by the competition met by operating companies and partly by the undertakings' general aim of profitability. The other part of the doctrine is meant to ensure that the adventure and expansion are on the one hand tempered by social needs and on the other inspired by commitment to the national interest. This doctrine has been described by its own exponents as a 'philosophy' and it is indeed pervasive and influential throughout both organizations as a way of life rather than as an impersonal and formal set of rules. In the case of ENI the 'philosophy' was almost political in nature in the way that it drew so much of its inspiration from the person of Enrico Mattei.[4]

Of particular interest for British observers is the fact that using this part of the public sector to further the public interest has not required extensive ministerial control of the affairs of IRI and ENI or their subsidiary undertakings. Both undertakings have deliberately adopted policies of their own accord designed to serve general social and economic ends approved by governments. In the case of ENI this took the form mainly of developing resources where the national interest was felt to be at stake but where private capital and initiative were not available. In the post-war period IRI took on two particular responsibilities which were vital to the country's social and economic well-being: first, the provision of employment (in particular by maintaining shipyards receiving a declining share of world trade) and, secondly, by managing to hold down prices in sectors such as steel and cement upon which other industries depended. More recently, IRI and ENI have welcomed formal obligations by statute to assist the Government's policy for the *Mezzogiorno* (they are required to make at least 40 per cent of their total new investments in the South). In spite of sustained political pressure to increase government control over IRI and ENI, the latter are subject to nothing like the ministerial intervention experienced by the British nationalized industries. The first major attempt to provide effective ministerial supervision of the two undertakings was the establishment in 1956 of a Ministry of State Holdings (*Ministero delle Partecipazioni Statali*). The Minister was given a number of statutory powers of control including the right to approve IRI's and ENI's general programmes of investment and their means of obtaining finance, as well as to see that these programmes were carried out. In addition the Minister is represented on the Board of IRI, whose Chairman is appointed by the President of the Republic on the proposal of the Council of Ministers with the advice of the Minister of State Holdings. The Minister also has some say in the appointment and conditions of other members and staff of IRI.[5] He also advises on the appointment of the Chairman of the board of ENI although the appointment is made by the Prime Minister by decree.

In practice the relationship between IRI and ENI and the Ministry of State Holdings has never extended beyond one of consultation.

Even though IRI and ENI seem to consider the government's endowments of finance as essential, this reliance has not weakened their independence. They tend to argue in fact that the state endowments (on which no interest is payable) should be considered as a return for the number of socially justified undertakings in which they have become involved. The government's usual justification for using public funds in this way is roughly that it enables economic objectives to be pursued more effectively, and in the longer term more cheaply than if the government tried to carry out these objectives itself. It is said that the existence of private interests in IRI's and ENI's undertakings expecting a financial return provides an incentive to enterprise and efficiency. Moreover, the scope and flexibility of IRI and ENI enables them to carry out holding operations which most privately-owned concerns could not perform and to pay the costs of co-ordination and technological innovation out of the return from more immediately profitable or more secure investments.

But by far the most telling defence of this practice of 'self-denial' by the government is that the state holding companies are a vital means of diversifying the forms of economic intervention. Public expenditure by the central government in Italy is notoriously 'counter-productive', not only because of the delays involved but also because there is an unavoidable lack of flexibility in the financial procedures of the central administration. The reasons have been thoroughly treated by Italian academic lawyers and economists.[6] For one thing the rights of the legislature in Italian government are protected by the maintenance of detailed and rigid legal controls of administrative activity. This is said among other things to make it difficult to employ modern fiscal and monetary techniques for managing the economy. In general it is felt that the financial procedures of the central administration were designed primarily with judicial rectitude in mind rather than modern economic policy. The *enti di gestione* have been welcomed as a substitute for modernization of the central administration itself – a task which would have taken more political will than was available in post-war Italy. One might almost say that in some ways IRI and ENI provide through their activities a means of bypassing the political system altogether, in that special social and economic demands have on some occasions been received directly from the public, and the Institutes have responded spontaneously without the need for government intervention, which would probably not have been forthcoming anyway.

Far from being inspired, then, by any positive collectivist faith in the natural superiority of public over private forms of enterprise, the doctrine which has produced the modern role of IRI and ENI is essentially a response to practical economic and administrative needs. In this respect the role of these bodies has clearly developed in conformity with what we have called a contingent approach to state enterprise. Their contribution to national policy has often been 'macro-economic', in the sense that it has been geared to general aims, such as holding down the level of prices in key sectors, and sustaining the level of employment. Thus it could be seen as an example of constructive control of 'commanding heights of the economy'. However, in the sense that other forms of intervention were probably not available in the circumstances of the place and time, then state enterprise was not being used here as an ideal but rather as a convenient and necessary instrument. Indeed the instrumental character of this form of intervention has been stressed again and again by those who hold to the 'philosophy' which pervades IRI and ENI.[7]

The fact that the actual manner of intervention by IRI and ENI has often seemed more appropriate to a positive attitude towards the role of government in the economy is easily explained and too much meaning should not be read into it. It is because the undisputed emphasis in post-war Italy has been on rapid economic development and restoration (in some cases creation) of the basic infrastructure necessary to a modern industrialized state. At the same time it was inconceivable that private capital could, unsponsored and undirected by some central authority, perform the task adequately. And, as we have seen, it was regarded as hopeless to rely on the conventional machinery of the central government. The point we are trying to make is that we in Britain may have failed to see the advantages of state enterprise represented by the Italian state holding companies simply because it has been associated with a positive approach to public intervention in general. Just because the doctrine of 'public entrepreneurship' grew out of a relatively *dirigiste* contingency is no reason to assume a necessary connection between its principles of organization and particular methods of political economy. Might those methods – and their particular relevance in post-war Italy – have obscured the general value of the principles of organization associated with them? At least, that is a thought worth pursuing. Before doing so we should take account of some recent criticisms of the 'philosophy' of IRI and ENI – criticisms which, although being made in the context of a positive approach to state enterprise, help a good deal in generalizing from the Italian experience.

ECONOMIC PLANNING AS AN ALTERNATIVE

The theme of a recent study by Posner and Woolf is one which seems to be very strongly supported on the Left in Italy. This throws doubt on the amount of 'entrepreneurship' provided by IRI and ENI and argues that they have not been quite as adventurous and enterprising as their 'philosophy' requires. It also questions the contribution made by this form of state enterprise to Italy's post-war economic growth. The authors are led finally to doubt the value of the 'philosophy' of 'public entrepreneurship' altogether, concluding that the main weakness in Italian national economic decision-making has been the absence of effective ministerial direction. Here an interesting contrast is drawn to British experience:

> '... while in Britain there exists no mechanism for centralized control (like the Institutes or the ministry), no agency (similar to the financial holding companies) for the spawning of new public enterprises, no experience (with the doubtful exception of British Petroleum) of joint public-private enterprise, no means of escaping the strait-jacket of Treasury finance, all these are to be found in profusion in Italy. And yet it is in Britain that the possibilities, for both centralized planning and Government technological intervention are fully recognized; in Italy, on the other hand, proper scope for the exercise of public policy through the agency of the State enterprises is thought to be limited to the aim of regional development. In Britain, we have the policy, without the machinery to put it into practice; in Italy, the machinery is available, but as yet no policy has been formulated.'[8]

This long quotation illustrates an argument met quite widely in Italian criticisms of 'public entrepreneurship'. This is that the pursuit of general economic and social objectives demands a coherent and determined government strategy which can be applied directly. The 'entrepreneurial' part of the 'philosophy' of IRI and ENI – that part which stresses their independence of the state – is more or less rejected. Paradoxically (at least in Posner and Woolf's presentation) the risk-taking and expansion associated with this part of the doctrine are vindicated. Indeed IRI and ENI are criticized for failing to show enough of these qualities: their past success in persevering with socially and economically important ventures is accounted for mainly by their ability to exploit a monopolistic position or to use the diversity of their undertakings to advantage. The companies' reliance on the private capital market, it is argued, has actually discouraged the taking of risks. Too few public funds have been made available to the undertakings. What is also interesting is that criticisms like this are combined with complaints about inefficiency and inadequate financial control. Too many decisions of IRI and ENI, it is implied, have been taken on the basis of unclear objectives, in particular in sentimental or politically-motivated responses to social need, or in pursuit of a vague criterion of profitability.[9]

Like many presentations of the positive approach to state enterprise, Posner and Woolf's study reads rather like Hamlet without the Prince. The argument is that more financial support and administrative control by ministers would have provided at one and the same time more enterprise and more efficiency. But this is not substantiated by any discussion of the forms ministerial direction and control might have taken. Among other things the authors neglect problems such as how to measure the performance of individual undertakings – an oversight typical of Left-wing economists. The role in IRI's and ENI's holdings of spontaneous and decentralized forms of control exercised by private investors and competitors is not treated. Indeed, the authors say that information was not readily available for them to do so (and even their downgrading of IRI's and ENI's contribution to Italy's postwar economic recovery is mainly impressionistic). It seems that the real purpose of their writing is simply to question the grounds for private intervention in a national policy for growth and development. At the same time they want to find reasons for their conviction that centralized political control by governments is a prerequisite of effective economic planning. These are both arguments familiar in the positive approach to state enterprise and it is important for our general theme to notice that the IRI and ENI style has been found undesirable from this point of view.

In Italy itself, certainly, determined steps have been taken in the last few years to centralize economic decision-making. It is not yet clear where these steps will finally lead, and they are still faltering ones. In 1965 new responsibilities were vested in the Ministry of the Budget and Economic Planning and the task of co-ordinating the whole public sector including IRI and ENI was vested in a new inter-ministerial committee (*Comitato interministeriale per la programmazione economica*, 'CIPE'). New formal procedures for approving the investment programmes of the *enti di gestione* and ensuring that these conform to the national five-year plan were introduced partly by law and partly by the Prime Minister's decree in 1967. Ministerial control of the policies of IRI and ENI now takes place in three distinct phases: first, approval when necessary of individual programmes for a particular sector or of individual projects modifying such programmes; secondly, five-yearly formation of general programmes defining the objectives and co-ordinating the policies of the undertakings; and finally, annual review of the achievement of programmes together with revision of estimates for the remaining part of the five-year period. It is up to the Minister of State Holdings to bring individual programmes or projects in the first phase to the attention of CIPE and this may involve producing details of individual projects of investment if these alter the general lines of the *ente's* five-year programme. The most widely discussed example where CIPE's approval was sought for an individual project in recent years was the 'Alfasud' project of IRI (the building of a new motor-car manufacturing plant near Naples). CIPE approves submissions of this kind if it judges them to be in conformity with the national economic plan and for this purpose the Chairman of the Institute concerned may attend meetings of the Committee. A fairly detailed and systematic time-table has been laid down for the two other phases of ministerial control and again the Minister of State Holdings acts as a go-between of CIPE on the one hand and the *ente* on the other. The five-year programmes for each *ente* are drawn up by the board itself in the first place and then submitted to CIPE through the same Minister.[10]

The central administration now has greater and more explicit powers over IRI and ENI than ever before. Perhaps most important of all, these changes have been accompanied by an attempt to bring new people into the administration from outside and to break down (at least in this sector) the cramping and cumbersome official attitudes which have characterized Italian central administration up to now. Many argue that the reform of the public administration has not gone far enough and that effective policy-making in this sector will depend on the transfer of still more power to a new kind of 'technocrat'. Just how far this would imply a diminution of the initiative available to IRI and ENI themselves is not yet clear. But it is clear that this is what many would intend. Of course the problems of the Italian Civil Service cannot be considered on the same plane as those of the British – but it is striking that the argument for a more positive approach to state enterprise points in the same direction in both countries – towards greater power, and therefore different procedures, in the central administration. The degree is totally different, but in essence the problem is the same. Certainly not everyone in Italy sees the solution in greater government control. However, the more IRI and ENI were required to conform to government-inspired policies in the interests of social policy or economic growth, then correspondingly the less realistic would be their commercial freedom. There is certainly a point beyond which entrepreneurial qualities such as risk-taking and initiative are no longer compatible with centralization and administrative control.

That point has probably not yet been reached with the Italian *enti di gestione:* IRI and ENI give no signs of objecting to the intensification of political control so far as it has gone. However it must be remembered that the very advantage of this form of organization was its independence from government control – even that which applied to ordinary public corporations like the railways and postal services – so that the economic argument for greater political control might well defeat itself.

The best conclusion for our purposes is to consider this an example of the limitations of public enterprise – at least of that which is truly commercial in its organization – in what we have called roughly a positive economic strategy for the central government. As far as Italy itself is concerned, different stages of economic development may demand different instruments of state intervention. There is evidence of increasing concern with the allocation of scarce investment resources and with the distribution of income both among classes and among regions, so that the extraordinary emphasis on growth might be giving way to another ranking of objectives. For example, it is complained that while funds cannot be made available for urgent public projects in fields such as education, health and housing, then the government is obliged to exercise stricter control over the public money which passes into the hands of IRI and ENI.

The emphasis on rapid economic development has tended to overshadow the problems which lead to anxieties about over-investment or misuse of resources – anxieties which have obsessed British central administrators since the war. At the same time, it should be stressed that this has been possible in Italy because the forms of parliamentary and administrative leadership available could not themselves provide the kind of economic policies required.

Indeed, the response of IRI and ENI themselves to such criticisms is to seek to expand into the very fields where development is said to be overdue. Thus, much of the *enti's* more recent activity has been in public utilities such as road-building and education. Their argument is that shortcomings in these areas arise from the traditional weaknesses of the public administration; having taken the place of government in stimulating economic growth and efficiency in manufacturing industry, IRI and ENI are offering to take its place now as providers of adequate and efficient welfare services. The question is of course whether that is a politically acceptable extension of the style of 'public entrepreneurship' and it leads us beyond our immediate theme. We are not now concerned with the general opportunities provided by commercial forms of organization for relieving a central administration of responsibility for public utilities and welfare services. However, that is a fascinating subject and its recent development in Italy deserves greater study from Britain.

At present our concern is with the value of different forms of state enterprise in reducing and simplifying the existing work of the central administration in industrial and commercial matters. It is clear that some kinds of economic policy might not be compatible with the style of state enterprise represented by IRI and ENI. That is not surprising, perhaps, and the only difficulty is that so many supporters of greater state intervention of a positive kind are unwilling to consider the means available to achieve their ends. In so far as they prefer the central administration to perform commercial tasks itself, and expect it to do so with efficiency and enterprise, their predicament is to explain why such qualities have not been typically found in central administrations before. Since we are not interested here, however, in finding means to expand the role of government in economic affairs we need not dwell on such problems. The main question for us is how well the Italian state holding companies provide for enterprise and efficiency in their industrial and commercial undertakings.

PROBLEMS OF EFFICIENCY

It is not difficult to find informed observers in Italy who are willing to challenge the bold claims of IRI and ENI themselves to enterprise and efficiency. It is indeed certainly not enough to listen to the arguments of undertakings which are after all self-consciously commercial organizations with generously-endowed facilities for public relations. We have not made it our job to test the assertions of either champions or critics of IRI and ENI but we shall mention some criticisms because we believe they illustrate problems of a general nature likely to arise in organizations of this type. We shall not try to assess the performance of IRI and ENI or their undertakings here.

The first problem is in fact the very difficulty of substantiating impressions about the performance of IRI and ENI or the undertakings they control. The financial control of companies in Italy is traditionally less formal and precise than in France or Britain, and it is said that the information supplied to shareholders is usually far less, even than in other European countries. It is certainly true that, when one asks representatives of IRI what controls of performance exist, they point to the chart at the back of the Institute's annual report showing numerous and often large patches of white illustrating the interests of private investors in individual undertakings. The critics maintain however, that, while IRI shareholders might well be content with the dividends they earn, this is no guarantee that profits have been gained efficiently. More revealing, they say, would be some examination of prices in relation to costs. One particular anxiety is lest the growing state endowments to *enti di gestione* are simply to provide private investors with an adequate return.

These complaints really imply that IRI and ENI and their holdings are not sufficiently competitive. This is said to be partly the effect of the size and complexity of the organizations of both IRI and ENI. It is feared that expansion might be valued simply as an end in itself. Critics point here to two rather different kinds of development: first the enthusiasm for entering into joint undertakings with large private enterprises such as Fiat and General Electric; secondly, the tendency (already mentioned) to diversify into the field of public utilities, where there is little or no competition. In general it is maintained that there are often no means of telling whether new undertakings have been inspired by commercial policy, by social needs or simply by political patronage and manoeuvre.

Growth has led to internal problems and it is maintained that both *enti* have become bureaucratic in their own procedures and organization. The pyramidical structure of IRI, for example, means that decisions of individual operating concerns have to pass through at least two levels of approval – the financial holding company concerned and the Institute itself. The intervention of the second-tier holding companies is often said to be wasteful and unnecessary, but it is clearly a consequence of a greater scale of operation from the centre. One leading director in an undertaking controlled by IRI remarked to us that in many ways the Institute had become as cumbersome and authoritarian in its attitudes as an ordinary government department would be.

How far do these criticisms, which we have only sketched here, point to conduct which is inherent to this form of state enterprise? Some almost certainly arise from problems which are peculiar to Italy – in particular, to the characteristics of private enterprise in that country. There are probably also general risks inherent in the state holding company as a means of controlling a variety of commercial undertakings, above all the danger of imprudent expansion. That problem would need to be studied in its own right as an aspect of diseconomies of scale. No doubt it could be avoided by careful policy. It is not our business to examine whether the growth of IRI and ENI has gone beyond a reasonable point. Indeed much depends on the purposes for which this form of state enterprise is used. Most British students of Italian state enterprise are looking for evidence to support or qualify experiments like the Industrial Reorganization Corporation in Britain. In other words, they are interested in the way in which IRI and ENI have given opportunities for expanding the state's share in industry and commerce to further economic policies in the national interest. We are not now interested in that particular approach to political economy, although the Italian experience may suggest that there are risks in it. What we have been trying to do is to describe a particular style of state enterprise, a manner of reconciling public ownership with qualities considered necessary in good commercial activity.

The aspect of the Italian state holding companies which has interested us is the way they have relieved the central government in that country of the need to adapt itself to dealing with business decisions (which it probably could not have done anyway). As we have seen some critics would maintain that the central government *should* have played a more prominent part in Italian state enterprise and that therefore the benefits we mention were deceptive. We have suggested that that view is important only if one takes a particular approach to the role of the state in the economy and interprets the economic problems of the country in a particular way. Neither these critics, nor those who point to the inefficiency and bureaucracy which we have just mentioned, seem to have any realistic alternative to offer as a means of organizing state enterprise and ensuring that it is both enterprising and efficient. It is difficult to see, for example, how transferring any responsibilities from holding companies to government departments would bring any improvement. (Whether increasing the role of the private sector would be an alternative we do not know.) We cannot tell from our own cursory examination whether IRI and ENI really do succeed in combining ends of national economic policy with the incentives and controls thought to be built into competitive private enterprise. In so far as they have succeeded in achieving any social and economic ends, however, it is remarkable and highly fortunate that they have managed to do so without making a near-revolution in the system of Italian central administration necessary, for that would almost certainly not have been possible.

Indeed it is striking that in neither Italy nor Britain has any practical alternative to the model of private enterprise been found for combining opportunism and enterprise with economic efficiency. Private enterprise and its methods have been attacked and found wanting in both countries. In Britain, however, although experiments have been made with intellectually derived economic principles as a substitute for practical incentives and controls, it is still broadly speaking the criteria of the business-man which administrators try to apply, if unsuccessfully. In Italy, although state intervention has been found essential to make up deficiencies in the private sector, Italian state enterprise has sought far more energetically even than the British to retain basic principles of private enterprise in its manner of functioning. This difference of degree is in fact the main lesson to be learned in this country from the Italian experience. There has been in the Italian *enti di gestione* none of the same antipathy to the profit-motive or doctrinaire hostility to private capital which have been such strong influences in the establishment and running of the British nationalized industries.

The question is whether a similar style could be adopted in the case of British nationalized industries. This does not mean that we would recommend the same use of state enterprise here as in post-war Italy, nor that we would suggest trying to transplant structures from one country to another, which would be absurd. We have been writing here not of a specific economic policy but of a manner of conduct, which we admire because it seems to have achieved ends of public policy in the industrial and commercial field without making extensive reforms of the central administration a necessity, and without interrupting the normal conduct of the activities it has affected. We are only too well aware of criticisms that it has succeeded only partially in this and we have been unable to substantiate or quash these. It is clear, however, that many of the criticisms are made by those who believe that the normal conduct of business *should* be disrupted and replaced by something else, and their criticisms are therefore irrelevant to our theme. It also seems as if IRI and ENI might have been used for unsuitable purposes in Italian political economy, that they might have grown too large or have wielded too much political authority or have outlived their usefulness there. That does not affect our argument because we are not trying to take them bodily out of Italy and put them in England, but to get an idea of what it is like to vest publicly-owned undertakings, not in monopolistic public corporations, but in commercial holding companies and for the state to own part, rather than the whole, of some commercial or industrial activity. In our conclusion to this book we shall try to see whether a similar style would be applicable here in view of the objectives of our own nationalized industries.

REFERENCES

1. See, for example, A. Shonfield, *Modern Capitalism*, Oxford University Press, London, 1965, pp. 176–92; M. V. Posner and S. J. Woolf, *Italian Public Enterprise*, Duckworth, London, 1967; W. A. Robson,

Nationalized Industry and Public Ownership, George Allen & Unwin, London, 1962 (2nd edn), pp. 494–8.

2. Three smaller and newer *enti di gestione* have been created to control a number of small companies belonging wholly or partly to the state but outside the scope of IRI and ENI. The most important of these is EFIM (*Fondo per l'Industria Meccanica*) which includes some mining and engineering companies.
3. Posner and Woolf, *op. cit.*, p. 150.
4. The first President of the Institute and a leading Christian Democratic politician. See Shonfield, *op. cit.*, pp. 184–5.
5. Decree-Law No. 51 of 12 February 1948 (as amended by Law No. 1598 of 22 December 1956).
6. See the conversation in '*Lo Stato non sa Spendere*', *Adesso*, Anno V No. 40, February 1969.
7. See in particular, P. Saraceno, *Lo Stato e l'Economia*, Cinque Lune, 1963; and G. Petrilli, *Lo Stato Imprenditore*, Cappelli editore, 1967. Note the following from the second of these sources: 'L'intervento economico dello Stato, anche nella sua forma imprenditoriale, è in fatti essenzialmente un fatto strumentale che non può essere valutato in se, bensì in ordine alle finalità che concretamente persegue' (p. 12). And: 'Cio che davverò importa è che in ogni caso gli interventi imprenditoriali dello Stato risultino indonei a raggiungere col minor costo possibile, e quindi con la massima efficienza, la specifiche finalità pubbliche a cui sono ordinati' (p. 14).
8. Posner and Woolf, *op. cit.*, p. 129.
9. *Ibid.*, *passim*, especially p. 68.
10. See, Ministero del Bilancio e della Programmazione Economica, *Programma di Sviluppo Economica per il Quinquennio 1966–70*, Rome, 1967, pp. 50–2, 209–14; I.R.I., *Annual Report 1967*, Rome, 1968, pp. 16–18.

Chapter 12

A NEW STYLE OF STATE ENTERPRISE

There are two reasons for wanting to know whether state enterprise is predominantly business or politics. First, there have to be standards by which those in charge of state-owned undertakings can set their own aims and choose their own methods and there have to be criteria by which the performance of undertakings can be judged. Secondly, it makes for the efficiency of government that tasks should be given to those most able to perform them, whether by training, aptitude or authority. We have seen that the disposition of rights and duties made by British nationalization between 1945 and 1950 (and by later statutes on the same model) satisfies neither of these needs. Now it could be that they can never be met fully and that the style of state enterprise embodied in British nationalization does as much as possible. Indeed writers on nationalized industry in this country have invariably paid more attention to state enterprise as a means of reaching general social and economic goals than to its effects on the performance of single undertakings or the efficiency of government. Sometimes they have done so quite honestly because their political convictions require it. Not only economists and party ideologists, but even students of public administration, have been known to regard the problem of effective and efficient organization as secondary, if not dull. We have tried to be equally honest, however, in seeing it on the contrary as important and fascinating. That, we hope, has made us neither callous, for we hope that the same desires might be fulfilled better in other ways, nor tedious, for we think that fresh ways of organizing state enterprise can be explored.

We are encouraged in this by recalling that the need to be clear about the purposes of state enterprise for the same reasons as those given here was recognized at the time of nationalization on all sides of politics. The question we have asked, then, is not a new one, nor is it unreasonable or irrelevant. Indeed the question is really why the intentions of those who brought about nationalization have been so poorly fulfilled in this respect. Partly of course the cause is their own at best confused, and at worst inarticulate, idea of why state ownership should take the form of nationalization at all. We have tried to make up for that by toying with a distinction among different approaches to state enterprise, in particular between a *positive* approach and a *contingent* approach.

A positive approach to state enterprise is to regard public ownership as an end in itself. To a large degree the aim is to abolish private ownership because it is thought to be evil. Ownership by the state is also seen, however, not only as an instrument for achieving specific social and economic goals, but as a unique and indispensable instrument. The solution to problems is the transfer of ownership itself, which is therefore positively desirable. When a contingent approach is taken, public ownership is seen on the other hand as being conditional. It is not a transfer of ownership which is considered important but the achievement of something ulterior to that. By itself it is thought to achieve little or nothing and may even be seen as a nuisance, but after careful study of the alternatives its costs are found to be less. There is nothing particularly new and certainly nothing sophistical in this distinction, we suggest, because it is well known that many people support or tolerate public ownership and state enterprise without liking or wanting British nationalization.

Our main argument therefore is that there should be a distinction between British nationalization (on the model of 1945–50), based as it seems to be on a positive approach, and state enterprise based on a contingent approach. British nationalization is characterized above all by the public ownership of the whole or main part of so-called 'industries', by consequent centralization of direction and control, by an abolition or at least discouragement of private ownership and capital, and by the organization of undertakings as public boards or agencies rather than as companies. In fact, it is these characteristics of British nationalized industries which are important, rather than the legal relationship between the boards of the industries and ministers, or their public accountability.

We are rather sceptical of the value of reforms to the statutory relationship of ministers with boards, considering the real solution to be in the organization of the undertakings and the policies of government towards them. Our general conclusion is that, if both the fixing of meaningful standards of performance and the efficiency of governments are thought to be of first importance then it is necessary to consider 'de-nationalization' as a practical step. That of course (as well as being infelicitous) is a troublesome and pejorative word and we would rather avoid it. The problem as we see it is not so much public ownership itself but the kind of organization peculiar to the British so-called 'nationalized industries'. And we wish to emphasize that, while there may be honest reasons for wanting nationalization in this 'positive' sense, it must be admitted equally honestly that this can increase the cost of running nationalized undertakings and diminish the efficiency of government. The only worthwhile means of reducing the costs is turning the nationalized undertakings into businesses, a task which we think is compatible with some degree of public ownership and with the achievement of many interpretations of the public interest, but not with nationalization. Nationalization, as we shall now argue in summary, is defensible only if the principles of commerce and business can be rejected on general grounds, if the capacities of political activity can be shown to be greater than is generally assumed, or if special justifications can be given for the type of organization and style of conduct found in existing nationalized undertakings.

ARE THE NATIONALIZED INDUSTRIES IN BUSINESS?

In a rather superficial sense the nationalized industries in Britain are obviously in business in that they are clearly engaged in commerce, that is, in the exchange of merchandise on a large scale. The organizations in which the industries are vested have many traits typical of large business concerns: they keep commercial accounts, seek in general to cover their current expenditure with the revenue collected from customers, and so on. In other ways, however, there are aspects not typical of business in the conventional sense: there are no shareholders or equity; the undertakings have extensive rights and duties defined by statute, bestowing in some cases a power of monopoly; in practice they depend for capital funds on the central government and the latter in any event virtually guarantees their financial viability by writing off debt from time to time. Above all, the nationalized industries are unlike 'ordinary' business in their relationship with ministers and Parliament. While they might enjoy certain rights and opportunities not belonging to a typical privately-owned business, the nationalized undertakings are subject to far more publicity and accountability than the latter. The very names given to the organizations – 'board' or 'corporation' – implying as they do something representative or administrative, something appointed and fixed, suggest a basic difference from ordinary commercial things like 'firms' or 'companies' or 'enterprises'.

As we have seen throughout this book, there has been a continuing effort to get the nationalized undertakings treated as ordinary, independent businesses rather than as agencies of the central government. The difficulty of doing so has led on all sides of politics to a certain disenchantment with the methods of nationalization. The nationalized undertakings themselves have been affected by this in a number of ways. Their financial obligations have been more defined and in some cases special account has been taken of social and economic obligations made by governments. A more 'business-like' type of member has been appointed to boards and sometimes salaries have been paid based on levels ruling in the private sector rather than in the public service. Quite recently some boards have had greater freedom to raise their capital on the open market and to diversify their activities. The expression itself 'nationalized industry' has become unpopular (if it was ever found attractive by anyone):

> 'I call them national businesses to avoid "nationalized", which seems to give a permanent emphasis simply to the process of public acquisition. Must we go on for ever implying that these great industries have suffered some traumatic change from their natural state instead of growing into it? The word "business" stresses that we are not simply discussing administration. Business is not the civil service. We are discussing the business world with its risk-taking and profit-making, its hurly-burly and its individual accountability. Business is more realistic than "public enterprise", which somehow sounds emotive and anachronistically distinct from "private enterprise". It really is time, in our mixed economy, to recognize that business is business, public or private, and it had better be good.'[1]

In spite of this a belief lingers on that in vital ways the nationalized industries are not in business in any ordinary sense. There are two respects in which nationalized industries – by the very fact of being nationalized – are thought to serve the public interest uniquely. First, they are thought to be necessary for achieving social and economic objectives and, secondly, nationalization is thought to promote efficiency.

1. *Social and Economic Ends of Nationalization*

The social and economic objectives for which nationalization is said to be a necessary instrument are themselves often obscure. They extend from providing social services, avoiding abuse of monopoly and responding to government requests for restraint in prices and incomes to investing in technologically advanced but risky projects, supporting domestic industries and ensuring essential supplies. It has long been recognized that using nationalized undertakings as special instruments of objectives like these might be incompatible with treating a single undertaking as a business. As a result governments have often been reluctant to articulate their social and economic objectives for nationalized industries or to admit their commercial consequences.

It has also long been recognized that social and economic objectives of government can and do affect industry in general, and that in a mixed economy the acceptance of obligations of this kind need not mean that an undertaking is any less commercial or business-like. It sometimes happens that a government falls short of its objectives and, deciding that its existing powers of regulation or subsidization or fiscal and monetary management have proved inadequate, takes a more direct control over a commercial activity by acquiring an owning interest in it. In the mixed economy, while any of these steps may be controversial and may be hotly scrutinized and challenged, they will be taken by either main political party – they are not considered unusual in countries similar to Britain. The puzzle is why nationalization is thought to be necessary to achieve any social and economic objective; or rather, given that nationalization exists, why it has to be retained. No one would deny that the nationalized industries are of great public importance. The same is true, however, of many large undertakings in the private sector. What is it that makes steel, air transport and telecommunications more important than chemicals, shipping and computers?

The fact that governments have not hesitated to intervene in the private sector is produced as evidence that the nationalized and private sectors are alike. The existing nationalized industries were, it is said, nationalized for special reasons (for example, because they were starved of capital under private ownership, or had to be 'rationalized' or were already largely publicly controlled). However, to all intents and purposes, the argument continues, they should be treated today like any large industrial concern. This view rests on a distinction between 'the public interest' (in the form of social and economic obligations) and 'the commercial interest' of a nationalized undertaking itself – a distinction which it is very difficult to maintain in practice. For example, when taking responsibility for getting boards to provide what are called social services, ministers are bound to influence the overall effectiveness of an undertaking, if only by becoming a major customer. Although intended to do so, this procedure does not, as we have tried to explain, reduce a minister's responsibility for the performance of the undertaking concerned. On the one hand, the minister must ensure that he gets a good service at a fair price from what is normally a monopoly supplier. On the other hand, because the undertaking is nationalized, the minister must continue to exercise an interest in its efficiency and viability.[2] Under nationalization what is called 'the commercial interest' of a board merges with 'the public interest'. No government could wholly separate its interest in a nationalized concern on social or economic grounds from its interest in its financial viability or efficiency as a single undertaking. Similar problems might arise when a government is a major customer of a private undertaking or supplies a company with a lot of capital. There are limits to the extent to which social and economic obligations can be imposed on any undertaking without its commercial interests being somehow affected. This may be a growing problem in the relations between government and industry in general. But it is particularly acute in the case of the nationalized industries because there a government has a direct responsibility as 'banker' and 'shareholder'. For this reason, governments are forced to go beyond identifying and justifying social and economic obligations and are obliged to find criteria of competent and efficient performance. This requires a kind of political control which is quite different from that required by other forms of government intervention in industry. As we have implied in earlier parts of this book it could be that nationalization actually makes the achievement of social and economic objectives more difficult.[3]

Of course some simply do not believe that the public and private sectors should be treated in the same way. This view is reflected in the tendency to recommend ideal rules of behaviour for nationalized undertakings. When these rules are seen, as they often are, as being superior to those thought to prevail in business generally, then there are clearly positive reasons for believing in nationalization, at least to the extent that it means that pricing and investment decisions can be influenced directly. A further stage in the same line of argument is reached when it is said that wider social and economic obligations should override, not just commercial objectives such as a financial surplus or expansion, but economic efficiency itself. One thing that has never been satisfactorily explained is why, if the standards adopted for nationalized industry are better than those thought to be accepted elsewhere, the present nationalized industries should be specially picked out in this way. On the other hand, if other means than nationalization are available for seeing that the good standards are observed, why not adopt these means in the case of the industries now nationalized? Is nationalization essential?

Is it indeed effective? For few would now suppose that on its own it ensures greater economic efficiency or more socially responsible conduct. In fact it is doubtful whether any set of rules for making socially and economically 'desirable' decisions at a commercial level could be found for nationalized industries and agreed upon at present. Most civil servants and members of boards of nationalized industries realize this, which is why they tend to be more sceptical than academics and select committees in accepting analytical and administrative notions of what is a good or bad business decision. What nationalization has meant in practice is a pragmatic approach where those responsible have had to work out principles of conduct as they have gone along. Among other things this has led ministers and their officials into business and caught the boards of the industries up in public administration. Was that intended and is it now thought desirable?

Nationalization is positively desired not only to spread vague intellectual notions of what is efficient or good commercial behaviour. As we have seen all governments have made use of it to further specific social and economic policies. Doubtless few officials would like the opportunities it provides to be withdrawn or reduced. Indeed even the Conservatives recommended special restraint of prices in nationalized industries as part of the economic strategy set out in their campaign for the 1970 general election. Public ownership in some form or other is now quite widely accepted as a tool of social and economic policy – the point being whether it could be used here, as it has been in Sweden and Italy, both for macro-economic and micro-economic ends without requiring the style of management, or the degree of government intervention, found in British nationalization.

One of the strongest arguments in favour of public ownership of whole 'industries' with a centralized organization has been that, in order to plan effectively, a government must control 'the commanding heights of the economy'. We have noticed the influence of this view on ministerial control of investment in the fuel and power industries. One might think that it followed from this argument that ministers should impose a forecast on particular boards (having taken their expert technical advice). In practice of course, at least in one of their many roles, ministers encourage boards to have their own commercial policies and their own estimates of future demand. Actually there are good arguments against governments imposing any forecast on industries whether nationalized or not. There is no magic quality in the forecasts provided by official sources in Britain, at least on past experience. Even if they did come to inspire more confidence, it might still be advisable not to determine investment in accordance with a ministerial view. However, while encouraging independence governments have gone on to control investment in British nationalized industries, not so much in accordance with some economic plan, as from anxiety about the commercial viability of particular undertakings or the short-term effects on public opinion or specific interest groups of pricing or employment policies implied by long-term decisions. It is as if nationalization had left ministers with embarrassing authority and had made them less able to do things (such as planning for a sector) which nationalization was meant to make easier.

It is not our purpose to enter a general argument here about the means chosen by governments to promote efficiency and growth in a mixed economy. However, there has been a reaction in many countries in recent years against government intervention in microeconomic decisions. In France those who are still champions of a positive government, which is sensitive to both social and economic needs and ready to act on them, now seek ways of decentralizing responsibility for industrial activity, in order to find the 'right level' for business decisions.[4] Nationalization on a model similar to the British (although what the French have is even more centralized) is often seen in France now as being irrelevant to positive government. Nationalization in France was a response to social pressure for a change in the control of industry, and a rescue operation for undertakings either nationally important or technically backward or both. Today the main challenge to the same undertakings seems to be different; it is essentially keeping commercial objectives to the fore both to avoid a waste of resources and to meet increased competition resulting especially from the Common Market. Under these circumstances, it is felt, much more authority needs to be returned to the directors of nationalized enterprises to seek goals of profitability.[5] The difficulty remains of reconciling profitability at the level of a single undertaking with long-term social and economic benefits. In recent French thinking as in British the solution seems to be sought mainly in developing techniques of decision-making and encouraging governments to be more articulate and definite in laying down strategies for management.[6] We have argued here that this solution may well be self-defeating. Indeed, as a leading British economic decision-maker has remarked:

> 'The solution to this dilemma may lie not, as some economists would instinctively suppose, in refining the criteria laid down from above, but in devising different structures of responsibility so as to leave greater freedom of action coupled with different incentives and a different training for those to whom it is granted.'[7]

2. *Nationalization and Efficiency*

However clearly and fully the social and economic obligations of nationalized industries might be expressed, there would still be a problem of finding criteria of performance for individual undertakings and translating these into practical managerial terms. In an earlier part of this book we saw that this concern with criteria of performance led to a continuing argument about the need to measure the efficiency of the nationalized industries. This argument dealt with efficiency from different points of view without always being clear why this might matter. Particularly in recent years, there has been an attempt to articulate principles for pricing and investment in nationalized industries in the hope of producing economic efficiency. But the kind of efficiency with which the board of a single undertaking are chiefly concerned is what we have called 'technical' efficiency. This is the efficiency with which the undertaking produces at a given price and in a given market. It is closely related to economic efficiency, because it is when prices and output are thought to be economically 'inefficient' (for example when affected by monopoly) that external inspection of technical or operating efficiency are thought to be so necessary. It is widely supposed that these conditions exist in the nationalized industries as well as in parts of the private sector. Indeed some people saw nationalization as a solution to the problems they present. Clearly it has not been a very satisfactory solution, because in itself nationalization provided no means of ensuring efficiency.

Of course the efficiency of both nationalized and private undertakings is meant, according to the orthodox view, to be measured by an undertaking's financial results. Thus financial objectives rather than economic rules or external audits are still the basic measure of the performance of the boards of the nationalized industries. It is interesting, however, that in both public and private sectors other ways of promoting efficiency are felt to be necessary. This is one explanation why the word 'commercial' used evaluatively raises so many problems. People disagree about the standards which are – or should be – observed in the running of large industrial undertakings generally. The minister and boards held responsible for nationalized industries do not seem to have come up with anything staggeringly original. As we have seen, in spite of much talk in favour of 'efficiency audits' and some practice in the shape of studies by the NBPI, there is no real substitute for financial results obtained over a period of years and even they are an unsatisfactory guide from many points of view under nationalization.

It will be argued perhaps that the objectives of most large undertakings in the private sector are unreliable as a means of ensuring efficiency. Even if we accept this, is the only alternative to increase the tasks of the central government in inspecting and auditing their behaviour? For one thing, there is a risk of getting efficiency quite out of perspective.

Although an undertaking's performance is sometimes easy to measure, there are vital aspects of it which cannot be expressed quantitatively at all. Take, for example, what has been the chief problem of some of the most problematic nationalized industries – industrial relations. Unemployment in industries undergoing painful changes (like coal) has, as we have seen, been not only a social problem for governments but a problem for boards as well. Increasing the productivity of labour sometimes calls for rates of growth or decline which may be undesirable by other standards. The existence of problems like mechanization in coalmining is one of the reasons why it was considered desirable to vest nationalized industries in boards rather than ministers. Efficiency cannot be an end in itself. It would be absurd to regard the end of business undertaking as maximizing output for a minimum input (although that might well be the goal of one part of an undertaking's management). Yet many of those who have worried about measuring the performance of nationalized boards have talked of efficiency as if it meant general commercial success and included such vital human functions as assessing risk, interpreting consumers' demands, and realizing the advantages of technical inventions. An undertaking's performance in this sense is more properly evaluated by expressions such as 'progressive', 'prudent', 'competent', or simply 'successful'.

Decisions about risk, about consumer preference and about employing labour are related in practice to decisions about the quantity of output, about prices, and about investment. Yet political economists might find a board's pricing and investment decisions efficient even though in fact its performance in other respects was unsuccessful. An undertaking's managers might, for example, make wild predictions about future demand or about future costs in setting prices, or they might fail to take advantage of a potential market by ignorance or timidity about new processes of production. Running a successful business may often depend on economically 'irrational' behaviour. Some decisions will be taken according to the principles of bargaining or politics which make up such a vital part of management of personnel. Others will be dictated by physical problems, such as economies of scale or unpredictability. Then there are decisions to spend on research and development, on public relations, on safety precautions and so on. As we have seen, what have become known as the social obligations of the nationalized industries invariably fall into the same category. In other words, they are activities which make an uncertain and indirect contribution to an undertaking's overall performance and the decision to provide them is in the last resort a question of judgement. The quality of that judgement depends in turn on the results of the undertaking. One way of taking account of the effects of such longer-term decisions is to have a corporate strategy embodying all decisions about objectives along with account of the restraints imposed by such factors as government policy. To be held responsible for management as we have thought of it here, the leaders of a business must be free to set prices and to make decisions to invest in accordance with a strategy which is their own. In other words, there could be a conflict between the strategy of a business and a government's view of what was economically efficient, but treating an undertaking as a business means that such conflict must be accepted.

One thing which this study has emphasized is that there are different levels of control in a commercial undertaking or business. There are, for example, the objectives of the organization, for which usually a group of men are made responsible called *directors*, who are made to answer to a wider public. This wider public is heterogeneous and most business strategies can be seen as a compromise among different needs and objectives, such as consumer demands, the interests of the workers, government policies, the financial rewards of shareholders and directors, the status and prestige of the organization and its members generally. The making of a strategy also has to include a number of practical judgements about the behaviour of competitors, technical costs and opportunities, management of labour and so on. Probably nowhere are the different interests to be considered or the skills employed in making a strategy combined to perfection. It is possible to question on the other hand whether ministers are able on their own, even with the assistance of independent advisory bodies, to represent and provide them adequately. Yet we have shown that the accountability of nationalized boards to ministers seems to include a sharing of many essential functions of direction.

At another level of control the achievement of corporate objectives is in question. This is the task of what might be called management and it is here that internal efficiency is at stake. But the function of ensuring that objectives have been met efficiently and effectively is another responsibility of the direction. As we stressed earlier, while the two levels of control can be distinguished, the total function of direction is essentially one which faces two ways. Not only does the strategy have to reflect the opportunities and obstacles facing the undertaking, but they must be realistic, and the strategy has to be communicated to the organization as a whole.[8] This two-way process of setting objectives is what people think of when they argue that the boards of nationalized industries should have 'commercial freedom' in day-to-day management and should be directed by business-men rather than by ministers or civil servants. It is of course possible that, however acceptable its plans, an undertaking's performance might turn out to be disastrous, and the board will have to be made to answer for that. But management cannot be assessed on its own without some strategy to which it can be related. Therefore a board which lacks freedom in setting, and seeking to reach, its own objectives cannot be expected to be able to get the most out of the resources available to it. As we have seen some would maintain that nationalization was and is necessary precisely for that reason, in other words because the nationalized undertakings are not of their nature businesses and cannot be allowed that freedom. The consequences of such a view are alarming.

DISADVANTAGES OF POLITICAL CONTROL

The main disadvantage of the relationship between government and the nationalized industries in this country as it has been so far is the way it leaves ministers with incongruous functions: incongruous because they go ill together and because they are not best performed by government departments. The incongruity has been at its worst in the role of sponsoring departments like the Ministry of Power, Ministry of Transport, Ministry of Posts and Telecommunications and the Board of Trade.

The sponsoring department has to be close to the nationalized and other undertakings it sponsors in order to carry out its general duties of 'co-ordinating' activities in its sector and trying to ensure efficiency and adequacy of supply. The department needs reliable, objective information about the industries concerned: about technical changes and difficulties, about the attitudes of labour, about consumer behaviour, about foreign competition, and so on. The department cannot hope to get this information entirely by its own independent means and must rely on the industries' own spokesmen. That is so, however the industries themselves are organized. Indeed the department's need is rather like that of any policy-making, directing and controlling body relying on technical, specialized advice, such as the board of a nationalized undertaking or that of a private firm. Nevertheless, as we know, the relationship between a sponsoring minister and a nationalized undertaking is not meant to be the same as that between a board of directors and their own firm or between the board of a nationalized industry and their undertaking. That is because the running of a business could not be entrusted to government departments. It is not just our view but that expressed by the statutes and seldom challenged openly. However desirable it was thought, then, for ministers to make policy for different sectors of industry and commerce, it was *implicitly assumed* in nationalization that ministers could not themselves enter into industry and commerce and would have to rely even in the case of nationalized industry on the facility and qualification of people who were so engaged.

One undisputable justification for this is that the sponsoring minister in making his sectoral policy should be concerned, not so much with the performance of particular business organizations or with the articles they produce, as with the adequacy of a particular good or service and with the efficiency with which it is provided. It is not the Coal Board or the Railways Board or, for that matter, coal or railways which are important in themselves, but fuel and transport. Now business-men might be supposed to take a similar view, and certainly a sensible business-man will not continue to produce a commodity for which there is no demand. The trouble is – we need not go into it here – that business-men are not always so quick off the mark in realizing such things and sometimes they are too quick off the mark for the good of the rest of the community. So it is thought desirable for the government of the day – on the grounds that it takes a wider view than business-men – to see to the ordering of markets for essential commodities like fuel, transport, food, housing, and so on. Few people today would object to political control in that general sense. But it has never yet been suggested in Britain in peace-time that any government should take over the provision of fuel or transport: should employ the men, invest the capital, distribute the goods and so on. Organizing industry and commerce – however essential its product – is still to our knowledge best achieved by having a number of undertakings each trying to sell a different set of products for financial return and by making groups of business-men answerable within each undertaking for doing this. The individual groups of business-men are interested in fuel policy, say, only in so far as it affects their business.

How then should sponsoring ministers see to it that the markets for essential goods and services supplied by nationalized industries are organized in the public interest? We have noticed that the viability of particular concerns is in itself of no importance to them for this purpose. This is particularly true where there is competition among different types of product or service, as there is now, for example, in the fuel and transport sectors in this country. Of course there might be a reason for inhibiting competition because of its secondary effects (congestion on the roads, air pollution, regional unemployment, and so on) – but even then the viability of a particular board is not itself at issue. Indeed, sponsoring ministers are presumably not concerned with the profitability of private firms under their care as an end in itself. On the other hand, if there were just one organization providing transport, then its performance and that of transport in general, and thus its prospects and the transport minister's, would be identical. Now many people obviously thought that nationalization would give an organization just like that (and perhaps it did in the case of the British Transport Commission). As things are, however, it is difficult to set boundaries to any sector or industry or market, and even so there are disadvantages in large scale and centralization. The creation of huge monopolies for supplying essential commodities has generally not been popular. Instead there are nationalized undertakings competing with one another and competing also with privately-owned firms. Under these circumstances there is simply no sense in a sponsoring minister promoting particular nationalized undertakings or for that matter restraining their growth. There is nothing interesting in the financial results of the National Coal Board as such (whether the Board is in debit or surplus) except in so far as public money is at stake and those results might measure the efficiency and competence of the Board. *In fact there are no 'nationalized industries', only nationalized boards.* The best frame of mind for a sponsoring minister who wants adequate supplies of a commodity produced efficiently is to put out of his mind any distinction between nationalized and other businesses.

Here is the chief incongruity in the sponsoring minister's position, for it is that mental exercise which nationalization has made so difficult. In the first place there is the nagging implication that nationalization made the ends of a publicly-owned undertaking and the ends of public policy the same, in other words that it made the relationship between minister and undertaking singularly close. In practice that is palpably not so and there are few people who would want the minister to be any 'closer' than he is. Indeed fearing that nationalization in that way has 'failed' the advisers of ministers have toyed with theories to express government policy in mechanical rules of general application. If the facts of industrial organization mean that the whole of an 'industry' cannot be brought together under one source of political direction, but must rather be diffused among different competing concerns each with its own narrow business objectives, then perhaps the perspectives of business-men can be broadened by getting them to follow rules of decision-making approved in advance. As we have seen the conviction that such rules could be applied is based on a mistaken view of the nature of business objectives and how these are formed and made effective. Moreover, the sectoral policies of modern governments cannot be adequately expressed in general rules to promote economic efficiency. Fuel policy and transport policy are, as we have seen, not about abstract pricing policies but about the provision of specific goods and services, the settlement of particular human problems and all the things which go to make up the management of a commercial or industrial activity. Governments cannot know in advance how to do these things so that they can be formulated in some technical manual or guide-book. Surely no one would seriously suggest that they could? Naturally modern governments try to ensure that markets are organized so that supplies are adequate and efficient. The question is whether that is best done by laying down some general instruction in advance. Or is the minister's job rather to attend to the organization of markets itself – the size of undertakings, their relationship with one another, the amount of competition and restrictive practice, the social costs and benefits and so on? If the latter, then some government interest – even an owning interest – in the activities concerned might be helpful but nationalization in the conventional British style has many disadvantages.

Another reason why the sponsoring minister has difficulty in treating undertakings in his sector alike, and another incongruity endemic to nationalization, is that the minister is bound to take a close interest in the performance of single nationalized undertakings as their 'banker' or 'shareholder'. According to the statutes the undertakings are vested in boards, but the latter are appointed by the minister and without him there is no one to tell that the board is doing an efficient and competent job. Moreover, huge advances of public funds are made to the boards and from time to time boards have gone virtually bankrupt and have been re-constituted by ministers. It matters not to a shareholder perhaps how his dividend is obtained (as long as it has not been obtained by reckless expenditure) or to a lender of capital how the money he receives in interest was acquired. But these things matter a great deal to sponsoring ministers in the case of nationalized industries. This fact is bound to raise doubt in people's minds whether the functions of 'banker' and 'shareholder' can be performed rigorously enough by the sponsoring departments. This is one good reason, no doubt, why the Treasury needs to be concerned with commercial decisions in nationalized industries. However, even the Treasury cannot look at this aspect of the industries unequivocally for it is also concerned with promoting an efficient allocation of resources, and must be tempted to make use of the nationalized undertakings to expedite its short-term policy for managing the economy. So political control is a weak form of insurance against inefficient and incompetent business, and not only for the popular reason that civil servants are not trained for that kind of work or are forced to have the wrong attitude of mind. Fundamentally it is because of the incongruity of the tasks given to ministers.

There is a view of course that this particular incongruity is unnecessary in that the performance of single boards should not be judged by ordinary business standards but by special criteria based on social and economic principles. Such a view has led to proposals for a special Ministry of Nationalized Industries or for an Efficiency Audit Commission. Indeed, in so far as the present nationalized undertakings cannot be treated as ordinary businesses, then devices like this might well be required. However, it should be remembered that the study of efficiency cannot tell one a great deal on its own about performance of a business undertaking. Those who propose greater study of efficiency in nationalized undertakings have never been precise enough and have never said exactly what it is they want to measure and what the criteria would be. Very often efficiency studies turn out either to deal with day-to-day managerial problems in a piecemeal fashion or to criticize the failure of boards to meet rather arbitrary financial criteria. Moreover, if the performance of boards is to be weighed mainly by means such as inspection and audit then it would seem rather pointless to employ business-men on them and to pay business-men's salaries. Finally, it was to avoid replacing commercial with administrative control that the nationalized industries were vested in commercial public corporations.

This is not meant to suggest that external inquiries into the performance of business – whether nationalized or not – should not take place at all. Indeed it is nowadays a mark of intelligence in business to encourage constructive criticism from outside. The point we are making is a different one: it is that 'efficiency audits' (or whatever they are called) are no substitute for financial results of commercial activity as a measure of performance, that is, as a guide to a minister that the board he appointed has done a good job. It is also to say that there are costs in efficiency studies themselves, especially in view of the arguments repeated *ad nauseam* and on all sides that the boards are engaged in an activity where risk-taking and enterprise must not be hampered by excessive parliamentary or administrative supervision. Even if there were not ample evidence to support that view already, the prospect of increasing competition in the Common

Market would provide even stronger ground, as it has done in France and Italy.

Political accountability does not even lead to a significant extension of parliamentary control of industrial activity. Probably the best example of woolly thinking in this respect is the argument that social services provided by nationalized undertakings should be ordered and paid for by ministers, who would thus be made answerable to Parliament for their provision. As we have suggested, this argument fails to take account of the general difficulty of ensuring that Members of Parliament have effective influence over public expenditure.[9] Parliamentary control of expenditure is itself a difficult subject currently being debated as in need of reform. It sometimes seems to be implied that, by making ministers responsible for deciding to provide certain services, the right to decide important social and economic ends will pass to the people or their elected representatives in Parliament. An additional benefit of this is said to be an economic one, in that the people who benefit from the service concerned (namely the public in general), would then also be responsible for providing it. This is an extremely ill-informed and unrealistic view of government and not just because the relationship between ministers and Parliament in this country is in some way peculiar. It has yet to be shown how the governmental process of any Western 'democracy' with its general elections and legislative debates and ministerial responsibility provides an adequate means of channelling demands for goods and services to suppliers and distributing resources to consumers. That is after all not the main function of government and one could even argue that it should not be its task at all.

One justification everywhere for making large-scale industrial businesses politically accountable is that competition and private capital have ceased to be a means of ensuring efficiency or of maintaining adequate standards of performance. It is often said, not only that the 'virtues' of the market economy have ceased to exist in many important industries but also that these 'virtues' would obstruct economic growth, even if they did exist. Modern methods of production require large-scale working, centralized 'control' of markets, and monopoly. In view of this, and in view of the importance of the government as a consumer and as a protector of welfare, large-scale firms wield on their own a kind of political authority. In consequence it is argued that some political control must be found to supplement the rapidly diminishing 'commercial' controls provided by competitive markets and private shareholders. Answerability to political authorities seems then to be the only means of keeping the ends of industry and technology subservient to the public interest.

This thesis has been presented recently in its most popular form by J. K. Galbraith, although the arguments have been heard here before and in support of nationalization just before and after the last war.[10] It is said that they do not apply with anything like the same force or breadth to British experience as to that of the United States. Nevertheless, very similar arguments have been presented in the positive approach to state enterprise in this country. We are not certain whether in this book we have used the terms 'political accountability' or 'control' in the same way as Galbraith would understand them. As we have seen, at least in the British context, answerability to political authorities tends to mean expanding the functions of the executive branch of government. It does not necessarily lead to an increase in political activity in the conventional sense of greater public participation. Galbraith himself emphasizes the role which should be played by an 'intellectual community' in upholding standards of industrial performance and in this respect perhaps he means that there should be an increase in the power of public officials or 'technocrats'. We wonder how far those who share the positive approach to public ownership in Britain have thought these consequences through in the same way. Where business decisions were concerned, articulating the public interest for application by state enterprises in Britain has become the right of professional advisers of governments. These are invariably qualified, not as representatives of the general public or of particular classes or groups, but as specialists primed in tenets or 'laws' of human conduct and keen to use them in making administrative prescriptions.

This is not meant to be an argument against government intervention in general. Our main concern is to point out that political control is not so simple a notion as some writers suppose. In particular, there has been very little attempt to follow up the argument for greater public accountability by examining what might be the political and administrative costs. Political control might not be the only way of overcoming the problems presented by the concentration of power in large industrial organizations.

THE NEW STYLE – NATIONAL BUSINESS

In allocating responsibility for the activities of the nationalized industries it might be worthwhile to remember that in the private sector too there are criticisms of excessive centralization, claims that too little power is given to shareholders and workers, assertions of the need for a reform of company law, questionings of the current wisdom that the economies of large-scale production always require control from the centre. The organization of the nationalized industries has been a less popular subject than the political relationship between ministers and boards and the techniques of decision-making. We should like to suggest as a result of the present study, however, that more attention to the organization and structure of nationalized undertakings would pay well in terms of constructive reforms.

For example there is a habit of referring to the largest publicly owned undertakings in this country as 'the nationalized industries'. This habit (which we have already criticized) partly reflects and partly sustains an inarticulate assumption that these undertakings are and should be monopolies and cannot be compared with other firms. We have already remarked that, although they are called 'industries', most of the present nationalized undertakings face substantial competition from suppliers of substitutable products. A nationalized industry such as electricity supply is, moreover, not a legal entity itself but a combination of entities (the Central Electricity Generating Board, the Electricity Council, the various Area Boards). Even in the case of an 'industry' like coal, where the statute recognizes only one public corporation, the National Coal Board, it would help to distinguish between the Coal Board itself and the 'Coal Industry'. At the purely legal level the statute does not give 'The Coal Industry' the power to mine or distribute coal, but a body called 'The National Coal Board'.

However, as we have seen, nationalization was often justified in this country by the alleged need to centralize control of whole 'industries' while at the same time avoiding private control. Again, we have seen that the concept 'industry' seems to be necessary to some approaches to economic planning. In so far as governments attempt to make decisions at a macro-economic level, then the concept 'industry' clearly has some important analytical usage. At the same time, it is woolly, glossing over the different levels of authority within an undertaking and confusing an economic concept ('industry') with a legal and commercial one ('board' or 'enterprise'). It tempts one to think in terms of symmetrical units which might not make sense in practice. Freed from this habit of thought governments could look at the problems of the so-called 'nationalized industries' in a new and constructive way.

First, a 'nationalized industry' might be broken down *horizontally* into a number of different undertakings at a similar level. Some 'industries' are already sub-divided into area boards recognized in the relevant statute and others have a regionally-based organization which is not so recognized. What is the reason today for considering any nationalized undertaking as a monolithic 'industry'? Indeed the more state-owned businesses were expected to pursue their own corporate objectives the more urgent would be the need to scrutinize their organization as independent units rather than as integral parts of an 'industry'. Among other things it would then be easier to accept competition among state-owned undertakings and also between the latter and private undertakings: (this already exists to some extent). Another and more immediately relevant way of subdividing a 'nationalized industry' would be to accept the fact that individual undertakings need not confine themselves to any one activity. Thus British Rail are currently developing an interest in the hotels and catering 'industry' and in coastal shipping. In this respect there has been growing support from government for distinguishing boards from industries. So far, however, the exercise has not been fully applied in the other way, namely allowing private undertakings to diversify into activities considered peculiar to 'nationalized industry' (except in the case of civil air transport).

Secondly, a 'nationalized industry' should be seen in its different parts on a *vertical* plane. The 'board' (whether one of the boards established by a nationalization statute or the board of directors of a private company) is only one part of an undertaking and should not be confused with the whole of it. Clearly it is difficult to generalize even among nationalized undertakings, and, although there is usually one such group of directors in any industrial organization, the accountability of boards in the private sector is a matter of some controversy which is a subject of study in its own right. But it would probably be generally accepted that the directors of any industrial undertaking act in response to other groups, whether these are consumers, investors, government departments, or workers. The function of directors is not just a technical one of applying certain administrative prescriptions. It is like the political function of ministers: obtaining support (not only by means of financial incentive) for policies in the common interest of the organization. Whereas they themselves might be strongly influenced by the arguments of ministers and civil servants about broader economic problems, the directors of an undertaking will at the same time have to bear in mind the needs of their employees. Thus a board's policies (in both public and private sectors) will be successful, not only because they are economically rational or even because they are designed to achieve a certain financial return or rate of growth, but also because they are supported by other groups – workers, managers, consumers, investors and so on.

When state enterprises face competition from other producers of similar goods and services and have to compete on the market with private undertakings for their capital then the setting of financial objectives to measure efficiency and competence becomes much simpler than it is in the case of British nationalized industries. However, it might make effective economic co-ordination of the activities concerned more difficult. The desirability of such a system also depends on how one values such things as competition, the profit motive, private ownership and so on. It depends again on the extent to which governments have overriding social ends. Some of these questions could be settled only by political decision – that is, putting a particular party into office. We hope to have given in this book some idea of how the state's modern responsibilities for managing the economy in the short term, stimulating efficiency and growth in industry, and at the same time smoothing the more harsh and chaotic changes involved, can be pursued without the need to create cumbersome structures like the British nationalized undertakings. In post-war Italy, for example, state enterprise has been used to keep down prices of essential commodities, encourage greater competitiveness in particular industries, promote regional development and other general social and economic ends, by relying on partial ownership of commercial undertakings, by preserving an element of private capital in them, and by largely keeping out of ministers' hands the difficult functions which go with ownership. This approach has not perhaps been as successful in Italy as its champions have maintained, but that can largely be explained by factors peculiar to the Italian economy and political system. In many ways that style of state enterprise might have been more relevant in Britain. There would surely be less anxieties here about mixing private with public sources of capital in view of the relatively happy experience of cooperation between private industry and government in this country? One could also expect there to be reliable and useful sources of information about commercial results in state enterprises organized in that way in Britain, at least compared with present experience, however inadequate these might be by ideal standards. The same incentive to unwieldy growth given to Italian state holding companies by the weaknesses of the political system would not be present here. It is true of course that there are already some examples of mixed enterprise in Britain, where the state's interest takes the form of a shareholding, but these are still the exception and the model has not been applied yet to the existing nationalized industries.

Of course it could be argued that the existing nationalized undertakings in Britain are organized as they are partly for sound technical and economic reasons and not simply from the vague preference for large-scale and public monopoly, associated with the positive approach to state enterprise. Arguments in favour of centralizing control of these undertakings and limiting or preventing competition were influential at the time of the 1945–50 statutes of nationalization. The technical or economic character of the present nationalized industries varies a great deal and the needs of government policy also vary. Some boards have needed protection from the market in the interests of full employment and regional policy, but others would perhaps have welcomed a better opportunity to face competition. In fact the main defence some boards give in their struggle for 'commercial freedom' is that they face competition from other suppliers, who are often private undertakings, and that they are engaged in taking risks just like private concerns. In so far as they are to enjoy 'commercial freedom', however, it follows that the challenges as well as the opportunities of that condition should be presented to them. While undertakings supplying the same good or service need not be expected to compete with each other in supplying the same consumers (like the Victorian railways), then at least the supply of fuel, transport, telecommunications and other nationalized services might be so organized as to allow useful comparisons to be made between the performance of different units. Futhermore, could there not be competition for the field if not competition in the field? Again, perhaps the generation of electricity could be entrusted to area boards along with distribution, and the telephone service organized in a similar way in the form of a number of regional undertakings?[11] As a general rule, it would also follow from our proposed new style that private competition with existing nationalized undertakings should be facilitated, not discouraged. And correspondingly it should be recognized more fully that there is nothing sacred in the products which a public undertaking supplies at any one time: this has already been done now in the case of the Railways Board, but without concomitant changes to make the Board more like a private business in the way it raises capital.

Above all it would follow from the new style that 'co-ordination' in the interests of adequacy and efficiency of supply should be the responsibility of commercial bodies rather than government departments. We have tried to show in this book that what is now known as 'sector policy' is in large part a commercial matter and cannot be made without deep understanding of, and influence on, the business decisions made by undertakings. One way of doing this would be to transfer much of the responsibility for this sector policy to public corporations organized as holding companies, as has already been recommended elsewhere.[12] That change would not on its own reduce the responsibilities of ministers for the functions of ownership and it might well make them more difficult to perform. So, in addition, changes would be needed in the way state enterprises raise their capital and in the way their ownership is settled.

The argument that the nationalized industries should be required to raise their capital on the market along with privately-owned industry has always been rejected by the Treasury on the grounds mainly of sheer inconvenience. The Treasury's case has so far been accepted by the Select Committee on Nationalized Industries.[13] The furthest past governments have gone in responding to the industries' demands for more flexibility in raising their capital is to allow a small amount of borrowing on foreign markets and to introduce a special kind of Exchequer dividend capital. It is also argued that boards would be unable to raise sufficient quantities of capital on the market. Again, therefore, it would be absurd to suggest a radical and total change of practice, but a change of principle would at least mean that the administrative costs could be estimated again in a different set of values. Moreover, we are far from convinced that the Treasury's real reason for not wishing the boards to go to the market is the one which they have always given. Do they not really fear a reduction in the government's influence on investment in the industries concerned? If so, and if the interests of economic management demand such a degree of political and administrative control, then what are they worth? The holding company, however, might well be a means to getting round many of the difficulties said to exist in supplying public undertakings with private capital.

This is related to the question of ownership and we feel that making a clearer definition of the rights of ownership would bring advantages on its own. We have already suggested that at present the boards of the nationalized state enterprises might be thought insufficiently representative and responsive on their own to be entrusted with settling their own corporate objectives.[14] On the other hand it is also highly undesirable that so much of the task of making them more representative and responsive should fall on ministers. These aspects of nationalization are so commercially harmful that it would indeed be surprising if many private investors were content to lend money to such enterprises without a guarantee from the Treasury. We wonder if their attitude would be the same if the structure of the enterprises allowed direct representation of lenders of capital. In other words, there would have to be an end to nationalization, and a different means of representing the state's interest (where this was still necessary) would have to be adopted. Could not the state's interest be represented through holding companies, established by statute as public corporations having much the same relationship with ministers as the present nationalized boards? The new public corporations would in some cases, however, be entrusted with responsibility for much wider areas of commercial activity than the present nationalized boards. Thus there could be one for the fuel sector, one for inland transport, one for the air corporations, one for steel and one for posts and telecommunications. And they would not themselves have the power to operate the undertakings now nationalized but would simply be vested with 100 per cent shareholdings in them. The main task of the new corporations (which could be written into their enabling statutes) would be to find the best way of dealing with the undertakings whose shares they held and of organizing the industrial sectors for which they were responsible. This would mean in some cases selling equity shares in the operating concerns. In other words the statutes should recognize the operating undertakings as companies (they would be the existing nationalized boards with different names and legal structures), the share capital of which could gradually be sold off to private buyers where the holding corporation thought fit and practicable. New capital could be raised by the operating companies by new issues of equity shares as well as by the issue of debentures. The holding corporation and the operating companies would be free to dispose altogether of any of their stock, or on the other hand to set up new subsidiaries. Capital for an operating company could also be raised by means of a loan from public funds, but this loan would come to the company through the holding corporation.

The legal relationship between holding corporations on the one hand and ministers and Parliament on the other could be much the same as with the existing nationalized boards, but its practical consequences would be quite different. For example, political control would not bear directly on operating concerns, and in so far as these became partly privately-owned it would not need to bear even indirectly so much as it does now. The holding corporations would begin life with complete power to appoint the boards of operating companies, to approve their programmes of capital investment and so on, but in time it would gradually begin to share this power with other shareholders. This structure would, we believe, enable ministers to divest on to a new and more suitably organized body many of their present functions in making sector policy, in taking responsibility for the efficiency with which the boards fulfil their social obligations, as well as in acting as the undertakings' 'bankers'. This would leave ministers better placed to decide what was the public interest in commerce and industry and to find arrangements for promoting it.

Monopoly, for example, is only part of the general problem of reconciling economic efficiency with the need for growth and development, and a government's industrial policy needs to be worked out for both public and private parts of industry. At the same time it needs to bring together the regulation of monopolistic practices by both employers and labour, the control of prices and incomes in the interests of economic stability, and the promotion of efficiency and technical progress. These aspects of policy should be more closely related to sector policy, which should become less interested in the viability of individual nationalized concerns and attend rather to the general structure and conduct of commerce in its sector. Under the sort of arrangements we have proposed it could benefit in this from the advice of a holding corporation to which directions could be given from time to time whenever the corporation's own policy for the sector seemed to the government to be inadequate.

As for the provision of social services, the new holding corporations could see to these by tendering schemes to the minister concerned for his approval and financing. A holding corporation could either pay one of its subsidiary operating companies to provide the service or could set up some new undertaking for the purpose. A minister should, however, be free to take his custom elsewhere if a corporation's tenders were unsatisfactory. The holding corporations would naturally be in close touch with their sponsoring ministers. The difference would be that in sponsoring holding corporations ministers would be dealing not so much with an operating business as with an agency managing public funds in accordance with their own policies.

In view of what has been said so far, under these new arrangements the sponsoring department, covering both public and private undertakings and concerned with both 'social services' and economic efficiency, should be retained at least in some form. If the functions of existing sponsoring departments were reduced sufficiently by the changes proposed here this would be quite compatible with their amalgamation in a new Ministry of Trade and Industry.[15] The Treasury would probably still have to seek to ensure an adequate return (both financial and otherwise) on the sponsoring ministries' (and therefore the holding corporations') expenditure, as it does now for all departments and their agencies. It is difficult to see how any re-casting of functions in the central administration could take that vital co-ordinating task away, unless it was the creation of a special Bureau of the Budget. However, the Treasury's need to control the operating companies would be largely removed. It could be concerned less with the 'profitability' of investment in those companies, with all the ambiguity which that implies, and more with the wisdom of the sponsoring departments' and holding corporations' expenditure for the social and economic objectives stated.

In order to avoid distortions to competition and to the financial measures of performance employed by all businesses, public or private or both, it is best that national economic policy-makers should treat commerce and industry as a whole and not select particular types for special treatment. Even if they were faced with a temporary shortage of public funds the holding corporations could make use of their subsidiaries' access to the open market, which would in itself encourage the makers of national monetary policy to co-ordinate their approaches to public and private investment. The private share in the profit accruing from the activities of the operating companies would serve to belay the impression that, by choosing to operate on public funds or on the open market, government policy-makers were choosing between public and private interests. In any event even if economic measures were especially punitive on public funds going into the holding corporations, the latter would enjoy enough flexibility and discretion with the finances available to them to maintain the supply of essential goods and services. They would also be able to prevent cuts in public funds damaging the financial results of their subsidiaries. Such a compulsion to treat all business as business would at least force into the open the reasons why governments want to control any commercial and industrial activity, and would present a clearer picture of the costs of doing so.

GENERAL CONCLUSIONS

There could be great gains for the efficiency and effectiveness of government if state enterprise in this country could be treated as a business. To treat the existing nationalized industries in that way, if it was to be at all meaningful, would require fundamental changes in policy.

A recent statement of the new Conservative Government's policy for nationalized industries (made while this book was going to press) suggests that a fundamental change might now be possible.[16] This could be seen as an intensification of party conflict over the issue of nationalization and, if it is that, then it would be in keeping with our view that there are important differences of approach to this question which should be brought into the open and settled politically. For our part, however, we should prefer to emphasize the general benefits which could be gained by adopting the style of state enterprise which we have recommended and which should make it appeal, therefore, to members of all parties. First, there are benefits in terms of increasing the efficiency of government. Secondly, the effectiveness of the undertakings themselves should be increased by providing clearer standards of performance for their boards of direction and their managers. Finally, the undertakings could be further protected against the direct effects of the political conflict which is unavoidable in this sector of government.

First, then, the experience of the nationalized industries suggests that the efficiency and effectiveness of government will not be increased simply by divesting the central administration of its tasks. As controls of one kind are removed from an activity, then others have to be found to take their place; withdrawing ministerial responsibility might simply make the job of protecting the public interest more difficult, indeed more bureaucratic, in that abstract and formal rules might replace personal and responsive guidance. In the field of commerce and industry the intervention of government has invariably come about because it was said that the existing controls of efficiency and performance were inadequate. We have looked at ways of lightening central administration, where nationalized industries are concerned, not by clumsily attacking intervention itself but rather by scanning better forms of control. We have borne in mind in doing this that replacing ministerial responsibility with pre-determined rules would be self-defeating. The alternative seems to be reviving the relatively spontaneous, voluntary controls belonging to most ordinary commercial activity where these have fallen away. If this cannot be done – and there are strong ideological and economic opinions against it – then the costs of an unwieldy, overweening central administration have to be lived with.

Secondly, the point of treating state enterprise as a business is that it could, by reviving many of those controls, lead to a better disposition of tasks. In the first place there is the internal efficiency of undertakings and all the qualities which make up 'good management'. The best level at which to provide these is the level of the managers in an undertaking and the best level at which to control the managers is that of the board of the undertaking or its 'directors'. Management in this meaning does not make sense anyway unless it is related to the objectives of an undertaking, which must among other things make possible a full realization of the opportunities facing it and a prudent awareness of the difficulties. The best level of setting those objectives is the level of the directors; the 'board' or whatever it may be called. There is a need to see that the tasks of the directors are adequately fulfilled and this is a function in most western, democratic countries which is shared among a number of different groups and persons, usually those with some financial stake in the undertaking but also those with another kind of stake such as consumers or workers. In the modern mixed economy one thing which also has to be taken into account in approving the objectives of industrial undertakings is the social and economic policy of the government, including a number of procedures, laws and regulations to ensure that the directors do represent the various groups which depend on them. The best level for making this public policy is undoubtedly that of government.

As far as the nationalized industries are concerned, it is only too evident that tasks are not disposed according to this ideal model. Ministers have been responsible at all levels. Naturally it would be impossible to expect the levels to be kept completely distinct in practice and this model is presented here as nothing more than an ideal. There would naturally be great advantages to both business and politics if government could be confined to the making of public policy for industry. However, in the case of certain important activities (such as those carried on by the present nationalized industries) there is a strong case for making government one of the interests to be represented at the level of direction. We have tried to suggest a means of doing this which is the use of public corporations as holding companies. But for government to take on the task representing all interests is surely undesirable, not least because as we have seen, it leads on to responsibilities at even lower levels.

The organization of state enterprise in Britain has suffered a great deal from the attempt to apply general doctrines to different activities with their own special problems. The original statutes of nationalization (and later statutes on the same model) seemed to assume that the same broad rules of political control should apply to all the undertakings, however great the differences among them. That assumption has been shown here to be quite untenable. Thus we have proposed that, at a level between ministers and operating concerns, there should be holding corporations (appointed by ministers) which would be responsible among other things for applying general social and economic objectives of the government in the light of each concern's circumstances and needs. An equally important reason for such an arrangement is that already some of these undertakings (above all, steel and road transport) have suffered a great deal from politically induced change. It should be remembered that there are costs in change itself and these must be weighed against the benefit of any desirable innovations. Indeed a third general benefit of the style of state enterprise proposed here is designed to protect the operational or productive side of state-owned enterprise from the worst effects of political vacillation and interference. Had this style been adopted from the beginning, rather than that contained in nationalization, then the costs of politically induced change would have been much less. Moreover, the structure we have recommended would by its flexibility avoid the pitfall of generalization and permit the practical differences among undertakings to be taken into account.

We would go so far as to claim that the arrangements we have proposed would actually facilitate the expression of doctrinal party political differences in this area of government, because the direct consequences on the operational side of industry would be far less disruptive. For we have come to the conclusion that the objectives of public ownership can be pursued by means other than nationalization, indeed that they can be more confidently pursued without it because then there need be less anxiety about the effects on management. Our proposed style of national business should, then, not only appeal to both main political parties, but should also make it easier for them to exercise their different approaches to state enterprise. The need is to find ways of switching social and economic objectives without disruptive effects on the operational side of industry. Nationalization in the conventional manner and total 'denationalization' are altogether too clumsy for that purpose and we have tried to find a more incremental approach.

Our general conclusion, then, is that for the purposes of setting objectives for individual state undertakings and judging their efficiency, there should be a much stronger guarantee than exists now that these undertakings are in business rather than in politics. Most people do argue that state enterprises should be treated as being in business, but we have seen that undertakings which are nationalized cannot be in that position. There is need for a clear recognition of the desirability of competition among state enterprises, both among themselves and with privately-owned undertakings, as well as of the right of state enterprises to diversify. There should also be ready access to the open capital market, combined with a mixture of public with private ownership. Above all, indeed partly to expedite changes such as those just mentioned, the rights of ownership in public enterprise should be clearly defined. They should also be allocated to an organization which is commercial in nature rather than to a minister and his officials, and it must be recognized that vesting a formal right of ownership is on its own pointless without at the same time bestowing a good measure of financial independence and providing a structure which is economically viable. For this reason we have supported the idea of creating holding corporations in place of the existing boards of the nationalized industries. These holding corporations would control the state's interest in the undertakings now vested in the nationalized boards while the undertakings themselves would be constituted as ordinary, joint-stock companies. We feel that this arrangement would provide better conditions for weighing the performance of individual undertakings, would bring about a substantial and desirable lightening of the tasks of government and would be healthy for the working of a two-party system of democracy.

REFERENCES

1. Peter Parker, 'Minding Our Own Businesses', *New Statesman*, 15 December 1967, p. 835.
2. As in the case of British Rail and grant-aided passenger services. See pp. 104–10.
3. By complicating the role of ministers. See pp. 102–18.
4. See, for example, Louis Armand and Michel Drancourt, *Le Pari Européen*, Fayard, Paris, 1968, pp. 198–200: 'Tout içi-bas a son niveau de régulation et, chaque fois que l'on fausse les circuits, on complique le problème.'
5. Groupe de Travail du Comité Interministeriel des Entreprises Publiques, *Rapport sur les Entreprises Publiques*, April 1967, Documentation françaises, *passim*. See also Michel Albert and J. J. Servan-Schreiber, *Ciel et Terre: Manifeste Radicale*, Denoel, Paris, 1970, pp. 74–89.
6. See *Rapport sur les Entreprises Publiques*, *op. cit.*, pp. 91–2, 101–2.
7 Sir Alexander Cairncross, 'The Managed Economy', *The Advancement of Science*, 26, 1969–70.
8. See pp. 65–66 above.
9. See p. 155 above.
10. J. K. Galbraith, *The New Industrial State*, London 1967, *passim*.
11. See, for example, David Alexander, *Dial ENTerprise 1971*, Conservative Political Centre, no. 425; Michael Canes, *Telephones – public or private?* Institute of Economic Affairs, 1966; Select Committee on Nationalized Industries, Session 1967–8, *Ministerial Control of the Nationalized Industries* HC 371–II, vol. II, Memorandum from Professor J. Wiseman p. 603.
12. See pp. 118 and 168–72 above.
13. *Ministerial Control*, *op. cit.*, vol. I, paras. 621–5. See also Committee on the Working of the Monetary System, *Report*, August 1959, Cmnd. 827, paras, 84–9.
14. See pp. 55–70 above.
15. In fact a new Ministry of Trade and Industry, including the former Ministry of Technology (itself including the old Ministry of Power

since 1969) and the Board of Trade, was set up by the new Conservative Government in autumn 1970, as this book went to press.

16. See speech by Mr John Davies, Secretary of State for Trade and Industry at 'Businessman of the Year' lunch, Monday 7 December 1970; see also speech by Mr John Davies at Conservative Party Conference, Blackpool, 8 October 1970.

Index

For Product Safety Concerns and Information please contact our EU representative GPSR@taylorandfrancis.com
Taylor & Francis Verlag GmbH, Kaufingerstraße 24, 80331 München, Germany

www.ingramcontent.com/pod-product-compliance
Lightning Source LLC
LaVergne TN
LVHW020641300926
849161LV00004B/765
9781041131229